THE
WONDERFUL
WORLD
OF
WALKING

THE
WONDERFUL
WORLD
OF
WALKING

by BILL GALE

 A DELTA BOOK

A DELTA BOOK
Published by
Dell Publishing Co., Inc.
1 Dag Hammarskjold Plaza
New York, New York 10017

This book is dedicated to Avia, Barbara, and Nina, who I hope will know the joy of walking all their lives.

CONTENTS

**PART IV / WALKING TOURS OF TWELVE
GREAT AMERICAN CITIES**

INTRODUCTION

I AM A *walkaholic*. I WALK MILES EVERY DAY. EXACTLY HOW MANY miles I can't tell you because I don't carry a pedometer, I don't count blocks. Walking is far too pleasurable for me to bother keeping track of the distance I cover in the course of the day. After all, you don't have to schedule it the way you do other exercises. It requires no equipment other than your own two legs. So it slips—nice and easy—into your daily lifestyle. Let's just say that I ride only when that is absolutely essential. For I know that walking enriches me physically, mentally, emotionally—and spiritually too.

Only once in my fifty-three years have I been seriously ill. At forty-one I had septicemia—blood poisoning. At times my fever raged to 106 degrees, and then my temperature would plummet and I'd shiver with chills to a point where my bed would shake. Later my doctor told me that I wouldn't have survived if my heart hadn't been so strong. And when I was finally recuperating and able to sit up, I'd look out the window into the street below and watch the people walking there. I envied them their good health. And how anxious I was to be part of their world again. The very act of walking seemed to me to be something quite extraordinary. I had always enjoyed walking (I believe that it certainly helped to make my heart strong), but now I thought it was the most exciting exercise in the world. For me sitting there in my hospital robe and slippers, it became the very symbol of life. And now, more than a decade later, I still regard it that way I simply can't take walking for granted. I feel a thrill each time I set out on a walk. For me it's not only the most natural, least expensive means of locomotion, but *essential* to my survival. And without meaning to sound pedantic, I think you should see it that way too.

New York City

BILL GALE

THE WONDERFUL WORLD OF *WALKING*

WHAT HAPPENS TO YOUR BODY WHEN YOU WALK?

"Walk every chance you get. Walking is actually one of the best all-around physical activities."

—President's Council on Physical Fitness and Sports

LITERALLY *every* PART OF YOUR BODY PERFORMS NATURALLY WHEN YOU walk. Muscles stretch and turn and knead with every step you take, as your lungs dilate with fresh, invigorating air. Legs, thighs, buttocks, spine, pelvis, rib cage—even your neck—move in one wonderfully coordinated rhythm. It's a marvel of simple engineering! And since no one set of muscles ever runs the risk of being overtaxed, it's impossible to walk too much.

Your leg muscles are the largest and most powerful muscles in your body. They were built to move and that way squeeze blood back toward your heart and brain despite the pull of gravity. Which is why in medical circles, our leg muscles are sometimes referred to as a "second heart."

If we were still ambling about on all fours, our hearts wouldn't have to work so hard. All our vital organs would be on the same level. But we stand upright and, as a result, our blood has to be pumped *up*. When you walk, the muscles in your thighs, calves, buttocks, abdomen, and feet give your heart a big assist as they rhythmically contract and release, squeezing the veins and forcing the blood along.

15

Of course, there are other benefits to be had from walking besides revving up your circulation (and improving your skin in the process). You not only feel more fit, you *look* more fit. Walking strengthens the leg muscles that give shape to your legs. Walking also strengthens the abdominal muscles—you can literally walk your stomach away. Your buttocks spread when you sit (*the adult American hip width has been increasing at the rate of one inch every generation*)—but contract . . . relax . . . and contract again as you walk. So you can quite literally walk off a middle-aged spread, too. And as we both know, the better you look, the better you feel about yourself and the world.

Walking is like giving yourself a transfusion of joy!

PART I

THE JOY OF WALKING

CHAPTER

1

WHY NOW?

"Walking is an idea whose time has come."

—C. CARSON CONRAD, executive director, President's Council on Physical Fitness and Sports

BACK IN 1964, WRITER-NATURALIST JOSEPH WOOD KRUTCH WAS ASKING in print, "Is Walking the New Status Symbol?" He thought it was, and so did a lot of other people at the time. President Kennedy had declared physical fitness a part of national survival. "We don't want a nation of spectators." And Robert Kennedy led a group on a fifty-mile hike.

Krutch saw a return to walking as part of a cultural revolution. "Americans have rediscovered nature," he wrote. "Books about animals, plants, mountains and oceans are being sought in unprecedented numbers. But you can't observe nature from an automobile."

Right on! as they used to say back in the 1960s. Krutch ended his piece on a high note of optimism: "Hurrah for what our fathers used to call shank's mare. Nowadays 'the man who has everything' is using his legs."

Ten years later Arnold Gingrich, publisher of *Esquire* magazine, was working the same "shank's mare" theme, if a bit more wistfully. Writing at the time of a national gasoline shortage, he noted:

There's only one possibly bright corner to this otherwise pretty dark picture. Some of us could benefit from getting a little more exercise than we have had sense enough to take. You'd be surprised how useful your two feet can be, when put to unaccustomed service. Also surprising is what a large number of places turn out to be within walking distance, now that this exotic possibility may suddenly present itself. Another old term, that many of us never had to know, and the rest of us have forgotten, is "Shank's ponies" or "Shank's mare"—terms once used interchangeably for the only truly dependable free transportation service there is.

Wouldn't it be funny if it took a crisis to teach a lot of us our first really good habit? To walk, for a change, instead of ride. As they say of that ethnic penicillin, chicken soup, at least "it couldn't hurt." And who knows, with our strange national propensities, but what it might take on the proportions of a sport?

Well, we've finally got the message. *Our feet were made for walking.* It certainly isn't a new idea. Hippocrates prescribed brisk walks, short walks, early-morning walks, after-dinner walks, and night walks. Thomas Jefferson wrote, "Walking is the best exercise of all." But I don't believe anyone ever put it to us with such gusto (and no little impatience) as Sam Austin, who, in 1883, at the time he wrote the following, was sporting editor of the *National Police Gazette*:

> It has always been my ambition to help perfect man through exercise. I have undertaken physical feats, just like this last one, to popularize walking, one of the easiest, most graceful and useful forms of exercise.
> People ought to get out on the road. Keep your legs and feet spry and limber. Pump your flattened chests with God's free air. Redden your blood, start it coursing through your veins. Purify your sluggish skin with honest sweat. Throw away your cigarettes and smash your cocktail glasses. Leave subways and the "L," trolley cars and autos to rheumatic old women and babes in arms—walk, walk, walk! Don't be afraid of the rain. It has its part to fill just as the sunshine has. It is a blessing if you take it right.
> Outdoors is our home; indoors an unavoidable evil which we must escape whenever we may. Stop thinking about ourselves—and *walk!*

Almost a hundred years have passed, and we're finally walking. But why *now*? Well, for one thing, today Americans are more interested in better health and physical fitness than ever before. And walking, the world's oldest exercise, is also an aerobic exercise, which makes it very contemporary.

And, as Joseph Wood Krutch noted in 1964, Americans have rediscovered nature. It was true then and truer today. The number who walk through the wilderness has more than quadrupled in the past decade. And it still holds that you can't observe nature from an automobile. Which brings us, I think, to an important point: the demise of the automobile. There is a touch of irony, and no little poetic justice, in the fact that the machine which did so much to encourage our limb lethargy has helped to put us back on our feet and walking. Bumper-to-bumper traffic. Gasoline shortages. As the joy of riding has decreased, we've returned to the oldest transportation mechanism: walking. What Oliver Wendell Holmes called "an immeasurably fine invention."

Back to nature. Back to the Greek ideal of a sound mind in a sound body. In a sense, we've been running the reel of man's development in reverse in our desire to simplify life, to get back to basics and out from under the weight of the unwieldy technology we've spawned. So it was inevitable that we would eventually rediscover the joy of walking, perhaps a primal instinct. And inevitable too, I suppose, that en route we would stop to run or jog.

There is no question but that jogging can be pleasurable, but too often there's pain mixed with the pleasure. The term *jogger's ankle* (sprains accounting for 75 percent of joggers' ankle injuries) has become part of our vocabulary. And in view of the fact that our feet contain one-fourth of our body's bones, as well as muscles, ligaments, and yards of blood vessels, it's not surprising that most medical men today favor brisk walking over jogging for achieving and maintaining physical fitness. Walking is risk-free. The oldest exercise is still the safest.

Five experts * in exercise and physical fitness, each with special interest in cardiac health, were asked to evaluate a number of popular physical activities. The following table summarizes their general opinions with regard to jogging and walking.

I won't belabor the conclusion one must come to on the basis of the opinions of those five medical men. But happily, as many men and women discover that they must abandon jogging, they turn to walking for their daily exercise.

For as we grow increasingly sophisticated about the maintenance of our bodies, there is more emphasis on less strenuous exercises and sports. And as the American woman continues to play a more active role in society, her influence on how America stays fit is going to increase. Since bulk and muscle power play no part in successful walking, women are at no disadvantage. And if the national birth rate hasn't increased by the year 2001, ours will be a middle-aged society, prompting Dr. David Bachman, a prominent Chicago orthopedist, to predict, "I think the major emphasis

* The experts consulted were: Dr. Samuel M. Fox III, director, Cardiology Laboratory, Georgetown University Hospital, Washington, D.C., and member, President's Council on Physical Fitness and Sports; Dr. Henry Blackburn, director, Laboratory of Physiological Hygiene, University of Minnesota School of Public Health; Dr. Ezra Amsterdam, University of California School of Medicine, and director, Coronary Care Unit, Sacramento Medical Center; Dr. Albert Oberman, director, Division of Preventive Medicine, University of Alabama Medical Center, Birmingham; Dr. Robert J. Murphy, Columbus, Ohio, internist and head team physician at Ohio State University.

ACTIVITY	AGE SUITED FOR	BENEFITS	CAVEATS
Jogging	All ages if fit, under 40 best.	Excellent conditioner. Increases cardiac & lung capacity. Builds leg strength. Promotes weight control.	Hard on joints & ligaments. Have checkup if beginning at 40 or older. Preconditioning necessary. Don't wear rubber or plastic sweat shirts. Don't overdo. Wear running shoes.
Walking	All ages.	Good all-around exercise for maintenance of heart & lung capacity & muscle tone. Excellent as a beginning exercise. Promotes weight control.	Very brisk pace (1 mile in 10–12 minutes) needed to have conditioning effect on heart.

will shift towards sports in which people can participate throughout their adult life."

So here we are walking again. Getting reacquainted with our first really good habit.

Walking is more than a sport, more than an exercise. It's a way of life for males and females of all ages. We were born to walk. Man is the only primate who stands erect and walks. Walking is both our achievement and our heritage. But let's not forget that it's also great fun.

CHAPTER

2

THE WORLD BELONGS TO WALKERS

" 'Tis the best of humanity that comes out to walk."

—RALPH WALDO EMERSON

AND WHAT A BIG, WIDE, WONDERFUL WORLD IT IS. WITH NO BOUNDARIES because no terrain is off limits. You can walk through the world as though it were a village.

In the walker's world there is no tyranny of the calendar, no one season for walking. It's year-round pleasure, with each season offering its own special gifts. In winter when the whole earth is in repose and the air nips, a walk is just as magical as it is in summer; night walking with its catlike quality and moon radiance is as stimulating as a walk in the blank-eyed freshness of early morning.

America is a walker's paradise where, as Sir Francis Head, lieutenant governor of Canada a century ago, wrote, "The sky is bluer, the air is fresher, the cold is intenser, the moon looks larger, the stars are brighter, the thunder is louder, the lightning is vivider, the wind is stronger, the rain is heavier, the mountains are higher, the rivers longer, the forests bigger, the plains broader." Add to that one more compelling fact: Every city in America still leads out into wide open spaces. The variety of experience open to the walker is limitless . . .

WALKING À LA CARTE

City. You can know a city only by walking it. And no two cities are the same. Even the same city seen at different times of day looks different as the sun rises or sets. So I can never understand people's willingness to go belowground and ride a crowded subway, or stand on a corner and wait for a bus or taxi, when they can simply take off and under their own power get to wherever they want to go.

The first thing I do when I arrive in a city is to check in at my hotel and then take to the street and walk. To get to know the city if it's my

26

first time there, or to reacquaint myself with it if I've been there before. Every city has its own very personal rhythm composed of its traffic noises and the sounds of its people on its streets. Seen from a car, a city is a blur. Walking is the only way to discover the life beat of a city.

"Walking around the city is a ritual with me," Charlie Chaplin once told Lillian Ross of *The New Yorker*. He was referring to New York at the time, but it could have been any city. He and his wife had just arrived there from Chicago, where she said he had got her to walk with him for four hours. Half her husband's age, she now chose to stay behind in their hotel while he and the writer went for a walk together. Out on the sidewalk, Chaplin took a deep breath and then off they went down Fifth Avenue at a brisk pace. "I like this kind of day for walking in the city," he said. "A sultry, Indian-summer September day. But do you know the best time for walking in the city? Two A.M. in the winter is best, with everything looking frosty. The tops of the automobiles. Shiny. All those colors." He said that sometimes when he had a whole day free, he walked the whole day. "I just go along and discover places."

I think Charlie Chaplin summed up the essence of successful walking anywhere when he said, "Every time I walk, I get a terrific exhilaration. Each new day is a day of promise." Thoreau, the prince of walkers, felt the same way. He considered every walk a sort of crusade. And writer Donald Culross Peattie believed, "To enjoy city walking to the utmost you have to throw yourself into a mood of loving humanity." What it boils down to, I think, is this: Cities are meant for walker-gawkers and people-watchers who combine their walking with the curiosity of the sightseer.

You, the walker, are free to walk and gawk all you want. Free to walk in and around a traffic snarl and be on your way while the drivers lean on their horns, crane their necks, and sputter with frustration. The driver is committed to the road. But you, the walker, have no commitment other than to cross on the green. Between crossings you are a totally free spirit. Look up occasionally, as you walk a city street, to the tops of the tallest buildings and beyond to the sky, and the buildings will seem to move back and the street grow wider.

Every city street has a story to tell if only you'll look for it. Some have their stories written on the faces of beloved and honored buildings—sometimes with an identifying plaque set in the stone or brick like a medallion, a coat of arms. Walk over and read it. You can; the driver of the car can't.

Some cities' stories have pages missing, often whole chapters, courtesy of the wrecker's ball, and you have to read between the lines. And that's when I suggest you take a walking tour and let a city-wise guide serve as your tutor. Happily, since we are starting at last to care almost as much about our cities' past as about their future, there is scarcely an American city of any size today where there isn't a museum, historical society, community group, or simply a clutch of dedicated walker-gawkers offering a walking tour. So no matter whether you're in a strange city or your native city, take a tour and learn what Charlie Chaplin meant when he said, "There are always parts of the city to explore. Always parts you haven't seen." And if you think you've seen them all, allow yourself the joy of seeing them again as though for the first time. That, you see, is one of the secrets of being a successful walker: to combine experience with the willingness to be surprised. T. S. Eliot, the poet, put it this way: "The end of all our exploring will be to arrive where we started, and know the place for the first time." And that you do best on foot.

Although I was born and raised in New York City, there is still much I have yet to discover about my city. Just as I am certain there's much you have yet to discover about yours. And when you've taken all the tours you think you want to take of your city, why not start creating your own tour? Perhaps something you saw on one of your guided tours piqued your curiosity. A trip to the library for some background material, and before you know it you're on your way to becoming your own guide, for one thing just naturally leads to another—rather like when you drop a pebble into a stream and rings form, larger and larger. The history of, say, the building you read about mentions another building in the area, and that story leads to another story about still another building, and soon, in your mind's eye, you begin to see a street—perhaps even a neighborhood— as it must have been a hundred years ago. It's then, when in your imagination the past links up with the present, that your personal walking tour starts to take shape. And I promise you that you'll experience the same sort of excitement discovering your city's roots—its family tree, so to speak— as the individual does who sets about tracing his own genealogy. No matter how much you love your city, you'll love it even more once you know more of its story.

That has been my experience, and a few years ago I wrote about it for *The New York Times*. "Buildings Nourish a Love Affair with the City," read the headline.

> Though I am devoted to New York, my affection for it has, like any romance, its ups and downs. But then, just when I begin to take my city for granted, I discover something surprising about it and I am enthralled all over again.

It happened recently during a stroll on Lexington Avenue. I spotted a plaque on an otherwise undistinguished building on Lexington Avenue between 28th and 29th Streets. Vice President Chester A. Arthur once lived here, it said, and it was here—on Sept. 21, 1881—that he took the oath of office upon the death of President James A. Garfield. And so President Arthur became the first Chief Executive since George Washington to be sworn into office in New York City.

What more appropriate time than now to recall the history of this and the other buildings that awakened my enthusiasm for the city and its past? Starting tomorrow, the city will be observing its 75th birthday—the birthday not of the founding of "New York," but of the great merger that created the city as we know it now. On Jan. 1, 1898, Brooklyn, Queens County and Staten Island merged into New York, giving the city its current boundaries.

It was to the New York Historical Society that I retreated to ferret out the history of the buildings that came to fascinate me—such buildings as the Arthur town house at 123 Lexington Avenue, the splendid set of millionaires' homes on Lafayette Street known as Colonnade Row and the remarkable old hotel where Abe Lincoln once stayed.

The historical society's microfilmed copies of *The New York Times* contain a vivid description of that historic morning in 1881 when the bells of St. Paul's Church tolled for nearly an hour as "the sorrowful intelligence was being sent with lightning speed throughout the country." Reporters collected outside Mr. Arthur's home at 123 Lexington Avenue, which was described as a row of plain brick dwellings with a veneer of brownstone.

"At 2:10 the light which had been burning in the library on the second floor was suddenly turned low," the account said, "and the gas in the front parlor was as suddenly lighted. The whole party repaired to the room and were joined by General Arthur's oldest son. At 2:15 o'clock Judge Bracy administered the oath which is prescribed in the Constitution."

The doorkeeper was asked if the general would give the press any information as to his probable movement. "I daren't ask him," was the reply. "He is sitting alone in his room sobbing like a child, with his head on his desk and his face buried in his hands. I dare not disturb him."

Not all Presidential happenirgs in the pre–Greater New York period were that dramatic. Downtown, on Lafayette Street, for example, President John Tyler had a quiet wedding breakfast one June day in 1844 with his 24-year-old bride, the former Julia Gardiner.

Originally, a group of nine Classic Greek Revival mansions along what is now Lafayette Street, they were called La Grange Terrace, after the country residence of General Lafayette. Some people called them "Geer's White Elephant," in recognition of the fact that their builder, Seth Geer, had chosen a site that was still considered open country when they were completed in 1838.

The area, then known as Lafayette Place, was enclosed by an iron fence, and the homes were unified by a superb colonnade of fluted Corinthian columns. Each home stood behind a 30-foot courtyard.

The stone for these buildings had been a subject of wide interest, for it had been quarried and hewn by Sing Sing convicts, and this had led to rioting by the city's stonecutters.

Geer's reputation as a shrewd builder was vindicated when John Jacob Astor, Stuyvesant Fish, Warren Delano, David Gardiner and other patricians of the period moved into the homes, which were considered to be among the finest in the city.

President Tyler was a widower and 30 years older than his bride, whose father had died only four months earlier as a result of an explosion aboard the steam frigate *Princeton*. Decorum dictated a simple wedding. The President made certain that his wedding plans were kept secret, so it was not until the next day that the country learned that it had a new first lady. The wedding took place at the Church of the Ascension, on Fifth Avenue at Tenth Street.

After a breakfast in the mansion of Lafayette Place, the couple boarded a ferry at the foot of Cortlandt Street and took a turn around the harbor, saluted by the guns of the fort on Governors Island and the warships *North Carolina* and, ironically, *Princeton*. By the eighteen-seventies, trade had moved uptown, and the fashionables of Lafayette Place left for mansions farther north. The Gardiner home joined with another to become a small, genteel hotel called The Oriental, and five others were turned into Colonnade Row. By 1912, only four of the nine were standing, and their iron railings and fancy stoop-like entrances had been cut away.

Today, these four buildings contain apartments, a restaurant and the Astor Place Theater. A commemorative plaque has been affixed to No. 432, from the balcony of which President Lincoln watched troops march off to the Civil War. In the vestibule is a notice from the present owner urging tenants, "For your own safety lock this door. Pull tightly." Next door, in the vestibule of No. 434, someone has scribbled on the wall, "Brenda Starr for President."

The Old Merchant's House at 29 East Fourth Street, practically around the corner from Colonnade Row, is another stunning example of Classic Greek Revival architecture, as well as a testament to the rugged individualism of Samuel Tredwell, the merchant who moved into it in 1835. At the time the area was so far from the center of the city that there were no bakeries for miles, which accounts for the kitchen's great wall oven. Probably the only house of the period retaining all of its original furnishings, it has been closed to visitors for months while repairs are made.

Mr. Tredwell died in 1865. He left a substantial fortune, but by the time his last child, Gertrude, passed away in 1933 at 93 her share had petered out, and the house had been heavily mortgaged. Then, the night before the house and its furnishings were to go on public auction, George Chapman, a distant Tredwell relative, bought them.

Mr. Chapman organized the Historic Landmark Society, which set up a small endowment fund to maintain the Old Merchant's House as a public museum.

In the same area, at Seventh Street and Fourth Avenue, is the Cooper Union Institute. It was designed, built and totally financed by philanthropist Peter Cooper, a New Yorker who began his business career as apprentice to a coachmaker for $25 a year and board. The school, the nation's first experiment in support of free education, opened in 1859, and Cooper, an old gentleman with a profusion of white hair, a white beard and green spectacles, visited it every morning, invariably carrying with him a rubber air cushion.

It was in the Great Hall of the institute on the evening of Feb. 27, 1860, that Congressman Abraham Lincoln delivered his famous "right makes might" speech. Perhaps more than anything else it contributed to his designation as a Presidential candidate.

He began speaking in a soft, high voice that drew howls of "Louder!" from the back of the hall. But by the time he concluded, according to a news account the next day, "three rousing cheers were given the orator and the sentiments to which he had given utterance."

That was Lincoln's first visit to New York City, and he chose to spend the night at the Girard House, a hotel that is still standing on the corner of Chambers Street and West Broadway. Now the Hotel Bond, it is the oldest hotel in the city, having opened in 1850.

As early as 1886, when the hotel was known as the Cosmopolitan, its ads gave a phone number (136 Murray), which was remarkable; in 1881, telephones were still such a rarity that word of President Garfield's death had to be delivered to Vice President Arthur by messenger. The Cosmopolitan, in fact, was the first hotel to install wall telephones in its guests' rooms, and Bernard Goldofsky, manager of the Bond since 1961, has kept one as a souvenir.

A native of Poland and a survivor of Auschwitz, Mr. Goldofsky is steeped in the history of his hotel and proudly escorts visitors to Room 100, "the room where Lincoln stayed." By today's standards, it is enormous with a 12-foot ceiling and four large windows with cheerful-looking paper curtains.

In the basement, which once housed the Cosmopolitan's barber shop (two fluted iron pillars are still intact, although the shop closed in the nineteen-twenties), Mr. Goldofsky shows off three ornate glass globes that once graced the ceiling of the hotel dining room.

Mr. Goldofsky, a short, eminently polite man, puffs with pride as he talks about the hotel. "We have people—very well off—who stay here a few nights each year for sentimental reasons," he says. "They stayed years ago, and they know the place."

The Siegel-Cooper Building, on the east side of the Avenue of the Americas extending from 18th to 19th Streets, is as well known as the Hotel Bond is little known. With land and building valued at $3 million, it warranted a page in *The New York Times* a full month before a department store opened its doors there in September, 1896. It would be, said the *Times*, "the largest and finest building ever erected in New York City for the retail trade."

The day Siegel-Cooper opened, 150,000 people turned up, and traffic was at a standstill. Drivers of horsecars got down from their platforms and led their horses through the crowd. "Even Fifth and Seventh Avenues had throngs bound for 'The Big Store,' " the *Times* reported, "and the streams of humanity choked the side streets leading to Sixth Avenue."

Yet once the shopper got inside, it must have seemed worth the effort. "Welcome" was spelled out in electric lights over the main aisle on the ground floor, where a 65-foot female figure symbolizing the Republic stood in the center of a vast fountain, an extravaganza that soon made "Meet me at the fountain" a New York byword. It was just what the owners had promised, "a magnificent temple of commerce." Furthermore, Siegel-Cooper gave trading stamps with every purchase.

In 1918, after Henry Siegel had encountered financial difficulties, the fixtures from the Siegel-Cooper store were sold at auction, and later that year the Army converted the building into a military hospital.

Businesses of various sizes now occupy the building. The Avenue of the Americas entrance has been sealed, and the main floor, with its columns and decorated ceiling intact, was until recently used by NBC to build and store TV stage sets. For the last 15 years the statue of the Republic has been standing majestically in Forest Lawn Memorial Park in Glendale, Calif.

While I was standing on the spot where the famous Siegel-Cooper fountain once splashed, an NBC employee mentioned that he liked to stand outside after lunch. Time and time again, people had stopped to chat about "The Big Store" and the building that housed it.

A retired vaudevillian had told him of the time in 1918 when he had played a benefit there for the disabled veterans, and of his shock when the lights came on and he stood looking out over an audience composed entirely of amputees. The young man looked pensive. When NBC moved to Brooklyn, he said, he would miss the old building.

Which is how it happens, you see. It just takes one glorious old building to do it to you. And you're hooked.

"The first turning to the left is the way of the heart. Take it at random and you are sure to find something pleasant and diverting. Take the left again and the piquancy may be repeated. But reason must come to the rescue, and you must turn to the right in order to save yourself from a mere uninteresting circle. To make a zigzag walk you take the first turning to the left, the first to the right, then the first to the left again, and so on."

—STEPHEN GRAHAM, *The Gentle Art of Tramping*

Graham wrote that back in 1926, but the idea is still sound. A walk, after all, should never be simply the locomotive act of getting from point A to point B. So when you have time, and especially when you're in an unfamiliar city, why not take Graham's zigzag walk and "let chance and the town take charge of you?" I did early one Saturday morning when visiting Los Angeles.

I started out in the vicinity of the famous Brown Derby restaurant on Wilshire Boulevard. I chose it at random, but it was extraordinarily appropriate considering that I was following the precepts of a book written in 1926, and this restaurant is, as a sign outside assures you, the *Original* Brown Derby and still under the original ownership of 1926. Following Graham's instructions, I headed up the street and at the corner turned left. In a few minutes, by following the left-right-left plan, I found myself in a pleasant residential neighborhood and outside the New Jerusalem Church ("The New Christianity . . . Eternity Forever"), where a rummage sale was in progress. In fact, though it had only just opened, there was a sizable crowd already inside poring over a collection of items that included everything from dishes and clothing to flashlights and small artificial Christmas trees. As I stood inspecting a pile of books tagged for sale, I struck up a conversation with a middle-aged Dutch couple from The Hague visiting the United States for the first time. They were charming people, and they told me that they were staying at a hotel despite the fact that their married daughter had a home nearby, because they suspected that if they were to stay in her home, she and her husband would insist on driving them every-

34

where and they much preferred to walk. "You see so much more that way," the woman said. The next stop on their American tour, her husband said, would be San Francisco, and then it was on to Oregon. The idea of seeing Christmas trees when the temperature outside was over eighty amused the woman, and as I left she was buying one of the smallest trees as a surprise gift for her granddaughter.

Outside, following Graham's master plan, I soon found myself in a Chicano area. In just a matter of blocks, I had entered another world of young mothers sweeping the sidewalks outside their homes while beautiful children clung to their skirts, and at the curb teen-aged youths stood poking around inside dilapidated cars with monkey wrenches. I moved on and passed a five-story hotel that looked as though it had been borrowed from a Hollywood movie set. The doors were wide open, and inside the gaunt tile-floored lobby sat an elderly man and, far at the other end, a young black woman, like a pair of murals painted on opposite walls with no relation one to the other.

Some more left and right turns and I was inside a coffee shop where a celebration was taking place. "Free Coffee for Everybody!" read the signs dangling from the light fixtures. A Korean family had just bought the shop and this was their grand opening. The father of the family explained to me that they had chosen a Saturday to be their first day because it wouldn't be as busy as a weekday and they would be less confused. His wife poured me a delicious cup of coffee, and then they introduced me to their two daughters, one of whom was married to a handsome young Korean in jeans who was working the cash register with considerable aplomb. I finished my coffee, wished them good luck, exited, and took the next left turn.

Again, in a matter of minutes, I was in yet another world, outside an elegant hotel situated opposite Lafayette Park. Two couples were standing on the sidewalk outside, surrounded by their luggage, waiting for a taxi. As I passed, one of the men asked if I would oblige them by taking their picture. He handed me an expensive camera, and then all four of them moved back from the curb to be sure to have a little of their hotel and its flowers in the background. I snapped the picture and moved on.

Another few turns and I was back on Wilshire Boulevard with its fine shops. It wasn't noon yet, but already there was an informal parade of the lovable eccentrics for which Los Angeles, like London, is known. An elderly, rotund woman, her white hair in pigtails and her bulk inside an elaborately decorated caftan, came padding along in her bare feet. Farther on a petite middle-aged woman in a black cocktail dress stood on the corner, her Kewpie-doll face all but hidden by an enormous salt-and-pepper wig extending about a foot on either side, as wide as the brim of a summer straw hat. And as I came within sight of the Brown Derby from where I set out on my zigzag walk and felt the noonday sun beginning to bake the top of my head, a distinguished-looking couple passed, he in a velvet-collared overcoat and she in an ankle-length antique mink, both looking implausibly cool and dry.

Now, while I certainly can't guarantee that every zigzag walk will offer the variety of a Los Angeles walk, I feel fairly secure in saying that Graham's principle has merit: *Let chance and the town take charge of you,* and you can't help but have an entertaining walk.

Beach. America's beaches are natural wonders, and walking them mustn't be limited to any one season. The difference between a summer beach and a winter beach is as vast as the difference between a night walk and an early-morning walk. And I think every serious walker should walk a beach in an off-season.

Walt Whitman used to stride the sands of New York's Coney Island in the winter, shouting his poetry to the winds. When you walk a winter beach, dress warmly . . . carry a thermos of hot soup . . . breathe in the crisp, tangy air . . . and study the wild patterns left in the sand by the wind.

One of the most beautiful beaches I've ever walked is along the Oregon coast between Florence and Coos Bay. Its majestic dunes—mountainous sculptures carved out of the white sand by the winter storms—are a Mecca for walkers. New York's Fire Island is a stunning white barrier beach thirty miles long, and somewhere around its narrow middle is a sunken forest nestling behind the dunes—an enchanted forest of pitch pines, ferns, beach plums, as well as holly trees, some growing as high as forty feet. And off the southwest coast of Florida is Sanibel Island, with a bird sanctuary, 4,700 acres of wildlife refuge, and sands so full of extravagantly beautiful seashells that it's rated one of the three best shelling beaches in the world.

River and canal towpath. My father was born and raised in a village in upper New York State where a river flows beside the main street like a guardian angel. The children can roam its banks just as my father once did, and imagine what it was like in the days when Indian canoes traversed its waters. And on the Fourth of July in the tiny park situated high above the river fireworks still explode while a band plays patriotic music. America's waterways are so much a part of our national heritage and personal history, in some instances, that a walk beside a river imparts a precious sense of continuity.

There are old canals across America whose towpaths have changed very little since the days of the mule-drawn barges and the elegant packet boats on whose flat roofs the passengers danced to fiddle music. The coming of the railroad, the "Iron Horse," made canal travel obsolete, but now citizen groups and government agencies have rediscovered our remaining canals, and their towpaths are once again being enjoyed by walkers.

I think the re-emergence of the canal towpath probably dates back to 1954, when there was a move on to convert a strip of the historic Chesapeake and Ohio Canal towpath into a scenic parkway. Supreme Court Justice William O. Douglas, a master walker, promptly challenged two editors of the *Washington Post*, who had championed the idea, to take a 185-mile walk along the towpath so that they might see for themselves that it was a stretch of country that was "a sanctuary for everyone who loves woods." They accepted, and what was soon known as "The Douglas Blister Brigade," a group of naturalists, newsmen, and the merely curious, set out from Washington, D.C., for an eight-day hike to Cumberland, Maryland. Justice Douglas made his point, and in the process also made Americans canal-conscious again.

Nature trail. Walking clubs of one kind or another are mushrooming all over America, and many of them publish notices in the local newspapers announcing Saturday and/or Sunday walks in the country. And rarely are these walks confined to club members only.

I was in Washington, D.C., last fall, feeling overworked and rather sorry for myself. And though I'm primarily a solitary city walker (few people I know share a writer's flexible schedule), I felt a real need to get out of the city and walk in open spaces with companions. The next day I was doing just that—walking along a nature trail with some members of the Potomac Appalachian Trail Club.

The walk, a five-mile hike through a portion of the Mason Neck National Wildlife Refuge across the border in Virginia, was described as follows:

Established to protect the habitat of the bald eagle in southeastern Fairfax County, this 2,800-acre refuge includes upland forest, a large marsh adjacent to the Potomac, and a few trails. Bring water. No reservations needed. Departure: 2 P.M. from Parking Lot No. 8 behind Dept. of Agriculture's North Building, on north side of Independence Ave. SW, 200 feet west of 12th St. Passengers pay driver $1.25.

I arrived early at the departure point, but there were already some fifteen people assembled there. It was a warm, sunny day and some of my fellow walkers were wearing shorts and hiking boots and looked dressed for vigorous walking, while others, like me, were more casually dressed, as though they'd been wondering what pleasant thing they might do on such a splendid day when, suddenly, they remembered reading that there was a hike scheduled. Despite the range of attire, I noticed that everyone was wearing sensible, comfortable-looking footwear.

By two o'clock the group had doubled in size and was gathered around Phil Stone, a bespectacled man with gray hair and a ready smile, who was to serve as leader. He wrote our names down on a pad and inquired of each of us in turn, "Do you need a ride?" A ride meant going in the car of another walker to the starting point across in Virginia, for which you paid the owner of the car $1.25. And that, it turned out, was the only fee involved in the day's outing.

I rode with a woman who introduced herself as Paula and who told me that she lived in Maryland, worked in Virginia, and devoted much of her spare time to the activities of the club in Washington. "Once you get the Potomac fever, it's hard to shake it," she said, laughing. Also sharing the ride was a small, deeply tanned Englishwoman wearing hiking boots and a shirt with sleeves rolled to the elbows, and a young married couple who had only just joined the club. In about twenty minutes we were in Virginia countryside, assembled around Phil once again, but this time we were at the starting point of our five-mile hike. "One of the joys of Washington is that you can get out into the countryside so fast," said Paula, leaning up against the back of her car as she changed into more suitable shoes.

Phil counted heads. There were thirty-one of us, of which only eight were club members. "It's a good crowd for a hot, sunny day, but then Phil's hikes are always popular," I heard someone say as we started the three-quarters of a mile through the woods to the trail head. We walked single file and Phil's wife was the rear guard, carrying a first-aid kit. In age we ranged from a twenty-year-old girl with backpack to an eighty-five-year-old named Charlie, an active club member since 1934. As we made our way into the comparative coolness of the woods, Phil called out, "If you have knowledge, particularly of plants, please share it." He said that he thought that today we'd probably see more plants than wildlife. The area where the bald eagle can be found was off limits for obvious reasons.

Phil carried a collection of cardboard arrows in his knapsack, and each arrow had the club's initials, PATC, painted on it. These he proceeded to drop on the trail whenever we came to a fork; on the way back his wife would reclaim them. That way, if anyone wandered away from the group, he or she wouldn't run the risk of getting lost. Meantime, an occasional car would drive down the dirt road we were walking, and each time it did, someone at the front or the back of the line would call out, "Car!" and we would all step to the side of the road. We hadn't been walking more than ten minutes, and already we were sharing a communal feeling.

At the trail head there was a sign reading, "National Wildlife Refuge." We paused for a moment, and Phil told us that the state of Virginia is currently buying more land "so there'll be lots of land and recreational opportunities in the years ahead." The trail we were about to walk, he said, was a new one—cleared only within the last couple of years. Since it was narrow, we would have to walk single file most of the way.

Early on we passed a great deal of holly growing along both sides of the trail, and Paula advised me that "this is about as far north as holly grows wild in this country." After we had walked about a half hour, the trail, which was mostly on flat land, took us up a gentle hill, where we stood for a moment. A woman's voice announced, "There's the river— that misty thing beyond." Several people produced binoculars, and then a girl from somewhere in the group cried, "There's a marsh hawk out there!" and the binoculars all turned in unison.

In a few minutes we resumed walking, and Paula said, "Let the runners go first, the ramblers next. I'm with the stragglers." The "runners" she referred to were some of the younger members of the group—college students, judging by the letters on their sweaters, who were walking rapidly. Paula, who, it turned out, has hiked in practically every state in the union, had obviously concluded a long time ago that a steady, comfortable pace is best.

We descended the other side of the hill and moved out onto a narrow wooden bridge extending across the marsh. Assorted walkers stopped midway to identify the plants they saw. Arrowheads. Wild rice ("that's the plumelike things"). Jewelweed. Red-centered mallow ("one of the hibiscus family"). We proceeded across the bridge and up a slight incline, where we saw some red leaves on the trees. The first vivid colors of fall. And then in a few minutes we crossed still another narrow wooden bridge, and this one started to sag in the middle. "Too many people," Phil explained as we gingerly made our way across to the other side.

Continuing single file along the trail, I overheard scraps of conversation. A young male voice confided to someone, "I enjoy sleeping out and listening to night sounds." Someone else, aware of the crackling sounds we made as we stepped on twigs and sticks, wondered aloud how the Indians were able to move so stealthily through the woods. A female voice replied, "They were tuned in to nature." It wasn't exactly clear to me what that meant, but it seemed to satisfy, perhaps because all of us were feeling so tuned in to nature ourselves at that moment.

As we passed beds of fern lining both sides of the trail, Phil suddenly shouted that a heron was flying by in the distance. Again the binoculars appeared, and the line in unison turned to follow the flight of the long-necked, large-winged bird.

We approached open land on the banks of a marsh. Phil went down to the water and pointed to a pickerelweed, an aquatic plant that he said produces a bright-blue flower in summertime. He fell silent, cocking his ear. "Hear the water moving?" And the girl who earlier had spied the marsh hawk said that there was a dam nearby.

We continued on and walked around a fallen white oak that was all but cut off at its base. One of the men identified it as the work of a beaver. Phil inspected the beaver cut and said, "They seem to know how to make it fall the way they want it to, but the tree was just too big for the beaver to do anything with it." He decided that it was an example of their instinct outwitting their common sense.

We had been walking steadily for one hour and fifteen minutes when we came to the halfway point. There was a small wooden pavilion there containing a giant map of the trail as well as some handsome full-color sketches of some of the birds to be found in the area. We rested for a few minutes, and Phil told us that he'd seen four deer on the road there last week at about ten in the morning. When we started walking back, I noticed that a few of the walkers had picked up long branches and were using them as walking sticks.

Halfway back to our starting point we stopped again, this time to allow those who had to relieve themselves to do so. The women remained where they were, while the men walked about a quarter of a mile ahead along the sun-dappled trail. I talked with Phil, who told me that he was seventy-one and retired. He looked at least a decade younger and appeared to be an unusually contented individual. He said he'd been a member of the Potomac Appalachian Trail Club since 1936, and that his love of walking began with family walks his parents used to take him on every Sunday the year round. Suddenly, we heard a female voice caroling through the tops of the trees, "Charcoal! Charcoal!" It was the women's way of announcing that they were moving toward us now, ready to resume the final stretch of trail.

At five-fifteen we were back at the roadside where our hike had begun. Phil opened the trunk of his car and produced a half-gallon jug of cold lemonade and paper cups, while his wife passed around a plate of home-made cookies.

On our ride back to Washington, Paula looked as refreshed as though she'd been away on a long, carefree weekend rather than merely a five-mile hike. When I told her so, she laughed and said that it was all mind over matter. "A walk like that . . . well, it replenishes me," she said. I looked at the Englishwoman and the young married couple, and they too looked relaxed and refreshed. There was, said Paula, another nice thing about walking with a group. "It's a true democracy. Nobody asks who you are. All that matters is who you are the day of the hike."

A few weeks later autumn arrived in full color and I was fortunate enough to be in New England. I checked with the Appalachian Club head-quarters on Joy Street in Boston, discovered that there was a Saturday-afternoon walk in the area of Walden Pond in nearby Concord—an easy half-hour ride from Boston—and I joined it. Here, too, you didn't have to be a member of the club. Simply show up . . . pay two dollars . . . and start walking.

We met in a school parking lot about one mile from Walden Pond, where over a hundred years ago young Henry David Thoreau retreated to a rustic cabin and immortalized the area with his writings.

There was a pleasant *déjà vu* quality about this second walk. Again, the ages of the walkers—twenty-three in all this time—ranged from the early twenties to a woman of eighty who wore hiking boots, carried a walking stick, and announced that she had been swimming—as she had every day since early summer—in Walden Pond. "Oh, it isn't so cold!" she replied to someone's question about the temperature of the water. She said that she hated swimming indoors. Our leader was Mark, a younger version of Phil Stone, and as we stood in a circle around him as he took our names on a pad, the conversation was easy and pleasant. Once again, this was a collection of kindred souls ready to enjoy a walk together. I had come by train from Boston and walked the mile from the station to the starting point here, and already three people, including Mark, had offered to drive me back to the railroad depot after we'd completed our walk. For the moment we were a family.

It was about another mile to Walden Pond, and again we walked single file, but in no way did this interfere with conversation. Some of the walkers apparently knew each other from previous walks, and others had arrived in pairs. Still, the solitary ones, like me, seemed to be instantly accepted. The joy of walking was our common bond. Approaching the pond, we walked over ground cushioned with a blanket of pine needles. "I feel as though I'm walking on feathers," a woman exclaimed from somewhere in the back of the line.

Standing alongside the western shore of the pond, Mark called our attention to the clarity of the water. The pond, he said, was 107 feet deep, just as Thoreau, who once measured it by dropping a plumb line through the ice one winter's day, said it was. We walked up and down some gentle and some not so gentle hills past hickory, maple, and white pine trees. A few of the walkers were naturalists, and at one point, stopping to inspect some wintergreen plants, one of them saw something rosy-red flowering about two inches above the ground, and they squatted to inspect it. Nobody was certain what it was, but one man suggested that it might be pinesap. When we moved on, everyone very carefully walked around this solitary sprig.

We stopped next by the shore of a stagnant bog, alongside a bush heavy with blueberries. A woman with a soft German accent said that in the month of June this area by the bog is always full of rose begonias. "They come out in the hundreds." A log lay in the water thick with fallen leaves, and most of the walkers took turns inching their way to its center, in order to get a closer look at the plants flowering on either side of it.

We proceeded up a steep hill, and to our right was a marsh with lily pads floating on its water, in which the reflections of nearby trees shimmered as though in a painting not yet dry.

Now the men and women separated according to custom, with the men walking ahead. This time, however, there was no announcement forthcoming from the women, and finally one of the men took a silver whistle out of his knapsack and blew on it. The women walked into view and we all resumed our hike.

We stopped just once more, this time on a cliff looking across the bay toward Lee's Cliff, which Thoreau often referred to in his writing. Some of the walkers stood in the shade of two huge white pines and studied a map of the area, while others sat on the ground, locked their arms around their knees, and gazed down at the bay, where a silver canoe stood on shore. One of the younger men came up to Mark with something in his hand. "Is this a coral mushroom?" he asked, and Mark said it was. "There's a good bit of it around," he explained. Then we all watched silently as two men and a girl in a pink blouse climbed into the canoe and paddled away on the diamond-splattered water.

Exactly three hours after we had begun our hike, we were back at the starting point, from where Mark drove me to the depot. Once again I had enjoyed with friendly strangers a classless, ageless nature walk. I still don't know much about plants and flowers, and probably never will. That doesn't matter. What did matter was that I had had a good walk in the fresh air, made pleasant contact with people with whom I felt a kinship . . . and now I was returning to the city feeling content, refreshed, and thoroughly satisfied with life. And that is no mean achievement.

> "But no weather interfered fatally with my walks, or rather my going abroad, for I frequently tramped eight or ten miles through the deepest snow . . ."
>
> —HENRY DAVID THOREAU, *Walden*

It was during my walk in and around the Walden Pond area that I learned of another walk created by a young woman, a naturalist employed by the Commonwealth of Massachusetts at the Walden Pond State Reservation. Her name is Dorothy Zug, and on Sunday afternoons she conducts what she calls "Thoreau Rambles," guiding walkers to the site of his house through the woods and around the pond, stopping to read from his works and that way fill in the now empty land with the spirit of the man who once lived there. Her group has on occasion comprised but herself and one walker. But most often she leads a group of about eight, and once she walked with seventy-five Harvard freshmen who were touring the Concord area during their orientation week.

Dorothy Zug advertised her first walk in the local newspapers and by posting notices at local historic spots, and scheduled it for July 4—133 years from the day Thoreau moved into his house in the woods. Now, in less than a year, her "Thoreau Rambles"—free of charge—are well known and attract people of all ages, many of them foreign visitors.

"When I woke up on July fourth and heard rain on the roof," she told me, "I was relieved . . . glad of another day to work on the walk. I spent the morning in my office at the pond, sure no one would appear to walk in the rain. When I returned after a late lunch, I was surprised to find a group waiting for me. A man dressed in shorts and a raincoat introduced himself as Walter Harding and explained that he was there with five of his students. I had heard about him and knew that he's a foremost Thoreauvian expert who each year conducts a series of week-long seminars in Concord. He and his students, of course, knew of the July fourth historical significance and were all prepared for a walk in the rain. I said to him, 'I don't know what I can tell your students that you haven't already covered,' and he said, 'You planned your walk; you must do what you had in mind.' So I began. One of them held the umbrella over my head to keep the books dry while I read, and we had a wonderful two hours together. That day I learned—though I never really doubted it—that there is something sig-

44

nificant about hearing Thoreau's words right here at the pond. As we walked that rainy afternoon, Walter added depth and insight, showing me where the Bean-Field was, finding the one dead tree still standing of the four hundred white pines Thoreau planted after he left the pond."

Of course, Dorothy Zug has incorporated it all in her walk, which, by the way, is never exactly the same each time. For example, the average walk lasts one and a half hours, although some have gone on for two and a half hours, what with the walkers requesting her to read their favorite passages, or a group discussion growing out of a passage some felt especially provocative. As she explains it, "Each walk is a unique experience and depends on the people, their needs, and their interests. I start the walks by having everyone introduce himself, adding where they're from and what their interest is in Thoreau. I make my position clear, stating that I'm a naturalist and view Thoreau from that viewpoint. I give some historical background, and then we're off. Our first stop gives an overview of the pond, and I tell the geological background, explaining that it is a kettle hole. Furthermore, it's spring fed, has no inlets or outlets, is 61 acres, 1.7 miles around, and 107 feet deep."

Now, imagine yourself there looking out over the pond with its crystal-clear water, surrounded by gentle hills and great trees of hickory and pine. And just ahead of you is Dorothy Zug, a tall, slender, sandy-haired young woman, with one thick book in one hand, and reading aloud from the open book in the other hand.

> I went to the woods because I wished to live deliberately, to front only the essential facts of life, and see if I could not learn what it had to teach me, and not, when I came to die, discover that I had not lived. I did not wish to live what was not life, living is so dear; nor did I wish to practise resignation, unless it was quite necessary. I wanted to live deep and suck out all the marrow of life, to live so sturdily and Spartan-like as to rout all that was not life, to cut a broad swath and shave close, to drive life into a corner, and reduce it to its lowest terms, and, if it proved to be mean, why then to get the whole and genuine meanness of it, and publish its meanness to the world; or if it were sublime, to know it by experience, and be able to give a true account of it in my next excursion. . . .

She pauses, and standing there you wonder how many times Thoreau stood on that very spot and drank in the serenity of that view. She begins to walk again . . .

> Our life is frittered away by detail. An honest man has hardly need

to count more than his ten fingers, or in extreme cases he may add his ten toes, and lump the rest. Simplicity, simplicity, simplicity! I say, let your affairs be as two or three, and not a hundred or a thousand; instead of a million count half a dozen, and keep your accounts on your thumb nail. . . .

When she stops again, you're suddenly aware of the fact that there are, incredibly, railroad tracks nearby. You can't see them, but now as she reads again you actually hear a train in the distance, and the sound intensifies, although, as if out of respect for the place and the moment, it never really splits the air but simply hurries by as she reads.

"The whistle of the locomotive penetrates my woods summer and winter, sounding like the scream of a hawk sailing over some farmer's yard. . . ."

That wasn't the only sound Thoreau heard, of course. "Late in the evening I heard the distant rumbling of wagons over bridges—a sound heard farther than almost any other at night—the baying of dogs, and sometimes again the lowing of some disconsolate cow in a distant barn-yard. In the mean while all the shore rang with the trump of bullfrogs . . ."

She walks closer to the pond and then turns off it to Wyman's Meadow, and manages meanwhile to go from one book to the other. Here in June, she says, the water lilies are in full flower . . .

Found two lilies open in a very shallow inlet of the meadow. Exquisitely beautiful, and unlike anything else that we have, is the first white lily just expanded in some shallow lagoon where the water is leaving it—perfectly fresh and pure, before the insects have discovered it. How admirable its purity! How innocently sweet its fragrance! How significant that the rich, black mud of our dead stream produces the water-lily—out of that fertile slime springs this spotless purity! It is remarkable that those flowers which are emblematical of purity should grow in the mud.

Now here is where Thoreau built his cabin. You're standing on its site as she reads:

I had already bought the shanty of James Collins, an Irishman who worked on the Fitchburg Railroad, for boards. . . .

I took down this dwelling the same morning, drawing the nails, and removed it to the pond side by small cartloads, spreading the boards on the grass there to bleach and warp back again in the sun. . . .

I dug my cellar in the side of a hill sloping to the south, where a woodchuck had formerly dug his burrow, down through sumach and blackberry roots, and the lowest stain of vegetation, six feet square by seven deep, to a fine sand where potatoes would not freeze in any winter. The sides were left shelving, and not stoned; but the sun having never shone on them, the sand still keeps its place. It was but two hours' work. . . .

I began to occupy my house on the 4th of July, as soon as it was boarded and roofed, for the boards were carefully feather-edged and lapped, so that it was perfectly impervious to rain; but before boarding I laid the foundation of a chimney at one end, bringing two cartloads of stones up the hill from the pond in my arms. I built the chimney after my hoeing in the fall, before a fire became necessary for warmth, doing my cooking in the mean while out of doors on the ground, early in the morning . . .

Before winter I built a chimney, and shingled the sides of my house, which were already impervious to rain, with imperfect and sappy shingles made of the first slice of the log, whose edges I was obliged to straighten with a plane.

I have thus a tight shingled and plastered house, ten feet wide by fifteen long, and eight-feet posts, with a garret and a closet, a large window on each side, two trap doors, one door at the end, and a brick fireplace opposite. The exact cost of my house, paying the usual price for such materials as I used, but not counting the work, all of which was done by myself, was as follows; and I give the details because very few are able to tell exactly what their houses cost . . .

And she reads the list, noting that Thoreau even included one cent for chalk and fourteen cents for hinges and screws. In all, his house cost him $28.12½.

"I intend to build me a house which will surpass any on the main street in Concord in grandeur and luxury, as soon as it pleases me as much and will cost me no more than my present one."

As for furnishings . . .

I had three chairs in my house; one for solitude, two for friendship, three for society. When visitors came in larger and unexpected numbers there was but the third chair for them all, but they generally economized the room by standing up. It is surprising how many great men and women a small house will contain. I have had twenty-five or thirty souls, with their bodies, at once under my roof, and yet we often parted without being aware that we had come very near to one another. . . .

But once the house was built, what was his life really like? For a moment turn your back on the people with you . . . face the opposite direction . . . and imagine you are living there alone.

After hoeing, or perhaps reading and writing, in the forenoon, I usually bathed again in the pond, swimming across one of its coves for a stint, and washed the dust of labor from my person, or smoothed out the last wrinkle which study had made, and for the afternoon was absolutely free.

Perhaps the sound of the railroad was comforting—a welcome link to the world outside. He made it seem so when he wrote:

The Fitchburg Railroad touches the pond about a hundred rods south of where I dwell. I usually go to the village along its causeway, and am, as it were, related to society by this link. The men on the freight trains, who go over the whole length of the road, bow to me as to an old acquaintance, they pass me so often, and apparently they take me for an employee; and so I am. I too would fain be a track-repairer somewhere in the orbit of the earth.

Dorothy Zug walks to where the Bean-Field once flourished, and reads:

Meanwhile my beans, the length of whose rows, added together, was seven miles already planted, were impatient to be hoed, for the earliest had grown considerably before the latest were in the ground; indeed they were not easily to be put off. . . .
My enemies are worms, cool days, and most of all woodchucks. The last have nibbled for me a quarter of an acre clean.

All right, you're seeing it all on a sunny autumn afternoon. But what about winter?

At length the winter set in in good earnest, just as I had finished plastering, and the wind began to howl around the house as if it had not had permission to do so till then. Night after night the geese came lumbering in in the dark with a clangor and a whistling of wings, even after the ground was covered with snow, some to alight in Walden, and some flying low over the woods toward Fair Haven, bound for Mexico.
At this season I seldom had a visitor. When the snow lay deepest no wanderer ventured near my house for a week or fortnight at a time, but there I lived sung as a meadow mouse . . .
But no weather interfered fatally with my walks, or rather my going

abroad, for I frequently tramped eight or ten miles through the deepest
snow to keep an appointment with a beech tree, or a yellow-birch, or
an old acquaintance among the pines . . .

Two young Japanese with the inevitable cameras slung over their shoulders announce to the group that in their country the young understand
and honor Thoreau's philosophy, and then one of them asks if Dorothy
Zug will read how Thoreau one winter's day measured the depth of the
pond. She obliges, starting with "I fathomed it easily with a cod-line and
a stone weighing about a pound and a half, and could tell accurately when
the stone left the bottom . . ." When she finishes reading, he and his
friend grin and applaud politely.

The walk is almost over. And Dorothy Zug collects all the loose pieces
and presents them to you as a sort of gift, facing you, standing with her
back to the pond:

> I left the woods for as good a reason as I went there. Perhaps it
> seemed to me that I had several more lives to live, and could not spare
> any more time for that one.
>
> I learned this, at least, by my experiment; that if one advances con-
> fidently in the direction of his dreams, and endeavors to live the life
> which he has imagined, he will meet with a success unexpected in com-
> mon hours. . . .
>
> I would not have any one adopt *my* mode of living on any account;
> for, beside that before he has fairly learned it I may have found out
> another for myself, I desire that there may be as many different persons
> in the world as possible; but I would have each one be very careful to
> find out and pursue *his own* way, and not his father's or his mother's or
> his neighbor's instead.

Then she closes the book and recites the last from memory:
"In the long run men hit only what they aim at. Therefore, though they
should fail immediately, they had better aim at something high."

I would say that that applies to what Dorothy Zug has aimed to do and
succeeded in doing with her "Thoreau Rambles." And it's not farfetched
to believe that you and I could do something similar if only for our own
enjoyment—something combining a walk with something else that gives
us pleasure. All it requires is your own two feet and a little imagination.
Meantime, and very fortunately, there are people like Dorothy Zug all
across this country of ours who will let us share what they have created.

CHAPTER

3

WALKING: THE COMPANIONABLE SPORT

"No matter how often I run the roads myself,
I am struck by how solitary my fellow runner
appears."

—Dr. George Sheehan, *Physician
and Sports Medicine,* November 1976

DR. SHEEHAN FURTHER EXPLORES THE SOLITARY CONDITION OF THE JOG-ger in his excellent book *Dr. Sheehan on Running*. "The runner is nobody's fellow man, and his fellow men know it. There is a metaphysical lawless-ness about running."

As he sees it, the runner or jogger "cares for little but the workings of his own mind and body," and "this calls for constant attention—attention to breathing, to arm movement, to the rhythm of the thighs, to the accelera-tion of the straightened leg. These details must continually occupy him, for only through this unnatural awareness can he attain the classical yet instinctual form of the champion." In response to the question *How will I know if running is my exercise?* he answers, "If you are a loner, have few friends, and have been described as a dreamer, you can go out and buy your shoes right now."

I know whenever I see a pair of joggers in action, I'm aware of their inherent separateness. It's rather like the so-called *parallel play* of very small children, who sit side by side but rarely interact with each other while playing. What they're doing for their enjoyment demands, at their tender age, all their powers of concentration. They have nothing to spare for the give-and-take of companionship.

Running is like that; it locks you inside yourself. Walking, on the other hand, releases you, stimulating your mind and giving wings to your imagi-nation. And what's more, Dr. Sheehan agrees. "Walkers," he notes, "have been the philosophers, the thinkers, the artists of their age." He sees the walker as an individual for whom "observation and thought dominate," and "if this suggests that walkers are mature men with a capacity for observa-tion, men with empathy for their environment, it is because it always has been so."

"The walker," he concedes, "has found the peace that the runner still seeks."

Small wonder. Walking is so natural an exercise it exerts no pressure, physically or mentally. There's no physical pain, no do-or-die discipline involved. You can walk to think—or walk *not* to think. You can walk alone—or walk with someone you enjoy. And if you choose to walk with someone, you can walk and talk . . . or walk together in happy silence, letting your closeness, the perfect rhythm of the walk you're sharing, speak for the two of you. You may hold hands or link arms, but whether you touch or not isn't all that important, either.

Hal Borland, essayist and naturalist, once wrote, "All walking is discovery." And walking with someone you like is one of the surest ways to get to know that person better and to discover still more reasons to like him even more. Sharing a walk is, I think, tantamount to sharing food; it's that basic and pure.

WALKING AS A SIGN OF LOVE

Since the beginning of time, walking has been an integral part of courtship. An "automobilized" America made that custom obsolete, but it's still very much alive in certain Mediterranean countries, and I think the people there are much the happier for it. And once they marry, the Sunday family walk—once an American tradition, too—is shared with their children.

You can tell a lot about a couple's relationship by the way they walk together. Sometimes they're not really together at all. One or the other is out front, while the other lags behind—often purposely. Sometimes even when side by side they may not really be walking as a couple. Again there is a similarity to the parallel play of the preschool child.

From my childhood, I remember a couple who walked together every Sunday, rain or shine. His name was Adam, and it fitted him. He was very tall and hearty. His wife, Jo, was barely five feet tall and prettily plump. And each Sunday they walked across Brooklyn Bridge into Manhattan and for several miles more before turning around and heading for home. And I remember marveling at how they managed to walk along so blissfully despite the great difference in size. He never seemed to be holding back, and she never seemed to be racing. They simply fell into step, maintaining an easy, effortless rhythm which I think now was symbolic of their happy life together.

I wish I had tender memories of family walks, but I don't, and I know I'm the poorer for it. My parents must have walked together at some time in their married life, but I can't remember when. They were unhappy together and often lived apart. My father was a silent man and not an easy person for even a son to know well. But I do remember that he and I sometimes took walks together, and on those occasions conversation or the lack of it didn't seem to matter much. We walked well together; despite the disparity in size, the nine-year-old boy easily kept pace with the tall man. I remember we would walk to a very small waterfall set somewhere in the park, and while I stepped across it, stone by stone, my father would sit and watch me. Two years later he vanished from my life, and four years after that we learned that he was dead. I will always be grateful for my memories of those father-and-son Saturday-afternoon walks.

I also remember walking with my grandfather, my father's father, who was a very vigorous, decent man who lived with his wife in a small town in upper New York State in a house on the banks of the Susquehanna River, where, during a summer visit, I would fish for carp from the back porch. I don't believe my grandfather ever got to know his only son very well either, but he and I were good friends despite the fact that we saw each other only during the summer months. My grandparents did not own an automobile—never did—and my grandfather was a great walker. On Sundays he would walk to his office just to check that everything was in order for the next day, and sometimes I would go with him and again I was able to keep pace. He was lean and erect, and as we walked down the streets of his town, everyone seemed to know and respect him. For a boy raised in the relative anonymity of a big city, the quality of life in a small town was especially warming, and that, too, I enjoy remembering from my walks with my grandfather.

Some years ago—twenty-three to be exact—I wrote a magazine article titled "What Makes a Child Happy?" The answer: A demonstration of affection. I wrote, "Any adult has what it takes to make a child a happy, contented little person—a pair of arms to hold him, lips to kiss him, and a hand to let him lose his own in." I had just returned from a trip to Mexico, where I had marveled at the children's serenity, their sense of well-being, their more or less perfect state of happiness. A poor country, Mexico nevertheless seemed to be a land of happy children. There were comparatively few automobiles and families walked, not only through necessity but even at times when they could have stayed at home and sat. But the parents chose to walk, with both hands full of little hands. And I noticed, too, that the big brother or sister almost always treated the smaller children with the same gentleness that they received from their parents.

"One of the loveliest sights I saw was on the Reforma in Mexico City," I wrote. "I watched a boy of perhaps seven walking with two little sisters, each clutching one of his hands. The boy was freshly scrubbed and brushed, and each little girl wore a shawl over her head. Their expression of happiness and utter satisfaction with the world as they traveled through it, hand in hand, was beautiful to see."

A few weeks after my article appeared in print, I received the following letter printed by hand:

Dear Mr. Gale,

I have just finished your article "What Makes a Child Happy?" I would like to thank you and show you the effect it had on my life.

My husband is twenty and I am twenty-one. We have a daughter three and a half and another due any time. I began to notice my daughter seemed to become too hard for us to handle more so than the average three-year-old.

Neither my husband nor I are quick to show any affection or love, this fault among others, such as impatience with our daughter started me wondering how to show our baby we loved her.

I began to listen to what she had to say and hug and kiss her, not the occasional peck on the cheek but a real honest hug and kiss. And I began to go walking with her. (Before that I had kept her in the yard most of the time.) She loved the walking so much that before long she would come to me and take me by the hand and lead me to the door.

The more affection, the more walking together we did, the more agreeable she became. She improved in her eating habits and came down to normal on whining. I am able to reason with her as far as reasoning will go with a three-year-old.

The point of all this is that I didn't know why this improvement came over my child until I read your article. I hope some day my husband will understand too.

Of course we still have a lot to learn. Our mistakes are plenty but your article has given us a big push in the right direction. Thank you very much.

That letter had been forwarded to me by the magazine along with this note from the editor: "If I were in your boots, I'd sure prize this letter. Anyhow, I got a thrill out of it."

And so did I. I have kept that letter and I sometimes wonder about that family. The three-year-old is now a young adult and perhaps a parent. I hope that she is demonstrative with her child and is taking it by the hand for long walks.

"Children divine those who love them; it is a
gift of nature which we lose as we grow up."

—PAUL DE KOCH

A friend of mine, a widow, was well past middle age when she decided
that she wanted to know the pleasure again of raising a small child. She
had been living abroad for years; her only son was married and living here
in America with his wife and family. My friend had plenty of money, and
in the years following World War II there were plenty of homeless children. Still, it wasn't easy for a foreigner—and particularly for a woman—
to adopt. By the time she had applied to the Madrinato Committee of the
Italian Red Cross for help in cutting the yards of red tape involved, she'd
decided that there was no way that she could ever enter an orphanage and
come out with only one child. And so she decided to build her own orphanage in the garden of her home in Assisi. She thought in terms of
twelve boys, and hiring a director to supervise the running of the orphanage. When she couldn't find a director willing to live so far from
Rome, she abandoned the idea and simply took on the care of three little
boys, the eldest of whom was five years old.

When the boys first came to live with her, they were petrified, and if
someone dropped anything they would tremble, thinking it was a bomb.
The eldest, an aggressive little fellow, kept his distance. He had very little
to say, and the more the other two boys adjusted to their new surroundings,
the more he withdrew, seeming to regard them as turncoats. After all, what
was this strange place? And who was this gray-haired old lady who spoke
Italian with the funny accent?

My friend didn't push, but when occasion offered, smiled encouragingly
across the abyss that separated them. Little by little she moved closer, often
extending her hand, which the boy steadfastly refused to take. Finally
my friend, who was a great walker, decided it was time to add something
more tangible to this approach. So each morning as she set out for her
walk down the hill to the ancient town of Assisi, she would come to him
and smile and offer her hand. Although he kept on refusing to take it,
she noticed that each morning as she walked to the gate his eyes followed
her. And then came the day when he took her hand and they actually
walked into town together. She later told me that he didn't speak even
once during that walk, and all she heard from him was a rumble coming

from somewhere inside him; he still didn't take to the idea of giving in to this strange new life after the memory of a life spent with other boys like him who didn't expect favors and slept huddled together like a litter of pups. But the following day he took her hand again. And as they walked into town together, she kept up a running commentary about the trees and flowers they were passing, and the cloudless sky overhead. By the fourth day he was asking questions and making an occasional comment. On the fifth day he slipped his hand out of hers, ran into a field alongside the road, and came back with a poppy he had picked for her. That afternoon at luncheon he dipped his hand into a bowl of fresh fruit, draped a cherry over each ear, and, with a grin, announced to her and his two "brothers," "I think I'll stay."

WALKING WITH A DOG

I've never cared for the expression "walking the dog." You don't walk a dog any more than you walk a child, that other very delightful walking companion. You walk *with* a dog. There's a difference.

In his book *A Walk Across America*, young Peter Jenkins refers at various times to Cooper, his dog, who started out with him on his walk across the continent, as "my best friend" . . . "my forever friend" . . . "my irresistible friend" . . . "that smart dog friend of mine" . . . and "my best pal." Again and again, the reader feels the special affection Jenkins had for his dog companion.

"Seeing him there in the pure forest, I couldn't help but think how fantastically beautiful he was. His glowing coat of creams and browns melted in with the other colors, and yet they made him stand out like a vibrant star in the night. To me, my forever friend was more real, truthful, and ultimate than anything . . ."

And "What memories! With all the many adventures and moments we shared on the walk, it was obvious why Cooper and I were such great friends. He loved me and I loved him and that love grew with every experience we shared. As I daydreamed about the years of fun and excitement ahead for us, I silently brushed Cooper."

And I thought of Cooper—"ninety-five pounds strong"—when I sat in the Southern California home of Siegfried and Susan Othmer, whose handsome Siberian husky, Sitka, though half asleep in a corner, nevertheless seemed to dominate the room. "Of course Sitka walks with me," Susan replied in answer to my question. Sitka walked with her in the suburban area of their ranch-style home, and walked with her and Siegfried and their two small sons on weekends when they went up into the Santa Monica mountains. "A dog is an appropriate companion when you're walking," she said, "especially in the mountains, where we can let her off the leash. That, I think, is a dog's natural environment. Sitka always looks at us like, 'Hah, now you've come out in my element!' She's just so happy sniffing around. It's as though she was saying, 'You've come to live with me now.' "

I had a dog all through childhood. My favorite of them all was Laddie, a toy Boston bull. We got him as a pup, not knowing that he was a miniature. And while I at age ten was growing at what seemed like the rate of an inch a week, Laddie at one year seemed scarcely any bigger than when we got him from the kennel at six weeks. We must have presented an amusing sight, the two of us, as we walked together: the tall, stringy boy and the adorable runt of a dog. And yet despite the difference in size, we walked well together. I was never aware of holding back, and Laddie never seemed to be straining to keep up. Perhaps his four legs did compensate, although I prefer to think that, like any tall-short couple who are compatible, my dog and I walked well together because we were so fond of each other.

Dogs, like small children, seem to know when a walk is an act of love and not simply the acting out of an obligation. And if the walk is in open spaces and the dog can be free of a leash, then I notice, as Susan Othmer pointed out, that the dog assumes the role not only of companion but of protector as well. Walking in the hills that rise above the river in New York's Hudson Valley with my friend Steve Kanfer and his dog, a Dalmatian named Becky, I noticed this change in Becky's attitude. It was as though roles had been reversed now that we were out of the house and walking through an open field. Although Steve seemed to know just about every square foot of the countryside for miles around, he—and I, too, by virtue of association with her master—were now the particular concern of Becky, who would run ahead and then, on the crest of a hill, stop and turn around and check on our progress. Then, once convinced that we were safe and proceeding according to plan, Becky would run on. On the way back, the nearer we came to Steve's home, the more Becky's protective instinct subsided, until at the door she was once again the caring companion who has learned to adjust to the loving demands of a warm, though still basically alien society.

I wish that every child could know the joy of walking with a dog. A good dog has natural dignity that is never so much in evidence as when he's walking free in open country. We adults see this, but a child *senses* it and responds in the same way he or she responds to the majesty of a great tree. The child and the animal are both pure spirits, and they respond one to the other in a way that our adulthood makes impossible. I envy them their unique kinship, and I work every opportunity I can to be a silent partner to their coupling.

Some years ago, I was a volunteer worker in a halfway house for boys coming out of a reform school in upstate New York. I helped them with their schoolwork and listened to their gripes, but I think the very best thing I did during those years was to take some of the boys walking with a dog.

The headmaster of the halfway house had bought a bird, a finch named Petey, that the boys liked to take turns holding. It never failed to impress me how extraordinarily gentle they were with the bird. Often a lad who had been fuming with rage and frustration only an hour earlier would sit on his cot with Petey in his hand, stroking the bird's head and wings with his finger. It was a kind of therapy, this soothing act of holding and touching a creature this small, soft, and vulnerable.

Weekends the boys were permitted to go home to visit their families, with whom they would eventually be reunited; that is, the boys who had families. Two of them didn't and were waiting to be placed in foster homes. On Saturdays and Sundays they were the only children in the house. When I learned of that situation, I got permission to take them to the country with me to visit a friend and his family of two small children and a collie named David. That first weekend we must have walked at least ten miles—the four children, David, and I—and I can still see the immense joy on the boys' faces when David would race after a stick one of them had thrown and bring it back and drop it at his feet; their wonderment at the gentleness he showed toward the smaller of my friend's two children, chasing after her as she wanted him to, but taking very special care not to catch up with her and run the risk of toppling her over. I know for certain that the two boys learned some very valuable lessons from walking with a good dog.

Novelist Thomas Mann had a dog called Bashan, a short-haired setter he had bought from the owner of a tavern in a Bavarian village. When he first saw the dog, it was "trembling . . . tied to a kitchen table-leg with a frazzled rope." But soon Bashan was Mann's favorite walking companion.

Standing on the steps which lead down from my front door, I give a whistle . . .

He stands and stares, listening intently to the tone of my voice. He finds that this tone is full of accents which decidedly approve of his existence, something which I am at pains to emphasize in my speech. . . .

Bashan is jumping because he actually knows that I take pleasure in his jumping. Often by means of calls and knockings upon the fence, have I encouraged him in it and praised him when he had fulfilled my wishes.

A good dog makes walking all the more companionable, all the more enjoyable—bringing out in us the part of us that is still innocent and simplehearted enough to enjoy a walk to its fullest. As John Burroughs wrote some hundred years ago, "The dog enters thoroughly into the spirit of the enterprise; he is not indifferent or preoccupied; he is constantly sniffing adventure, laps at every spring, looks upon every field and wood as a new world to be explored, is ever on some fresh trail, knows something important will happen a little farther on."

And that, I think, is the spirit we should have each time we go out for a walk, whether alone or with a companion. Every walk is a potential adventure.

CHAPTER

4

WALKING AS TRANQUILIZER,
ANTI-DEPRESSANT, STIMULANT

"A vigorous five-mile walk will do more good
for an unhappy but otherwise healthy adult
than all the medicine and psychology in the
world."

—DR. PAUL DUDLEY WHITE, cardiologist

WALKERS ARE USUALLY MORE STABLE EMOTIONALLY, MORE SELF-CON-
fident, and less anxiety prone than non-walkers. It just seems impossible
to walk briskly and brood at the same time. And while we can't literally
walk away our worries, we can often walk them off and return home with
a feeling of buoyancy and relief.

Supreme Court Justice William O. Douglas has maintained, "The subconscious carries a heavy burden of our worries, concerns, and problems.
On a long hike it functions free of additional tensions and pressures. The
mind is lost in a world far from office or professional routine. As a result,
magical things happen. The process is a mystery, though I have experienced it again and again."

Douglas speaks of a long hike in the wilderness, but I've known people
to take a relatively short walk on city streets and have the same "magical
things" happen to them, too.

How does a sense of emotional well-being come from such a simple
physical exercise? According to Dr. Edward Greenwood of the Men-
ninger Clinic in Topeka, Kansas, "The physical stimulation induces an
intellectual stimulation through the central nervous system. The ego is
strengthened, accompanied by a greater feeling of self-confidence, stability,
and calmness."

To be fit is to be happy. There is a definite correlation between physical
fitness and emotional well-being. And regular vigorous walking is nature's
antidote for stress and strain.

It's certainly not a new idea. The ancient Greek physicians, one of
whom was Hippocrates, believed long walks were a good tonic for healthy
living. The Greek ideal was a sound mind in a sound body, and the
philosopher José Ortega y Gasset wrote, "The body is the tutor and
policeman of the spirit."

Dr. John Prutting, a New York internist, substitutes *mind* for *spirit*.

62

He says, "I am always amazed how often persons who are depressed walk without having been told to. The body is driven to it. If you let it, your body will dictate what's best for you. And I feel that for stress . . . for the control of the emotions . . . there is no exercise better than walking."

Dr. Herbert A. de Vries of the Gerontology Center of the University of Southern California finds that a vigorous fifteen-minute walk reduces neuromuscular tension more effectively than 400 milligrams of a tranquilizer.

What's so special about walking that it can work such wonders for the psyche? What makes walking so therapeutic?

I think it's because a vigorous walk is such a comfortable coupling of rhythmic motion *and* aggressive action. There's nothing passive about the act of walking. It's active, positive, and the feel of one's feet hitting the ground as the miles glide by gives a sense of power. Walking is the safest, most effortless way to get rid of anger and anxiety that I know of. Any aerobic exercise is superior in this regard to the stop-and-go sports of, say, golf and tennis (and far superior to a bruising physical-contact sport), but no sport reduces tension as effectively, as safely, as walking.

Certainly no other exercise is as diverting and as visually stimulating. In 1923, Dr. Alvah Doty in his book *Walking for Health* advised the walker, "Look about you—become interested in things that will bring about pleasurable mental reactions." And that advice is as valid today as it was then. To walk is to escape. Every city pavement, every country path, has vistas to offer you. Be selective. Concentrate on what will nurture and cheer you. Lift your spirits with every walk you take.

Whenever I hear someone speak of New York City as cold and impersonal, I think of something I have seen here while walking early on a Sunday morning in a small business section, home of many lofts and factories. It was obviously once a respectable residential neighborhood, but now on weekends its streets are fairly empty, except for the forlorn-looking men who lean up against the buildings or squat in the doorways. Each Sunday morning, a short, stocky man parks his car in front of his place of business, where he spends an hour or two, but before he goes upstairs he has a routine he faithfully follows: He takes out a pack of cigarettes and walks the length of the block, giving one to each man and lighting it for him. Some of the men smile, some shake his hand, and a few simply stare their gratitude. It's a small gesture on his part, but if you've ever seen a man scavenge for a butt, then you know what this gift of a cigarette means. My spirits lift every time I think of that simple act of kindness— the sort of thing one can see only when walking.

Make it a point to take a brisk walk every day, and your morale will improve and so will your productivity. A vigorous walk increases your "oxygen-transport capacity"—the amount of oxygen that each heartbeat delivers to the rest of the body. Mental alertness improves when larger amounts of pure oxygen are delivered to the brain cells. Lack of exercise, on the other hand, reduces one's "oxygen-transport capacity" and results in mental fatigue.

Wise men have always known the wisdom of walking. Fifth-century Greeks believed that walking made their minds lucid and helped them crack problems of logic and philosophy.

"Walking has something in it which animates and heightens my ideas," wrote the eighteenth-century philosopher Jean Jacques Rousseau. "I can scarcely think when I stay in one place; my body must be set a-going if my mind is to work."

Marcel Proust was a walkaholic who referred to the "poetic pleasure" he found in long walks. They made him feel totally alive again after long hours spent over his writing ("My mind, which in the long spell of enforced immobility had stored up an accumulation of vital energy, was now obliged, like a spinning-top wound and let go, to spend this in every direction"), and picked up his spirits, restored his self-confidence, when he had doubts ("I must abandon all hope of ever becoming a famous author").

The philosopher Immanuel Kant walked for an hour every afternoon. The poet William Wordsworth covered some fourteen miles a day on foot. His writer friend Thomas De Quincey said of him, "To walking he was indebted for a life of unclouded happiness—and we for much of what is excellent in his writing." Once when one of Wordsworth's servants was asked where her employer did his work, she replied, "Here is his library, but his study is out of doors."

Most of England's great nineteenth-century poetry was written while the poets were walking. Albert Einstein strode miles across the rolling country around Princeton University. And the great physicist Helmholtz on the occasion of his seventieth birthday said of his most important discoveries, "So far as I am concerned they have never come to me when my mind was fatigued, or when I was at my working table. They have come particularly readily during the slow ascent of wooded hills on a sunny day."

You don't have to be a poet, philosopher, or physicist to walk away from a problem and come back to it with your disposition improved, energy renewed, and self-confidence restored. All of us have jobs to do and problems to solve. When I was a copywriter with a Madison Avenue advertising agency I had no knotty problems of logic and philosophy, but I had plenty of job-related problems. And time and time again I chose a long solitary walk over attending what was called a "brainstorming session" inside the agency. And I never failed to come back to my office far more refreshed mentally and physically than I ever felt after an hour spent sitting around a conference table with a group of nervous advertising people.

Intense concentration demands that you escape for a period of time. And walking *is* escape, which is precisely why, when we feel the pressure of a problem bearing down on us, we often get to our feet and start pacing the room . . . rather like a caged animal. But we aren't caged. We can and *must* escape if we want to keep a clear mind and remain productive.

If you're in an office and can't leave the building to take off down the road, do the next best thing: leave your office and walk briskly down the corridors. The point, you see, is to substitute for the basically passive act of concentrating on something you *have* to do the doing of something you *choose* to do.

The simple interaction of mind and body tells us when it's time to escape. I regard it as the instinct for survival. And when someone as exquisitely talented as Virginia Woolf obeys that instinct and afterward writes about it, then we have a permanent record of the sense of relief a walk like that can give.

No one perhaps has ever felt passionately towards a lead pencil. But there are circumstances in which it can become supremely desirable to possess one; moments when we are set upon having an object, an excuse for walking half way across London between tea and dinner. As the foxhunter hunts in order to preserve the breed of foxes, and the golfer plays in order that open spaces may be preserved from the builders, so when the desire comes upon us to go street rambling the pencil does for a pretext, and getting up we say: "Really I must buy a pencil," as if under cover of this excuse we could indulge safely in the greatest pleasure of town life in winter—rambling the streets of London.

The hour should be the evening and the season winter, for in winter the champagne brightness of the air and the sociability of the streets are grateful. We are not then taunted as in the summer by the longing for shade and solitude and sweet airs from the hayfields. The evening hour, too, gives us the irresponsibility which darkness and lamplight bestow. We are no longer quite ourselves. As we step out of the house on a fine evening between four and six, we shed the self our friends know us by and become part of that vast republican army of anonymous trampers, whose society is so agreeable after the solitude of one's own room. For there we sit surrounded by objects which perpetually express the oddity of our own temperaments and enforce the memories of our own experience. That bowl on the mantelpiece, for instance, was bought at Mantua on a windy day. We were leaving the shop when the sinister old woman plucked at our skirts and said she would find herself starving one of these days, but "Take it!" she cried, and thrust the blue and white china bowl into our hands as if she never wanted to be reminded of her quixotic generosity. So, guiltily, but suspecting nevertheless how badly we had been fleeced, we carried it back to the little hotel where, in the middle of the night, the innkeeper quarreled so violently with his wife that we all leant out into the courtyard to look, and saw the vines laced about among the pillars and the stars white in the sky. The moment was stabilized, stamped like a coin indelibly among a million that slipped by imperceptibly. There, too, was the melancholy Englishman, who rose among the coffee cups and the little iron tables and revealed the secrets of his soul—as travellers do. All this—Italy, the windy morning, the vines laced about the pillars, the Englishman and the secrets of his soul —rise up in a cloud from the china bowl on the mantelpiece. And there, as our eyes fall to the floor, is that brown stain on the carpet. Mr. Lloyd George made that. "The man's a devil!" said Mr. Cummings, putting the kettle down with which he was about to fill the teapot so that it burnt a brown ring on the carpet.

But when the door shuts on us, all that vanishes. The shell-like covering which our souls have excreted to house themselves, to make for themselves a shape distinct from others, is broken, and there is left of all these wrinkles and roughnesses a central oyster of perceptiveness, an enormous eye. How beautiful a street is in winter! It is at once revealed and obscured. Here vaguely one can trace symmetrical straight avenues of doors and windows; here under the lamps are floating islands of pale light through which pass quickly bright men and women, who, for all their poverty and shabbiness, wear a certain look of unreality, an air of triumph, as if they had given life the slip, so that life, deceived of her prey, blunders on without them. But, after all, we are only gliding smoothly on the surface. The eye is not a miner, not a diver, not a seeker after buried treasure. It floats us smoothly down a stream; resting, pausing, the brain sleeps perhaps as it looks.

How beautiful a London street is then, with its islands of light, and its long groves of darkness, and on one side of it perhaps some tree-sprinkled, grass-grown space where night is folding herself to sleep naturally and, as one passes the iron railing, one hears those little crack-lings and stirrings of leaf and twig which seem to suppose the silence of fields all round them, an owl hooting, and far away the rattle of a train in the valley. But this is London, we are reminded; high among the bare trees are hung oblong frames of reddish-yellow light—windows; there are points of brilliance burning steadily like low stars—lamps; this empty ground, which holds the country in it and its peace, is only a London square, set about by offices and houses where at this hour fierce lights burn over maps, over documents, over desks where clerks sit turn-ing with wetted forefinger the files of endless correspondences; or more suffusedly the firelight wavers and the lamplight falls upon the privacy of some drawing-room, its easy chairs, its papers, its china, its inlaid table, and the figure of a woman, accurately measuring out the precise number of spoons of tea which— She looks at the door as if she heard a ring downstairs and somebody asking, is she in?

But here we must stop peremptorily. We are in danger of digging deeper than the eye approves; we are impeding our passage down the smooth stream by catching at some branch or root. At any moment, the sleeping army may stir itself and wake in us a thousand violins and trumpets in response; the army of human beings may rouse itself and assert all its oddities and sufferings and sordidities. Let us dally a little longer, be content still with surfaces only—the glossy brilliance of the motor omnibuses; the carnal splendour of the butchers' shops with their yellow flanks and purple steaks; the blue and red bunches of flowers burning so bravely through the plate glass of the florists' windows. . . .

Passing, glimpsing, everything seems accidentally but miraculously sprinkled with beauty, as if the tide of trade which deposits its burden so punctually and prosaically upon the shores of Oxford Street and had this night cast up nothing but treasure. With no thought of buying, the eye is sportive and generous; it creates; it adorns; it enhances. Standing out in the street, one may build up all the chambers of an imaginary house and furnish them at one's will with sofa, table, carpet. That rug will do for the hall. That alabaster bowl shall stand on a carved table in the window. Our merrymaking shall be reflected in that thick round mirror. But, having built and furnished the house, one is happily under no obligation to possess it; one can dismantle it in the twinkling of an eye, and build and furnish another house with other chairs and other glasses. Or let us indulge ourselves at the antique jewellers, among the trays of rings and the hanging necklaces. Let us choose those pearls, for example, and then imagine how, if we put them on, life would be changed. It becomes instantly between two and three in the morning; the lamps are burning very white in the deserted streets of Mayfair. Only motor-cars are abroad at this hour, and one has a sense of emptiness, of airiness, of secluded gaiety. Wearing pearls, wearing silk, one steps out on to a balcony which overlooks the gardens of sleeping Mayfair. There are a few lights in the bedrooms of great peers returned from Court, of silk-stockinged footmen, of dowagers who have pressed the hands of statesmen. A cat creeps along the garden wall. Love-making is going on sibilantly, seductively in the darker places of the room behind thick green curtains. Strolling sedately as if he were promenading a terrace beneath which the shires and counties of England lie sun-bathed, the aged Prime Minister recounts to Lady So-and-So with the curls and the emeralds the true history of some great crisis in the affairs of the land. We seem to be riding on top of the highest mast of the tallest ship; and yet at the same time we know that nothing of this sort matters; love is not proved thus, nor great achievements completed thus; so that we sport with the moment and preen our feathers in it lightly, as we stand on the balcony watching the moonlit cat creep along Princess Mary's garden wall.

But what could be more absurd? It is, in fact, on the stroke of six; it is a winter's evening; we are walking to the Strand to buy a pencil. How, then, are we also on a balcony, wearing pearls in June? What could be more absurd? Yet it is nature's folly, not ours. When she set about her chief masterpiece, the making of man, she should have thought of one thing only. Instead, turning her head, looking over her shoulder, into each one of us she let creep instincts and desires which are utterly at variance with his main being, so that we are streaked, variegated, all of a mixture; the colours have run. Is the true self this which stands on the pavement in January, or that which bends over the balcony in June? Am I here, or am I there? Or is the true self neither this nor that, neither here nor there, but something so varied and wandering that it is only when we give the rein to its wishes and let it take its way unimpeded that we are indeed ourselves? Circumstances compel unity; for convenience' sake a man must be a whole. The good citizen when he opens his door in the evening must be banker, golfer, husband, father; not a nomad wandering the desert, a mystic staring at the sky, a debauchee in the slums of San Francisco, a soldier heading a revolution, a pariah howling with scepticism and solitude. When he opens his door, he must run his fingers through his hair and put his umbrella in the stand like the rest. . . .

It is always an adventure to enter a new room; for the lives and characters of its owners have distilled their atmosphere into it, and directly we enter it we breast some new wave of emotion. Here, without a doubt, in the stationer's shop, people have been quarrelling. Their anger shot through the air. They both stopped; the old woman—they were husband and wife evidently—retired to a back room; the old man whose rounded forehead and globular eyes would have looked well on the frontispiece of some Elizabethan folio, stayed to serve us. "A pencil, a pencil," he repeated, "certainly, certainly." He spoke with the distraction yet effusiveness of one whose emotions have been roused and checked in full flood. He began opening box after box and shutting them again. He said that it was very difficult to find things when they kept so many different articles. He launched into a story about some legal gentleman who had got into deep waters owing to the conduct of his wife. He had known him for years; he had been connected with the Temple for half a century, he said, as if he wished his wife in the back room to overhear him. He upset a box of rubber bands. At last, exasperated by his incompetence, he pushed the swing door open and called out roughly: "Where d'you keep the pencils?" as if his wife had hidden them. The old lady came in. Looking at nobody, she put her hand with a fine air of righteous severity upon the right box. There were pencils. How then could he do without her? Was she not indispensable to him? In order to keep them there, standing side by side in forced neutrality, one had to be particular in one's choice of pencils; this was too soft, that too hard. They stood silently looking on. The longer they stood there, the calmer they grew; their heat was going down, their anger disappearing. Now, without a word said on either side, the quarrel was made up. The old man, who would not have disgraced Ben Jonson's title-page, reached the box back to its proper place, bowed profoundly his good-night to us, and they disappeared. She would get out her sewing; he would read his newspaper; the canary would scatter them impartially with seed. The quarrel was over. . . .

. . . Into each of these lives one could penetrate a little way, far enough to give oneself the illusion that one is not tethered to a single mind, but can put on briefly for a few minutes the bodies and minds of others. One could become a washerwoman, a publican, a street singer. And what greater delight and wonder can there be than to leave the straight lines of personality and deviate into those footpaths that lead beneath brambles and thick tree trunks into the heart of the forest where live those wild beasts, our fellow men?

That is true: to escape is the greatest of pleasures; street haunting in winter the greatest of adventures. Still as we approach our own door-step again, it is comforting to feel the old possessions, the old prejudices, fold us round; and the self, which has been blown about at so many street corners, which has battered like a moth at the flame of so many inaccessible lanterns, sheltered and enclosed. Here again is the usual door; here the chair turned as we left it and the china bowl and the brown ring on the carpet. And here—let us examine it tenderly, let us touch it with reverence—is the only spoil we have retrieved from all the treasures of the city, a lead pencil.

> ". . . my extraordinary new awareness of the land and animals, opened by the pace of walking. I feel that I am literally seeing everything for the first time."
>
> —CAROLYN BENNETT PATTERSON, *National Geographic*, October 1978

THE SENSORY WALK

Mrs. Patterson commemorated the one-hundredth anniversary of Robert Louis Stevenson's legendary twelve-day walk through the Cévennes in France by retracing his steps. On the second day of her odyssey she wrote of this "extraordinary new awareness" she felt. And it is, exactly as she wrote, *opened by the pace of walking.*

Motion is the great purifier—the rhythmic motion of the limbs clearing the mind and freeing the walker to look around and really assimilate what he sees. In the proper environment, a good walk acts as a catalyst for the senses. And under the proper circumstances, the everyday can suddenly become *extraordinary*.

"Cows?" wrote Mrs. Patterson. "How fabulous they are, swinging bags of milk with little spouts, and kind eyes. . . . Horses? How was it I never saw how aristocratic they look."

To experience this heightened awareness, this amazing feeling of discovery and wonderment, you don't have to travel to some exotic place. But you must walk somewhere that's quiet and open—and you must walk alone, eye to eye with nature. As Robert Louis Stevenson saw it, "You must be open to all impressions, and let your thoughts take color from what you see." If you can't get out of the city, then walk through a park that will shield you from traffic noises and crowds.

Walk erect, breathe deeply, and really look at the world around you. The American Indian held that man is not outside nature, but *in* it. That it's a community to which we all belong. Experience it. Feel the air on your skin. Reach out and touch a tree. Look up at the sky. And as your senses awaken, that sense of well-being will very gradually start building, step by step, to a feeling of such peace and exhilaration that—no matter what your age or degree of sophistication—you will, quite literally, begin to see everything about you as though for the first time.

71

Runners speak of the particular "high" they experience when they pass over the threshold of pain and a feeling of buoyancy takes over. Walking, of course, involves no pain. The walker's "high" grows out of the ease and naturalness of what he's doing.

Feet and legs were made for walking. When they move as nature intended them to, the entire body responds joyously. The brain signals its approval, and as you drink in the sights, sounds, and smells that surround you—enjoying a veritable feast for the senses—your entire being seems to gush with vitality. That's the walker's "high."

Stride a beach early one morning or off-season when it's relatively empty. Taste the salt in the air, feel it quivering at your nostrils and freshening your face. And soon you'll become aware of the majesty of *small* sounds—the flap of wings overhead, the splatter of spray on the top of the surf.

Walk through the woods and both hear and feel a branch resisting your attempt to press past it. Move on and out of the shade of the trees into sunshine, and there you may well see, as though for the first time, the color green.

You can't predict which of the senses will respond first. Ideally, when one sense responds it sets off a chain reaction. And when that happens, I've known people to stop walking and stand perfectly still for a moment like someone who, suddenly, miraculously, has had sight or hearing restored. And at times like that I'm often reminded of passages from *Blindness*, a novel by the celebrated British author Henry Green, in which the principal character is a young blind student. The author, a young student then himself, conveyed quite brilliantly the world of sensory awareness that one lives in when the other senses act in concert or alone to compensate for the loss of one.

"Every wind was different, and as he listened to their coming and to their going, there was rhythm in their play. . . . The long grass copied the trees with a tiny dry rustling."

When a walker has a similar sensory experience, I've heard it described as an "almost religious experience," and at other times as "mystical."

I remember when I was in college I had some difficulty with my hearing. It was some sort of stoppage in the ear canal that a visit to an ear specialist cleared up. And I can still recall how I reacted to the "miracle" of sound as I walked back to school through a park. In particular I remember touching the branch of a tree that seemed to fairly explode with the crackle of its leaves. At the same time I became aware of their smell—sweet and, oddly enough, rather like fresh milk. The unplugged ear had awakened more than my sense of hearing.

I imagine in none of us are all five senses equally developed. I know that mine aren't. My sight, my hearing, my sense of touch are the most developed. And perhaps because I live in a big city, I am especially sensitive to quiet. In fact, you might say that I travel in pursuit of it, and it never fails to deliver me my walker's "high."

I've walked on Inishmore, the largest of the rocky Aran Islands off the coast of Ireland. All three islands are sparsely populated and you see few people. On Sundays you can imagine yourself to be on a deserted island; after church the people ride off in their carts to disappear for the rest of the day behind the brightly colored doors of their cottages. Except for the occasional clip-clop of a horse's hooves on a road over a hill somewhere, the quiet is so intense that it fairly envelops you. There were times I felt I might reach out and touch it. I had never known a quiet like that before; it was both eerie and beautiful. Like a faithful companion that walks with you and never leaves your side.

More recently, I was on the Isle of Mull, one of the Inner Hebrides off the coast of Scotland. Here, too, a hush settles over the island on Sundays. On this particular Sunday morning, the only sounds were the gulls wheeling and twisting in the air. I walked up into the hills above the village and sat on the grass and listened to some lambs bleating. I walked on and after a while sat again, this time with my back against a stone wall that separated me from a thick clump of trees. It was while sitting there that I heard a sound like a flute being played. I turned around but there was no one there. And still the silvery sound continued. I climbed on top of the wall and peered in among the trees, and there it was—a babbling brook. I had never heard one before. I had an urge to go to it and dip my hands in it, but the trees were so thick there was no way I could do that. So I sat on the wall and listened to it—for how long I don't know, but it was late afternoon and the air had turned cool by the time I came down from the hills. For me a sensory walk invariably starts with my sense of hearing.

Not all my friends are walkers. Some prefer to sit rather than stand, ride rather than walk. Last year one of them was so overworked and testy that his wife insisted they leave the city for a long weekend in the country. She chose New England, and he drove through a snowstorm, protesting and complaining most of the way. They arrived in the evening, and the next morning, according to his wife, "It looked like Christmas. Icicles hanging from the trees, and snow without a footprint on it." She suggested a walk, and he went with her, again protesting and complaining. But then something happened to him after they'd gone a respectable distance: he began to walk taller and faster, taking in great, healthy gulps of the clean, fresh air. They walked for over a mile, the longest he had walked in years.

Late that evening he insisted on walking again, and alone this time. He put on a pair of snowshoes, and my friend, the tired businessman, went out and experienced his first walker's "high." And to hear him tell it now, he knew what he was doing.

"I don't know how to explain it, but as we walked that afternoon I felt almost light-headed. Where I was dead tired the day before, now suddenly I felt full of pep. I felt so good that I felt foolish." And he wanted to go out again to see if he could recapture that feeling of exhilaration and see where it would lead. And he did. This man who usually looked no farther than arm's length, or the distance from his armchair to the television screen, was standing now on a deserted country road, in a foot of snow, staring up at the sky, marveling at the clarity of the atmosphere, and counting the stars the way he used to when he was a boy back in Michigan.

Walking awakens the child living inside each of us. Make walking a way of life and the child in you will never let you grow old or bored. When you feel that you're slipping, he'll bring you to your senses—all five of them. And that's the essence of the walker's "high."

5

WARNING: WALKING CAN BECOME ADDICTIVE

"Man is not man sitting down; he is man on the move."

—STEPHEN GRAHAM, *The Gentle Art of Tramping*

THE WORLD'S MOST DEDICATED WALKERS ARE NOT AMERICANS—AT LEAST not yet. The most dedicated—the most addicted—are living and walking in Scandinavia, Germany, and the British Isles. For them walking is a kind of religion. They are walkaholics.

Arriving in Copenhagen for the first time some twenty years ago, I followed my usual *modus operandi*. I checked in at my hotel and then promptly went out for a walk. Listening to the pleasant, almost singsong rhythm of the Danes' voices and their lighthearted steps on the pavement, I knew that I was in a city of happy walkers. And I discovered the Swedes and Norwegians to be every bit as energetic too. It wasn't unusual for me to see a Stockholm pedestrian, standing on a curb waiting for a traffic light to change so he could get on with his walk, slowly rise up on his toes to give his calf muscles some impromptu exercise. And any Swede of middle age in that city today still has fond memories of seeing the extravagantly tall King Gustav V during one of his daily walks about the city, ramrod straight at ninety-plus.

During intermission at the opera or ballet, the Scandinavians walk. They take themselves to a long room where they buy a sweet or glass of wine, and then walk around and around the perimeter of the room as though on parade. They simply can't get enough of walking!

I came home from Scandinavia to write a book about how the people there stay so vital and healthy. Inspired by the walkers I had seen in Scandinavia, I did a chapter titled "The Most Natural Exercise in the World," and in it I wrote, "Walk to go shopping. Walk to visit a museum. Walk every chance you get and you'll help control your weight, stimulate your circulation, and keep your heart in good condition. Walking is a natural exercise available to all of us every day of the year."

I suspect that it sounded rather eccentric at the time. Americans, after all, were going to gymnasiums and health spas for their exercise then. Walking was still too simple, too accessible to be taken seriously.

At about that same time here in New York, I had become increasingly aware of two other daily and solitary walkers in my area: one was a short, silver-haired, and immensely energetic man with the kind of perennial suntan common to many serious walkers; the other was Greta Garbo. I grew accustomed to seeing them—and I imagine they grew accustomed to seeing me—but that was all there was to it. We never spoke. We didn't even nod. Each of us was a solitary walker who recognized the other two as members of the walking fraternity. And then one day I saw them together, standing just outside Central Park, chatting. She was wearing trousers, a felt hat, and tweed coat, and he, a book under his arm, was looking up into her face because he was quite a bit shorter. I remember wondering at the time if he had simply gone up to her, introduced himself, and engaged her in conversation. Or were they friends, acquaintances? In any event, while I continued to see her, after that he disappeared from the scene.

Until a few years later when, walking through a park in Munich one sunny Sunday afternoon, I saw him again. I stopped and introduced myself. After all, I was in a foreign city and his was a familiar face from back home.

His name was Heinrich, and Munich was his native city. He had fled from Hitler in 1938 and settled in New York, but now he was home and, quite naturally, he was walking in order to reacquaint himself with his hometown after so long an absence. He recognized me (yes, he knew Garbo "but not very well"), and we walked together after that every day of my stay in Munich.

Heinrich was past seventy and as trim and physically active as most American men in their thirties. He walked at least five miles a day. He belonged to both a walking club and a hiking club, and consequently he had friends of all ages who were enthusiastic walkers, too. One young couple I particularly remember had recently completed a thirty-mile hike around the Starnbergersee in Bavaria. He was a banker and she a fashion model, and they spent as much of their free time as possible hiking through the woods.

Heinrich explained the German passion for walking to me this way: "Our fathers and grandfathers walked before us with their children toddling by their sides. So naturally we grew up as confirmed walkers too. It's in our blood."

Still, I think the greatest walkers of all are to be found in the British

Isles. It's not that they walk more miles than anyone else; it's that they walk with such a sense of fun. "It is indeed astonishing with what ease and hilarity the English walk," wrote John Burroughs over a hundred years ago. And I don't think it's any less true today. The English enjoy walking so much and it's so much an accepted part of everyday life that, despite their reserve, they are practically giddy about it. London is a walker's city, and I recall one group, "Off-Beat Tours of London," that, true to its name, conducts escorted walking tours of such places as Baker Street ("On the Trail of Sherlock Holmes"), Whitechapel ("Jack the Ripper's Here!"), and Tower Hill ("City Ghosts and Bloody Sites"). The firm's emblem, fittingly enough, is a bare footprint.

I agree with the Detroit doctor who, a few years ago, told a health seminar that "it is impossible to walk too much," but if I ever came close to overdoing it, it would have had to be in London, where sometimes I've started walking early in the morning and returned in the evening, having interrupted my walking only once for a light lunch. Yet for all the walking I've done around that city, until recently I'd never walked in the district behind St. Paul's Cathedral, where remains of the Roman wall still stand. Last summer I decided to remedy that oversight, and once again I enjoyed the kind of walk that is uniquely British.

I set out from my hotel in Mayfair and walked past Trafalgar Square, where a coed band wearing white shirts and red ties played "Don't Take My Sunshine Away," while spectators sang and a barefoot girl in a leopard-stenciled leotard moved among them passing out pamphlets carrying the title "Meet the One World Crusade." I proceeded along the Strand, where big-fisted workingmen were celebrating their day off with a noon-day pint at keg tables set up outside the Charles Dickens Restaurant; moved on to Fleet Street past the Guild Church of St. Dunstan-in-the-West with its statue of Queen Elizabeth I standing in a niche above the door (carried there by an alderman of the ward when the gate where it had formerly stood was taken down in 1760); and took a detour off Fleet Street through a courtyard to Dr. Johnson's house at 17 Gough Street, where he lived from 1765 to 1776. Then it was back to Fleet Street past the offices of London's principal newspapers, by now feeling quite smug as tourist buses passed by en route to St. Paul's while I continued there on foot.

Finally I arrived at the cathedral and walked behind it and down Cannon Street toward the Mansion House station of the Underground, where unexpectedly I found myself standing opposite a city dig. On the wooden wall in which giant circles had been cut for sidewalk viewing, there was a notice that read:

Department of Urban Archaeology has been excavating this site since the beginning of June. From work on nearby sites it was known that Roman ruins were likely to survive beneath the Victorian cellars.

To the right of the notice was a partial list of the findings made by proper archaeologists aided by a volunteer work force: a fourteenth- or fifteenth-century building; a first-century residential building with a courtyard and corridor; debris associated with a fire during Hadrian's time; and a Roman town house with one room covered with the period's best black-and-white mosaic.

I peered through one of the viewing holes in the wall and saw several people, men and women, working there with ladders and wheelbarrows. I decided that my search for the Roman wall could wait while I went down into the excavation. One of the women looked up as I approached, and grinned. We chatted, and I learned that she was an artist who had answered the call for a volunteer work force. It was, she said, a very rewarding way to spend a Sunday. "There's an element of treasure hunting in it," she explained, "and it's a good open-air exercise as well." Further on, I talked to a man and his sixteen-year-old son who were visitors from New Zealand. Standing on a ladder, the boy, stripped to the waist, was very obviously having an adventure.

I moved on in the direction of the Roman wall, down picturesquely named streets: Ironmonger Lane. Bread Street. Cat Lane. Honey Lane. Threadneedle Street. Past a church just inside the ancient city walls in whose courtyard I caught sight of a mini-sized palm tree. Turning left on Noble Street, I came upon the remains of the Roman wall joined with those of a fort built around 100 A.D. before the wall. I wanted to touch the wall and in that way enjoy one of the luxuries open to the person who approaches it on foot. Two men were asleep on the grass, and I walked around them and went over and pressed the flat of my two hands against the wall, while a cat sitting on the wall watched.

The Scots, too, are intrepid walkers. And since they are known for their thrifty ways, they've managed in the city of Edinburgh, in the space of only one mile, to contain what surely must be one of the world's most fascinating walks. The "Royal Mile" it's called, because it begins at Edinburgh Castle high on a cliff overlooking the city, winds through the cobblestoned streets of the old section, and stops at the gates of the Royal Palace of Holywood House, where the Queen resides on state visits to Scotland.

Nearby are eight-hundred-foot heather-flecked hills that are being walked on at any hour, any season, by kilt-clad Scots accompanied by their favorite companions: a dog and a walking stick.

Now, happily, increasing numbers of Americans are becoming walk-aholics too. Once a person begins serious walking and sees the difference it makes in the way he looks and feels, he starts looking for new ways to enjoy what has become his favorite exercise. And the variety of ways he can extend his walking pleasure is extraordinary: there's something to suit every personality type, every life-style: Backpacking. Bird watching. Race walking. Long-distance walking. Orienteering.

The urge to fit the joy of walking into the tapestry of one's life seems to me to be as natural as man's drive to explore. It is his nature.

On July 2, 1976, a panel discussion, "Why Man Explores," was held at the California Institute of Technology in Pasadena, under the sponsorship of the National Aeronautics and Space Administration. It was a five-man panel, and I was particularly taken with the remarks of Jacques Cousteau, the oceanographic explorer.

"For young animals the world is to be explored and discovered from their birth on," he said, "and that exploration only ends with death; for the young fox, wilderness is unlimited; for a tuna, the oceans are infinite. Still, in the animal world, the physical need for exploration develops as well in individuals as in collectivities—tribes, schools, swarms, packs. In fact, if the baby human being shows the same motivation as a young cat, to explore with all his sensors the strange environment he was born into, the big difference is that the little baby soon stands erect"—and *walks*.

Cousteau concluded with the thought that "the exploring part of a plant, of a creature, of a crowd, is always the most vigorous, the most enterprising."

"Thousands of tired, nerve-shaken, over-civilized people are beginning to find out that going to the mountains is going home; that wildness is a necessity; and that mountain parks and reservations are useful not only as fountains of timber and for irrigating the rivers, but as fountains of life."

—JOHN MUIR (1838–1914), naturalist and crusader for national parks and reservations

BACKPACKING

For some 25 million Americans this is their way of exercising man's instinct to explore. All walking is discovery; backpacking is exploration. By taking to the open spaces with all our daily needs carried on our backs, we recapture a little of the American pioneer spirit. And backpacking is also a very pure way for us to reaffirm that we, and our children, are creatures of nature.

As with all walking, you can go backpacking alone, with your family, or with a group. It's a relatively inexpensive way to spend a weekend or vacation. Even a baby can go backpacking, carried in a canvas sling. And stamina is seldom a problem with child hikers. At age three, Brian, the son of my California friends, Susan and Siegfried Othmer, had his own hiking boots; at nine his own fifteen-pound backpack.

There's no one backpacker type, although a Yale professor who researched the subject concluded that the typical backpacker is well educated, middle class, and somewhere between twenty and thirty-five. But I've met backpackers of all ages, all temperaments. One young father told me that backpacking with his family had been "a discovery of nature, beauty, and, most important, ourselves," while the chief of a giant blue-chip corporation assured me that there was something wonderful and even meaningful about "filling a quart jug with cold mountain water for your instant coffee." And an artist of my acquaintance regards the lushly green forests, blue streams, and mountain summits as "my center, my cathedral. I go there and it just takes over and gives things a natural order." So it would seem that nature gives you what you look for—no more and no less.

81

There are a hundred thousand miles of foot trails in America, and the Appalachian Trail is the world's longest marked one. Yet to pinpoint it as a foot trail is rather like referring to the Eiffel Tower as another steel structure. The Appalachian Trail winds 2,025 miles from Springer Mountain, Georgia, to Mount Katahdin, Maine, passing through farms, eight national forests, two national parks, wilderness areas, and small towns. It is also, and most important, America's first National Scenic Trail, and some part of it is within a day's drive of 60 percent of the American public.

Not surprisingly, walkers everywhere consider a hike along the trail a high point, the ultimate in *extended walking for pleasure*. Some even walk the entire 2,025 miles; they're called the "2,000 Milers." In 1960 four hikers qualified; in 1970 ten; in 1973 eighty-eight; and in 1978 two hundred hikers registered in the logbook which is kept at what is considered the halfway point, in historic Harpers Ferry, West Virginia—although there's no way of knowing exactly how many completed their hike. Still, 926 miles is an impressive distance to cover on foot.

Myron Avery, a Maine man of pioneer stock, was the first hiker to walk the entire trail. He did it in sections, starting in Maine in the 1920s and finishing in the fall of 1936. Many years later he wrote a report of his hike, and the following excerpt is often quoted as a kind of definition of the Appalachian Trail: "Remote for detachment, narrow for chosen company, winding for leisure, lonely for contemplation, it beckons not merely north and south but upward to the body, mind, and soul of man."

Emma (Grandma) Gatewood, a farm woman from Ohio and a legendary trail character, hiked the entire distance three times with a denim sack slung over her shoulders that contained clothing, bouillon cubes, chipped beef, raisins, peanuts, powdered milk, salt, Band-Aids and Mercurochrome, hairpins, safety pins, needles, thread, buttons, and matches in a plastic matchcase. She was in her late sixties the first time, and seventy-six when she completed her third hike. Until Grandma Gatewood no woman had ever walked the trail in one continuous journey, from one end to the other. And she was the first person, man or woman, to hike the whole trail a second time. She sometimes logged as many as twenty-seven miles in a single day, and at various times en route she was bitten by a German shepherd, molested by a bobcat, and lost.

Twenty-nine-year-old John Avery holds the record for the fastest hike: from Springer Mountain to the Katahdin summit in just 65 days, 21 hours, and 15 minutes, while a man named Norman Greist of Hartford, Connecticut, took forty-three years to hike every step of the trail. The average hike from start to finish has generally taken from four to five months.

A young man from Tennessee who wrote the following in the trail's log-book rather capsules the sentiments of most of today's backpackers with regard to their sport: "I have walked 926 miles, but I didn't conquer the terrain or the weather. I walked in harmony with them. This is a way of life in which you find out who and what you really are." And Bill O'Brien, one of the "2,000 Milers" of 1969, wrote:

> Lots of times I would say, "Nice place you got here, Lord." I seemed to have an increasing awareness of a "presence"—that is the nearest word I can think of to describe the feeling of oneness with nature that I felt. Traveling alone made me more aware of everything around me. During the hike I had a feeling of friendly companionship with my Maker. I don't consider myself a religious person, at least in the sense of being a regular churchgoer, but this trip was giving me a lot of feel-ings that were essentially religious. It was a sense of being one with the mountains and the scenery, as though I was a part of the universe rather than just a viewer of it.

There is a delightful book that contains what it calls "The best stories of hiking the Appalachian Trail." It's titled *From Katahdin to Springer Mountain*, and, as that suggests, it is a collection of mostly first-person accounts of eight "2,000 Milers." Each story has its own adventures and misadventures, but some things are common to them all: the wildlife en-countered en route, and the profusion of berries that flourish along the trail.

> One morning I awoke to the unbelievably lovely song of wood thrushes. Like silver music. Surely nightingales couldn't sound any more exquisite.

> A catbird calling awakened me, and in the background I could hear the usual towhees. A wood thrush song cheered me so much that I stuck my head out of the tent.

> The owls woke me the next morning to a clearing sky.

> The next morning a crazy whippoorwill awoke me at 5:00 A.M. He had a terrific volume and he varied the speed of delivery, too, which was fascinating.

> I found a deer drinking at the creek, and followed his example.

> About that time I noticed a big male moose looking at me from the trail about fifty feet away. I wondered what would happen next. If I ran, would he run after me? . . . How long we might have stood gazing at

each other I have no way of knowing, but in shifting my weight, something metallic in my gear hit another metallic object, and at this sound the moose snorted, turned, and ran up the trail.

I saw a gray deer with white eyebrows. It stood in the trail until I was about twenty feet away and told it to move off. It moved a little way and then just stood and looked at me as I walked by. I never saw another deer just like it.

As I was going up a woodland road I stopped in my tracks. Here came a rabbit bouncing down the trail in three-foot bounces like a Walt Disney character. He looked as if he was having a really happy spring morning. I felt better now. That bunny looked so happy! He seemed to be trying for height as well as distance with those big bounces.

The day was beautifully clear and crisply invigorating. We saw a pair of martens investigating the possibilities of a squirrel dinner. We passed within fifteen yards of an eight-point buck. With a small pair of binoculars I watched a three-toed black-backed woodpecker, and in the same vicinity I saw two yellow-bellied sapsuckers and a family of flickers.

It was a day of sunshine and showers. The pheasants with their broods were out along the edges of the newly cut hay fields.

"Next morning I found strawberries ripening everywhere along the trail." . . . "Ripe strawberries were growing on the hillsides in unbelievable profusion." . . . "Among all the black raspberries that were ripening everywhere I found one late patch of strawberries and picked about a cupful." . . . "On Mt. Wilcox I found unbelievable blueberry fields. Large fat berries weighed the bushes down to the ground. I picked and ate and ate. Then I picked more to carry along for breakfast. A mile past Mt. Wilcox Lean-to I pitched my tent, built a fire, and made pancakes and blueberry sauce." . . . "The next day I found my first black raspberries and some cherries." . . . "Just before reaching Dalton, Massachusetts, I found the best highbush huckleberries so far. Huckleberries will be my downfall; I just can't pass them by."

But long-distance hiking (most of the "2,000 Milers" were alone) has one drawback: loneliness. And Jim Leitzell, who walked from Katahdin to Springer Mountain in four months to the day back in 1971, wrote of it in the journal he kept:

I have suffered much loneliness on this trip. After several days devoid of contact with mankind, one develops a positive craving for company of any sort. A brief encounter on the trail or in a town gives one a psychological boost which lasts for an hour or two afterwards. Then one settles gradually, inevitably, back into his loneliness and depression. Increasingly I miss the familiar, stable things in my life—close friends, casual friends, acquaintances, my cats, musical evenings, my own bed, my own apartment. . . . Sometimes I even miss the bleak, unfriendly medical center and the frustrating, harassed life of a medical student.

Still, Dorothy Laker, writing of the first of her three hikes along the trail, found that once she came into a town there was no lack of human contact.

I was a sensation in Duncannon, one of the largest towns the trail goes through. Evidently not many women with packs walked through Duncannon. Cars stopped, people came out on their porches, children ran after me, and dogs barked. . . . As I walked the long bridge over the Susquehanna, many hands waved in greeting, car horns were blown, and friendly comments were shouted by passing motorists.

I recommend *From Katahdin to Springer Mountain* to anyone who would like to walk vicariously the trail regarded as the zenith by seasoned hikers. It isn't to be had in any bookstores so far as I know. It must be ordered directly from the publisher, Rodale Press, Inc., Emmaus, Pennsylvania 18049. A soft-cover edition sells for $4.95.

At least half of America's backpackers are female, and many of them, especially those who grew to womanhood during the years when it was thought unladylike to engage in a physically strenuous exercise, equate backpacking with equality of the sexes.

Nancy Cator, for example, grew up in Portland, Oregon, at a time when to be athletic meant to be masculine. Today the mother of four young adults, Nancy's a backpacker who "immortalized" a recent five-day hike in needlepoint on a linen napkin, which she's planning to frame. The unlikely marriage of delicate needlepoint and hardy backpacking amuses her.

Nancy's been a backpacker for the past ten years. She has hiked Yosemite National Park and the Swiss Alps in the company of women friends, who, like her, were raised to do nothing more strenuous than drive a car or push a baby carriage. Her home in Palo Alto, California, has a commanding view of the hills, and she speaks feelingly of the regional park behind the hills which all the peninsula cities are funding in order to keep the green space from being taken over by builders. Meantime, the five-mile road running at a right angle to her home is full of early-morning walkers, and she's usually among them, walking with her two golden retrievers. Backpacking, says Nancy Cator, gives her a religious feeling—"not in a church context, but it's there and it leads to my well-being."

Paula Strain, a past president of the Potomac Appalachian Trail Club, is another woman who grew up at a time when it wasn't wise for a female to do anything more vigorous than sit in the bleachers and cheer the local football team. "Anything more active was considered a masculine thing," she remembers. "So those of us who were interested in something more strenuous than, say, croquet, would conceal the fact." But nowadays she hikes practically every weekend. "If I don't, I feel jaded by Tuesday," she says. "I get a lot of relaxation from the quietness of the woods. Getting out and hearing nothing but the birds sing is a wonderful relief."

Paula Strain has backpacked in Scotland, Austria, Norway, and Alaska. "I wanted to get out into the real wilderness," she says of the Alaskan hike, "so I went with a group of twelve men and women, and a bush pilot flew us to a place called Bettles beyond the Arctic Circle about five hundred miles due north of Fairbanks. There we hired another plane and flew another two hundred miles into the Brooks Range, the farthest northern section of the Rocky Mountains. Go any further and you're into the Arctic Ocean. The plane put down on what was really nothing more than a pond, and we walked three days and camped for seven—and then hiked out to where the pilot met us and flew us back out again. It was what I wanted: real wilderness. It's just you with your group and a map. I carried a pack that weighed fifty-seven pounds. We'd hike as long as we could every day, and when we came to a suitable camping place we'd stop. We'd hike ten to twelve hours usually. In July there's no night in Alaska, so I'd go out and find myself a nice peak of a mountain and I'd just sit and 'mountain watch.' I sit and I watch for the mountain to move; I figure in a few years it will. Meantime, you can see birds and trees and animals. Sometimes I take a botany book along on a hike and identify the wild flowers I see. I just like to look and see what I see. There are people who bird-watch, and people who photograph. There are all kinds of things you can do."

Alice Butler is what she calls "a finder of routes"; in short, a walker-explorer. I knew her when she worked in a New York advertising agency. Today she lives in the Austrian Tyrol. Alice is just a little over five feet tall and extremely slender. When she lived here, she walked miles every day. Now she walks in the valleys near her chalet, and then goes on and up into the mountains, where she keeps an eye out for deer, chamois, and marmots. She wrote me recently after one of her hikes, "I sat on a rock and gazed around at the beauty. The flowers are everywhere: tall white daisies, short yellow daisies, wild violets, orchids, the most purple clover I've ever seen, and deep-red rockroses. Austria is a walker's paradise!"

A confirmed backpacker is a walkaholic fired with a missionary zeal to convert walkers, and even non-walkers, to his way of life. One backpacker surfaces in a family and eventually the entire family is hitting the trail. I think you'll enjoy reading the following article written by Wanda Maxey, a Washington woman who says she "caught the craze for backpacking from my teen-aged son."

I surprised even myself the day I first hoisted pack to back and took to the trail with my teenaged son, Craig. The source of my inspiration, Craig had been a serious backpacker for five years and after each excursion would entertain the entire family with accounts of sleeping under the stars or watching deer drink from waterholes.

Craig's stories made backpacking sound like so idyllic a pastime that I found myself wanting to try it. Finally, I asked my son if he would plan a relatively unstrenuous trip for the two of us. When he recovered from the initial shock, he looked at my proposal as a worthwhile challenge.

Together we pored over Craig's collection of maps and trail guides, eventually deciding that our destination would be Goat Lake in the Cascade Mountains of our home state, Washington. Craig assured me that the trail leading to the lake was ideal for a beginner, starting off fairly level but with enough of a climb at the end to guarantee a genuine sense of accomplishment.

Once our itinerary was set, we began to select the provisions and equipment necessary for the trip. Like many other beginning backpackers, my first inclination was to take along everything but the kitchen sink. Craig promptly brought me to my senses, however, by pointing out that even on a gentle climb there would be times when I would heartily resent every extra ounce in my pack.

So when we shopped for food, we kept the menus simple. Actually it was quite easy to plan lightweight, well-balanced meals. Many foods, such as powdered fruit juice, oatmeal or cream of wheat, cocoa, and freeze-dried soups and stews, are transformed into tasty fare with the simple addition of hot water. We also included candy for quick energy and beef jerky for protein.

When the great day arrived, Craig and I made an invigorating preliminary hike from our car to the campsite. Here, my son showed me how to spread one tarp on the ground and then stretch a second overhead in case of rain. We stashed our sleeping bags and other gear between the tarps. With our camp thus secure, Craig led us as we hiked around the lake. The trail grew progressively narrower, ending at a rock shelf where we could sit and look across the lake to the year-round glacier which fills the valley at the end of Goat Lake. Far above, waterfalls tumbled over the cliffs.

Later on, back at our campsite, Craig and I cooked supper over a butane stove. It came as a surprise to me that the campfire, so integral to my preconceived notion of camping out, is virtually a thing of the past among today's responsible hikers. Heavily traveled trails are by now practically devoid of dry firewood. And aside from posing the threat of forest fires, often campfires do serious damage to the ground cover of a campsite. Much more convenient and considerate of the environment are light cookstoves.

In a welcome reversal of roles, my son showed me how to fry a potato in hot oil. Sliced thin (peel and all), with a bit of seasoning added, it is delicious fare. And I was so famished that our freeze-dried beef stew tasted as good to me as if it had been simmering all afternoon. Supper done, we carefully burned our paper garbage and packed up the rest to take back with us.

As I snuggled down into my sleeping bag that first night out the possibility of bears and other nocturnal predators lurking just outside our camp suddenly loomed as very real to me. When I confided this fear to Craig, he solemnly told me that the percentages were against our being bothered. (Craig has always been comforted by proving things mathematically.) He then added: "On the whole bears are less aggressive than people." Somewhat reassured and thoroughly exhausted from the day's exertions, I fell asleep.

The following weekend Craig was to return to college, but I went back to Goat Lake, accompanied this time by my husband, Carl, and our fifteen-year-old daughter, Robbin.

Since these early ventures our family has spent many hours on the trail. There we've met honeymooners, couples with infants strapped in cradle-boards on their backs, and whole families equipped with packframes. The most unusual backpacker we have encountered so far was a German shepherd dog with saddlebags slung across his back. His master told us he thought it was only fair that the dog tote his own grub.

On one arduous hike we stopped for a rest, panting for breath. A few minutes later, however, up the trail came another hiker moving along at a hearty clip. He slowed down only to tip his hat to us and then resumed his pace. "Boy, he must be in good shape," was Carl's wistful comment. And, "I'll bet he'll never see sixty again."

We have by now made friends with rangers, naturalists, Boy Scouts, professors, and others who represent a variety of ages, races, and political beliefs. By a sparkling mountain stream or alongside a steep trail any gaps in ideologies or generations cease to matter, particularly when the stranger smiles, says "Hi," and offers a drink of water.

Our own values seemed to become more basic with a pack on our backs. Away from the telephone, television, and pressures of work, school, and social obligations, we suddenly discovered the luxury of time. Time to daydream, to lie back in a meadow and watch clouds drift by. Time to truly listen to one another. Or to be quiet and watch the birds, insects, or other animals.

Family backpacking is one of the best ways I can think of to renew body and spirit. I heartily recommend it for children and parents alike.

"How can you explain that you need to know that the trees are still there, and the hills and the sky? Anyone knows they are. How can you say it is time your pulse responded to another rhythm, the rhythm of the day and the season instead of the hour and the minute? No, you cannot explain. So you walk."

—*New York Times* editorial, "The Walk," October 25, 1967

How to Be a Successful Backpacker. While you certainly don't have to take lessons, backpacking does ask for more preparation and know-how than does a walk on level pavement with traffic lights cuing you as to what to do and when to do it. The following blueprint has been rated wholly sensible for the beginner by every experienced backpacker I've encountered:

1. *Start walking*. Backpacking demands stamina and endurance. Walk every day without fail to get your legs into shape and test your staying power. Gradually increase the distance while maintaining your pace.

2. *Join a local hiking club*—one that sponsors group hikes led by experienced volunteers. Most such clubs grade their hikes: Easy . . . Moderate . . . Strenuous. Start with a day hike, preferably within a three-hour drive from home, since you're not planning to stay overnight. And don't push yourself. Observe how the experienced hikers maintain a steady, even rhythm. Ask questions of the veterans. That's the best way to learn what equipment you should buy for your overnight and weekend camping trips. After all, there's a whole world of packs, frames, and tents to choose from.

Clubs can be divided into two main categories: hiking clubs that are primarily interested in building and maintaining trails (the Potomac Appalachian Trail Club in Washington, D.C., for example), and clubs whose chief interest is conservation but who also maintain year-round local hiking activities (the Sierra Club and the Appalachian Mountain Club are the two biggest in this category).

To give you some idea of the variety of outings offered, here are just a few of the types of hikes available through the Sierra Club chapters throughout the country, most of which have regional offices:

Base-camp trips.   The group settles in a fixed campsite and participants are free to hike or climb in the area so long as they report back to camp for dinner.

Burro trips.   Hikes with about fifteen backpackers leading burros which tote food and tents.

Family trips.   Several families—often as many as fifty adults and their children, many of whom have had little or no wilderness experience—establish camp at what's called a *threshold* camp far enough from a road to give a taste of real wilderness, and yet close enough so even two- to four-year-olds can hike in comfortably on their own. This, like all the trips, is a cooperative venture with adults sharing cooking, baby-sitting, hauling water, scrubbing pots, and so on.

3. *Hike into the wilderness.* This you can do under the auspices of a hiking club, or by joining one of the wilderness backpacking treks organized by a reputable pack- and trail-ride outfitter. "Wilderness Backpacking Adventures" is how outfitter L. D. Frome advertises his backpacking trips into the wilderness of Wyoming, Utah, and Arizona, promising, "We'll cut your backpack weight by 50 percent." This promise is kept by providing a string of mules or burros carrying everything (tents, food, other heavy items) but the hiker's own personal clothing and sleeping gear —the latter is furnished along with packs. The trek into the wilderness also comes equipped with a trail guide, a camp cook who prepares meals over an open fire, and a portable toilet that's set up at each camp.

This is what I call "dude backpacking," and the first day on the trail is easier than average to give hikers a chance to get used to the elevation and to walking with even a lightweight pack on their backs. This may not be the most realistic way to introduce yourself and family to the rigors of wilderness backpacking, but it's pleasant, the scenery is fabulous, and the food is first-rate, and though you're being coddled, it is a way of giving the concept a try without taking any risks. For a free color brochure that describes his program, write L. D. Frome, RFD, Afton, Wyoming 83110.

"The opportunity to see wild geese is more important than television, and a chance to find a pasqueflower is a right as inalienable as free speech."

—ALDO LEOPOLD, conservationist and forester

BIRD WATCHING

Hike along almost any nature trail and you'll see birds, but if you're a "birder," this, of course, won't satisfy you. Nor does it have to. The National Audubon Society has more than four hundred chapters across the nation with a membership of four hundred thousand dedicated bird watchers—many of whom are also dedicated walkers who are combining their two favorite sports.

When I was in California recently, I met with members of the Santa Monica Bay Audubon Society and got some idea of the walking they do while bird watching. A weekend camping trip, for example, through Yosemite National Park, which is one of the most spectacular birding (blue grouse, great gray owl, three-toed woodpecker) and scenic spots (7,200 feet elevation) in all California. A three-mile New Year's Day Bird Search was described in the society's newsletter as follows: "Are you looking for a new and different way to spend New Year's day? Are you tired of roses and football on January 1st? Last year we compiled a total of 122 species seen . . ."

There are also an increasing number of museums and private packagers who offer guided bird-watching expeditions through advertisements placed in birders' journals, in particular the two publications of the National Audubon Society: *Audubon* and *American Birds*. Many of these tours involve walking, in some of the most beautiful settings imaginable, where there are nesting sites. A New York–based birder I know joined a tour that flew to Anchorage, Alaska, and from there by a smaller plane to Homer, 225 miles away, and then took a motorboat to a lodge in China Poot Bay surrounded by trails that snaked through coniferous forests to high bluffs bounded by snow-capped mountains. And since the sun doesn't set until 11 P.M. or so in the summer in Alaska, my friend, who is as rabid a walker as he is a bird watcher, had plenty of time for still another hike after dinner.

"The key reason for knee problems in distance runners and other athletes is that the knee is flexed at contact."

—Dr. Steven Subotnick, after analyzing films of race walkers

RACE WALKING

I met my first race-walker shortly after I graduated from college in the 1940s. He was a middle-aged man of medium height and wiry build, and I had only recently seen him in a newsreel sports segment devoted to a race in which some hundred or more men, wearing T-shirts and shorts, walked ten or fifteen miles through the streets of New York City, using a stiff-kneed, heel-toe gait that drew snickers and giggles from some of the movie-house audience. I had never seen anything like it before myself, and when, through sheer happenstance, I met the winner of that race a few weeks later, I was surprised that he seemed no different from anyone else. But since he proved to be an extremely nice man, I assumed that, like us all, he was entitled to do something silly once in a while.

Since then I've matured. I've also had the great pleasure of meeting a number of race walkers, a few of whom you are about to meet here. And while you may never become a race walker, I think you should know as much as possible about a sport that is finally coming into its own and which, because it is more taxing than regular walking, and more technical, may well become the next sport for the more competitive among us. Certainly it is becoming the sport for many joggers who want to give up jogging without losing face altogether. It is, after all, as Dr. George Sheehan said in his book *Dr. Sheehan on Running*, "the perfect sport for recuperating from some other sport. . . . The ailing athlete who turns to race walking will soon find himself on the mend." Furthermore, as you are about to discover in the pages beyond, substantial numbers of teen-agers are taking up race walking. Very possibly they will prove to be part of a ground swell that may become the wave of the future.

"My quick-stepping, good-sporting career as a race-walker."

—ELLEN MINKOW, seventeen, Port Washington, New York

When you tell people you race-walk, it's like telling them you eat prunes for breakfast every morning. They just giggle. Once in a while someone will realize that you're serious and then want to know "Just what *is* race-walking?" I don't try to give a definition; I demonstrate. But when people ask my mother what she means when she says that her daughter is a race-walker, she tells them: "You know, you wiggle your shoulders and hips and walk very fast." "Oh, yes," they'll often answer, "I've seen men doing that. Do you mean girls race-walk too?"

I began competitive walking in April of last year. I was a freshman and undecided about whether to try out for tennis (I played on our junior high's team) or track. I talked the dilemma over with my mother. I enjoyed tennis, I told her, but felt that I'd never be more than second string. The other girls came from "gung-ho" tennis-playing families, took private lessons, and went to tennis camp. Our family spent summers sailboat racing. Also, the captain of the track team was a friend and there weren't as many girls vying for places. My mother thought that tennis was a sport I could enjoy all my life and "a very good way to meet nice boys," but agreed that I probably did have a better chance with track.

One afternoon at practice a friend and I were clowning around, imitating men race-walkers we'd seen in movies. It was all in a spirit of fun, but Bruce MacDonald, a teacher at our school and a veteran race-walker, was watching us. Was I interested in really learning to race-walk, he inquired. According to him, I had natural ability; that is, "the motion of the hips follows the knees, allowing the walker to have one foot on the ground at all times" (one of the rules). I thought he was kidding, but I accepted the offer.

The next thing I knew, we were driving to Philadelphia so I could compete in a real meet "just to see what it's like." The women's event was one mile along the grassy esplanade of the Schuykill River. My time, without any training, was a very respectable 11:18. I felt elated; I'd always wanted to be good at something. So I started working out—

94

mile warm-ups in baggy sweat suits; then, wearing shorts and T-shirt, 220- and 440-yard walks, followed by sprints for speed. One to two hours, every day. With Mr. MacDonald striding along to coach: "Pull more from the knees. Relax—keep those shoulders low!" I ached all over, but especially in the backs of my legs.

At my first serious race, an exhibition at a neighboring high school, I came in first—a half-mile in 4:48. But arriving at the finish nauseated, I learned the hard way not to eat for several hours before a meet.

At that exhibition a coach from Greenwich, Connecticut, who wanted to introduce the girls at his school to the sport, invited several of us to visit. In the demonstration race we held, I came in first once again, but one of the Greenwich girls emerged from it so enthusiastic about walking that she has become my biggest rival.

Sometime later, after a string of other victories, I went to a walking clinic for coaches and found that Greenwich walker there ready to challenge me. During our race I was out ahead but heard my newest competitor huffing and puffing and pushing hard behind me. I felt so sorry for her I slowed down to let her pass me and, of course, she came in first. When I told my parents, they gave me a lecture on competition. "When you compete," they said, "you work to win and don't give way to anyone. But play fairly, and if you lose, we hope you'll do it graciously."

I remembered their advice at the Metropolitan AAUW Senior Meet in New York City. It was a hot, muggy day; the kind that makes you feel totally drained after the least bit of effort. I pinned my braid up on top of my head. Racers in bright shorts and white T-shirts buzzed restlessly around the starting line. We were tense because the huge stadium on Randall's Island was jammed with spectators. I let my Greenwich rival stay ahead of me for one lap but just before coming around the last turn, I passed her and kept picking up time. I was first by half a lap with a half-mile time of 4:14—my best yet. Later when my father boasted to all his sailboating friends that I'd taken "a first," they all asked him what the name of my boat was!

Then my coach went out of town for the summer and without anyone to work out with (it's not exactly the most refreshing way to spend a summer afternoon) I became sluggish. I wasn't in the greatest condition for my first meet of the fall season on September 19. During the race I was ahead of a girl who said she'd spent her summer hard at practice and had even gone to Denver to work out with the Men's Olympic team (as yet, there is no women's team). I felt I was doing well. We were battling for first position when she told me she didn't know the way for the rest of the course. While we raced, I pointed out the direction. She came in first and sent me a note of thanks, saying that I should keep up the good work, that she wished me continued success, and that I was a really beautiful person. I guess that's what good sportsmanship is.

Then I got bogged down with physics labs and stopped working out regularly. A few weeks later Mr. MacDonald asked if our family would put up a girl who was coming from Boulder, Colorado, to compete in the Annual Coney Island Walking Meet. Our house guest wanted company to work out with, so I joined her and decided to enter the two-mile marathon walk myself. I came in second in a field of ten, twelve seconds behind my old Greenwich rival. I'd been ahead, but the girl right behind me (the one who'd sent me the note) tripped and I stopped to look back.

I did receive a beautiful silver bowl though, and my name appeared in the papers. I'm excited about race-walking again (nothing like a trophy to boost sagging spirits) and work out for an hour almost every day. It's sometimes rough fitting this in with schoolwork, violin and art lessons (I'd like to be an architect), and my part-time job. Plus dating. But now I have a goal. My best walking time will be sent to the national secretary in Detroit. If my time ranks among the five highest, I'll make the honorary U.S. Women's Team. The U.S. times will be sent to a clearing house in Copenhagen to be rated with those of other nations. Then the top country will be declared winner of what has come to be known as the International Postal Meet!

Ellen Minkow is now a young married woman. She's no longer a competitive race-walker, but several times a week she goes over to her former high school and walks around the big track there at least twice. And if her former coach, Bruce MacDonald, sees her, he makes it a point to come over and walk at least part of the way with her.

MacDonald still teaches at the school, and is still coach of the girls' cross-country team as well as the school's walking team. A handsome, soft-spoken man of about fifty, he was a star athlete in college, and it wasn't until after graduation in 1952 that he took up walking as a serious amateur sport. He did so well in his first race walk that after a year he gave up all other sports to concentrate solely on competitive walking. He subsequently competed as a race-walker in three Olympic Games: 1956 in Melbourne; 1960 in Rome; 1964 in Tokyo.

I visited with Bruce MacDonald at the high school in Port Washington. Our conversation began in his office—a small, cluttered room whose walls are covered with pictures of the young race-walkers he has coached—continued in a classroom across the hall where he had scheduled a meeting with members of his walking team, and concluded in the grandstand overlooking the track around which his walkers were training. An eight-by-ten grainy print of the seventeen-year-old Ellen Minkow walking into the "eye" of the camera hangs on the wall directly above his desk. He recalls that like many another race-walker she began as a runner on the track team before she discovered her natural talent for race walking.

Walking, says MacDonald, is one sport where a female is decidedly not at a disadvantage when competing with males. Ellen Minkow, for instance, held the boys' state record for the one-mile walk indoors and outdoors. She was also the first female allowed to compete in the Intercollegiate American Amateur Athletic Association competition. At that time she was a college freshman, competing against college men, and she won the indoor one-mile championship. Girls, he believes, make natural race-walkers for the reason that they are usually less tense than men, especially in the hip area, where it's very important to be loose. Still, he says, a race-walker can be any build. Tall or short. Heavyweight or lightweight. But, he says, being light is an advantage the same as it is in running, because "you're carrying less weight, and therefore you don't have to use as much energy to move your body from place to place. To be tall and lanky should be an advantage, but some of the best race-walkers in the world are on the short side."

The chief ingredient for success as a competitive walker, he feels, is the desire to do well. "This is even more important than ability. Great ability without desire and you won't go anywhere."

MacDonald is a member of the Walkers' Club of America, sponsor of an annual race that he says is the oldest continuous footrace in the country, if not perhaps in the world. It was first run in 1911, and in those days the walkers set out from City Hall in downtown Manhattan and walked across Brooklyn Bridge and through Brooklyn clear down to Coney Island, the famous seaside resort some ten miles away. Today, what with heavier traffic, the race is confined to the boardwalk at Coney Island, and since the boardwalk is less than two miles end to end, the ten miles are done in two round trips plus a little more. Women started entering the competition about six years ago, and a sixteen-year-old high school girl by the name of Ellen Smith won in 1975, completing the ten miles in 1 hour, 37 minutes, 15 seconds. She was the only female competing among forty-six men.

Race-walker training, MacDonald explains, is exactly the same as that of a distance runner. You walk *every* day, the idea being to work up to as many miles as possible and that way get a good strong base. And, of course, a balanced diet is very important. A race walker should avoid fried foods,

MacDonald says, because "they're hard to digest and that can mean pains in the abdomen that feel sometimes like a knife going in."

What a race-walker eats or doesn't eat before a competition depends on the individual; there are no set rules, at least not so far as Bruce Mac-Donald is concerned, and he's regarded as one of the best coaches in the country. "Some people with nervous stomachs can't eat eight hours before a race," he says, "because the nervousness seems to keep the food from digesting properly. On the other hand, I've seen people eat just before going into a race." Many race-walkers, like long-distance runners, have certain favorite foods they believe give them quick energy. Honey, for example, is popular with some. As MacDonald sees it, the only effect it can have is a psychological one because it takes the honey time to digest. Sure, it's quicker than sugar and it's better than sugar because it's natural . . . but it still takes time. Honey the night before a race would be fine.

"The popular diet now for distance running and walking is three days of overloading on protein, and then four days of overloading on carbohydrates before the competition. You can continue with the proteins, but you go heavier on the carbohydrates so that the body stores up energy. That diet does seem to help. As for bread, I'd advise whole grain because it's better for you. There's a controversy about milk because it contains lactic acid, and when muscles work they build lactic acid, and too much of it is said to cause pain and, as a result, causes the body to slow down. Not everybody agrees that this is the case, but I figure the best thing to do under the circumstances is to stay away from milk at least twenty-four hours before a race."

In international competition, he says, they have tables situated along the route—usually every five thousand meters or so—where they offer the race-walker a choice of liquids. "It can be any liquid that's been approved by the organization sponsoring the competition, but it's almost always water, tea, a fruit juice, or a soft drink. I used to take Coke and that would give me a lift very quickly—I think it must have been psychological."

When talking on the subject of race walking, Bruce MacDonald sounds like a missionary on the lookout for possible converts to his sport. He's also constantly searching for new ways to improve training methods. He showed me a sleeveless canvas jacket that ties around the waist like an airplane life jacket, and carries removable ten-pound steel plates in the hem. It wasn't new, he said; the newer models carry metal filings or sand instead of steel plates, although the effect is the same: to give the body added weight while training so that when the jacket is removed for competition, the walker finds it much easier to move because muscles have got accustomed to the added weight.

"One of the great things about walking—whether it's for pleasure or for competition," MacDonald says, "is that you're using your body to build up your body, using your muscles to strengthen your muscles. Walking and swimming are the two best exercises because they involve your *entire* body." But walking, he maintains, has still another benefit. "Each time your foot hits the ground, you're getting rid of hostilities and frustrations."

Among the papers on his desk was recent correspondence received from the Department of Medicine at Case Western Reserve University in Cleveland, where researchers are participating in a project designed to evaluate the physical fitness of competitive race-walkers. An earlier test of members of the Lake Erie Racewalkers Club found that their heart and lung fitness was comparable to that seen in highly trained marathon runners.

The meeting with his race-walking team was held in a classroom across the hall, and the mood was very low-key and convivial. A pretty fourteen-year-old named Joan, and Martha, a very tall, slender sixteen-year-old, stayed behind to talk with me before going out to the track for training. Joan told me that Bruce MacDonald spotted her "jogging around the hall between classes one rainy day about three weeks ago, and he invited me to join his walking team." She said she's always been a walker. "As a kid, my mother would ask, 'Can I drive you?' and I'd say, 'No, I'd rather walk.'"

Martha said that her mother, on the other hand, "has always been a tomboy. She's a great walker." Martha has been a race-walker for one year; before that she'd been on the track team. "The best I've ever done this past year was to finish third in a fifteen-kilometer race. I'm not an especially competitive person. I just like to exercise in the outdoors." Both girls agreed that race walking has given them more energy and they sleep better now.

Later, I sat in the grandstand and watched the team walking around the track under the watchful eyes of their coach, while not too far away two groups of cheerleaders, each with pompons fastened to their white sweaters, ran through their paces. Sean O'Neil, a slender, hard-legged sixteen-year-old, and the only male member of the team, sat down next to me. He said that he'd asked to join the walking team. Up until then he'd been a member of the track team. He's glad he switched. "I feel walking is easier for me than running. When I run I feel more exhausted. When I walk my body is more relaxed and I can pace myself better."

He confided that some of his friends on the track team think that race walking is a strange sport, but he said that that doesn't bother him. He trains early in the morning before classes, and "You should see all the people who're on the track at six and seven in the morning. All ages—some walking, some jogging."

Sean left to take a turn around the track just as fourteen-year-old Joan walked by. "Keep your chin down, Joanie!" Bruce MacDonald shouted. "Keep your chin down!" He walked over to me, leaned against the grandstand, and watched her do as she was ordered. "I could tell by the way she was holding her chin that she was straining," he said. "It's very important to be as relaxed as possible." Without taking his eyes off his team as they made their way around the track, he managed to tell me what the proper position of the body should be while race walking: "Head over the shoulders . . . shoulders over the hips . . . hips over the ankles." That, he said, makes for a balanced body.

"You don't have to be lazy to enjoy race walking but it helps. You have to learn to relax. Straining and fighting yourself is wasting energy. Race walking is a combination of body alignment, balance, and relaxation. Many walkers make the mistake of dropping their heads. That's energy going into the ground. Drop your *shoulders*, and use your arms as if you were pulling a rope. Lean from the ankles and think about moving your kneecaps. Every muscle is working in race walking, and so the tough part is learning to be relaxed.

"Race walking has no age limits. A man named Larry O'Neill from out West began when he was fifty-eight. When he was sixty, he set a record by walking a hundred miles. Little kids are very loose and so they pick up race walking very quickly. Amateur race walking isn't new. It was in the first Olympics. Beginners should try to walk at least two days a week and work themselves up to four miles. The beginner can expect to walk a mile in about thirteen minutes. The novice seeking to enter his first competition should get his time down to about ten to eleven minutes. You take endurance and turn it into speed.

"Race walking is on the upswing," he says, adding that now he conducts classes that are attended by housewives and businessmen delighted to discover how easy it is to learn. He also conducts clinics for people interested in coaching or judging race-walking competitions. For the latter, he's worked up a list of pointers. For example:

"Ideally, on a 440-yard track there should be at least four judges who rotate around the track, to assure good judging of each walker. The judges go clockwise toward the walkers and the head judge goes counterclockwise.

"A judge should stand or, better yet, kneel or lie on the outside lane of

Two of the world's most celebrated walkers

Greta Garbo walking in New York City
("w," A FAIRCHILD PUBLICATION)

Harry S Truman enjoying an early
morning walk in Independence, Missouri
(WIDE WORLD PHOTOS)

A determined Dr. Barbara Moore being interviewed on the road during her coast-to-coast walk in 1960.   (WIDE WORLD PHOTOS)

A twelve-year-old backpacker lending a hand to a six-year-old backpacker. Hiking is a companionable sport for all ages.

(SIERRA CLUB PHOTO BY CAROL DIENGER)

Ron Laird has competed in four Olympics and is in the *Guinness Book of World Records* for most national championships won by a race-walker.

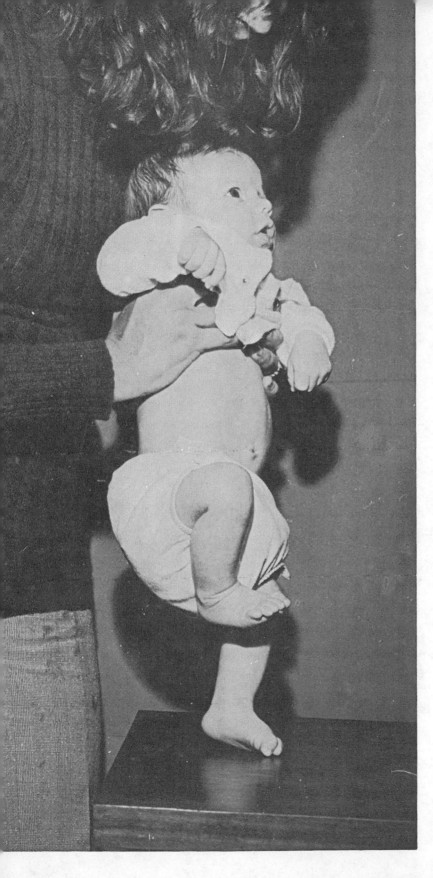

A six-week-old infant
exercising his stepping
reflex.

(PHOTO COURTESY OF
DR. PHILIP R. ZELAZO)

"Thousands of tired, nerve-shaken, over-civilized people are beginning to find out that going to the mountains is going home. . . ."
John Muir (1838–1914), naturalist.

the track to watch each athlete as he or she goes by. A judge should give his utmost attention to the athlete when he or she is within twenty-five feet and until he is approximately twenty-five feet away. Before and beyond the twenty-five-foot mark, the judge does not get a clear picture of the athlete's feet."

And when he has that clear picture, exactly what should he be looking for? Well, *lifting* for one. Which means when both feet are off the ground at the same time; in other words, the rear foot has come off the ground before the front foot has touched the ground. *Unbroken* contact with the ground must be maintained at all times.

Keeping one foot on the ground at all times isn't as easy as it may sound. During the heat of competition, there are a number of things that can cause a walker to defect. MacDonald cautions a potential judge to pay special attention when he sees a walker's head and shoulders bobbing; it's often a sign that he's not maintaining unbroken contact with the ground. Under those circumstances, he recommends that the judge block out his view of the walker's upper body and concentrate on his feet; the best way to do that, he says, is to shield his eyes with his hand or a piece of card-board. Another possible clue that the walker is breaking the cardinal rule of one foot on the ground at all times is a sudden burst of speed. When a walker suddenly picks up speed, there's often a tendency to push off with the back foot.

MacDonald advises his would-be race-walkers not to start out being concerned with speed, but rather with form and stamina; that way, he says, there's far less chance of walking illegally. He also tells them that it's best to do their training with at least one other person; it's more pleasant that way and the beginner is more apt to train faithfully. But always MacDonald gets around to the subject of staying loose, relaxed. He tells the new walker to continually think of relaxing at the shoulders, elbows, hips, and knees. Those, he says, are the pivotal anatomical spots, and thinking of them while the body is in motion is the best way to get those muscles to relax.

Although in race walking there is nowhere near any of the physical dis-comfort associated with running, Bruce MacDonald and other coaches advise the beginner to expect that progress will hurt a little. After all, the competitive heel-and-toe gait isn't the natural gait we were born to use, and it takes time for muscles to adapt. Warm-up exercises are recommended. The following three exercises are the ones I discovered race-walkers rate highest and practice faithfully before taking to the track, whether for training or actual competition:

1. Sit on the floor with one leg bent at the knee and tucked under you,

and the other extended straight out in front. Bend over *slowly* and s-t-r-e-t-c-h from the waist, meanwhile trying to clutch the ankle with both hands. When you do, hold that position to the slow count of six, all the while gently tugging at the ankle. Then sit straight, reverse legs, and repeat the exercise.

2. Sitting or standing erect, close your eyes and drop your head forward as far as possible. Then, gently move it to one side as far as possible . . . back, and around to the other shoulder . . . and continue until you've made a complete circle several times.

3. Standing erect with feet about ten to twelve inches apart, knees locked, raise both arms straight above your head. Bend slowly to the left as far as you can go without bending your knees or raising feet off the floor. Return to starting position, and repeat this bending movement to the opposite side.

> "The distinction between running and walking is very complicated. A man gets three warnings and then is waved off. If the knee of his front leg isn't locked when the leg touches the ground, if he doesn't place his forward heel on the ground before his rear toe leaves the ground, or if both feet are up in the air at the same time, then he's *running*."
>
> —HARRY RAPPAPORT, *The New Yorker*, June 19, 1948

The Talk of the Town editor of *The New Yorker* attended the 10,000-meter walking race that was the only track-and-field Olympic tryout held in New York that year. Of the forty-two starters in the contest, five were disqualified for illegal walking by chief judge Harry Rappaport, once a middle-distance walker himself. While he was chatting with Rappaport, Henry Laskau, who finished the tryout in first place, joined them. He was later described as "a dark-haired young man, with horn-rimmed glasses. He came to this country from Berlin in 1938 and he learned English at night school and as an infantryman in the army. Difficult though this may be to believe, he also learned to like hiking in the army and after his discharge took up the sport in earnest. 'Walking doesn't tire a man as much physically as it does mentally,' he says. 'The mental strain can be very wearing especially if you worry about keeping that forward knee locked.' "

Henry Laskau's time for the 10,000-meter tryout (10,000 meters work out to 6 miles, 376 yards, 4 inches) was 49 minutes, 29.4 seconds. The Olympic record for the 10,000-meter walk was set in 1912: 46 minutes, 28.4 seconds. Laskau went on to compete in the 1948 Olympics in London and, along with two other American walkers, was disqualified in a dispute over their walking styles. Two years later he competed in Madison Square Garden and set an indoor record of 6 minutes, 22.7 seconds for the mile walk. By 1954 he had won the AAU 10,000-meter championship eight years in a row. Today, with forty-three national championships to his credit, Henry Laskau is still referred to by some sportswriters as "the dean of this nation's race-walkers" and "one of the greatest figures in the history of American race walking." Now past sixty, an avid walker though no

109

longer a competitive walker, his body is slender and hard and he actually looks fifteen years younger than his calendar age.

He recalls that in his day race walking was mostly regarded as an old man's sport. But then younger men like him got interested in it, and the sport revived.

Laskau had been a middle-distance runner before World War II, and he resumed running after the war. "But I never amounted to anything," he says now. "I usually finished eighth or ninth. Then one morning I was running in McCombs State Park across from Yankee Stadium, and a fellow who knew me from the sport came up to me and said, 'Why don't you start race walking?' I said, 'Not interested, it's much too slow.' But he persisted and suggested that I try one lap walking. I said, 'No, it looks awkward to me.' Well, he was a race-walker himself, a national AAU champion, and so he dared me. We walked one lap together and he told me, 'Henry, you're a natural walker. You have more chances to compete in race walking and get a prize than in running. I bet you a hundred to one that in 1948 when we have the Olympic Games in London you'll be on the team!' I laughed at him. But he wouldn't take no for an answer, and he invited me to come out and walk with him the following Sunday. I agreed, and I came home that day and told my wife, 'I've adopted a new sport. It's walking— fast walking.' And I wasn't so young at the time. I was thirty-five.

"Well, in a matter of weeks I'd entered a race and won a beautiful big trophy, and from then on I competed in race walking. I walked a mile in Madison Square Garden and finished a very close second to the national AAU champion. I had a year and a half to go for the Olympic tryouts and so I started rigorous training: two to three miles during the week but distance only on weekends. Sundays I covered ten to twelve miles. In those days distance in the Olympics was ten thousand meters or six and a quarter miles on the track. In 1947 I won my first national AAU championship, and the next year I won the Olympic tryout and made the team."

President of the Walkers' Club of America, sponsor of the race walk held each November in Coney Island, Laskau has competed in ten of the races and won two. Today regarded as a kind of Bernard Baruch of race-walkers, he takes special pride in "having gotten some very famous athletes interested in race walking. Ron Laird. Bruce MacDonald. The Israeli champion Shaul Ladany, who competes all over the world." One of Laskau's protégés is Todd Scully of Virginia, "a fierce competitor. He's the man to watch in the twenty-kilometer event in the 1980 Olympics." (America has yet to win a gold medal in the Olympic walking event. Closest was a third place in the 1972 games held in Munich.)

Training has changed since Laskau was competing. "Nowadays," he says, "they train every day, sometimes twice a day. That's the new method. In my day, the training was not so rigorous. Today for the Coney Island race, you should start three months prior to the day of the race."

He has often served as a coach. Some years ago he accompanied the American team to the prestigious Lugano Trophy Race in Switzerland. It takes place every two years, and champions from all over the world come to compete. "The entire distance is about two hundred kilometers, starting at one of the highest points in Switzerland and ending near Lugano. It's a relay race, so each competitor walks about twenty-five kilometers. But it's a very tough course and a man has to be in top shape. He must train all year—speed training, distance training. If any race-walker wants to compete, he's got to be ready to walk hills. There are plenty of hills in Switzerland."

A walker's technique must change as he takes a hill in his stride. Steps, says Laskau, must be made smaller. "And going down you have to be very, very careful so that you're not off your heel. You might skip going down a hill and if a judge with binoculars—judges are placed . . . some in cars . . . a mile apart, a half mile apart, it all depends—sees you skipping, it can mean a disqualification. The racer is under surveillance at all times."

He and his wife went hiking in Switzerland a few summers ago and were much impressed with the Swiss technique for walking the hills. "My wife and I were young in comparison. Many were really elderly people, but they had a system for walking up the mountain. An easy, steady pace. They go step by step up the mountain path, bypassing us like we were standing still. *Amazing.* They simply bend their knees and lean the torso forward—all nice and relaxed. They don't breathe hard. It's a very relaxed attitude.

"And that, you know, is the secret of race walking. You are completely relaxed. When jogging you're pushing all the time. *Exerting.* In race walking you are coordinating with your arms and legs and hips. Personally, I have nothing against jogging, but for older people it's a very hard exercise for the body."

Laskau dropped out of competition after winning a gold medal in the 1957 Maccabiah Games in Israel, but in 1965 he came out of retirement to win his fourth gold medal in that event. Today he's perfectly content to walk a recreational mile in about eight and a half minutes. "Today's race-walkers are very, very fast," he says. "They're all breaking my old record now. Walking is much more popular because they start younger and that makes it very competitive. I'm quite happy at the growing interest in it."

* * *

Many years passed between the time I met my first race-walker—the man in the Fox Movietone newsreel—and my second, Otto Wenk. Otto came to America in the late 1950s and settled in Little Rock, Arkansas, where he continued walking with the same passion as he had back in his native Germany. On a visit to Little Rock, I heard about him; his prowess as a walker had made him a minor celebrity. When I met him, he'd just come back from a vigorous walk around the campus of the University of Arkansas. A small man with the narrow lines and grace of a whippet, Otto exudes vitality and good cheer.

About the time I started writing this book, I received a letter from him. He'd just got back from competing in the Senior Olympics held that summer in Santa Ana, California. He had won the 5,000-meter walk for the sixty-five-and-over age group. He wrote that he had also entered the 10,000-meter event and won that too, in the time of 1 hour, 2.52 minutes. And knowing that I was about to leave for California, he added that he had walked the whole ten thousand meters with Lori Maynard, whose time was the same as his, "but we were walking in different age groups since she is only forty-two. She paced me the whole race and was the reason I walked such a good time. She's a very friendly person and would be happy to talk to you about walking."

So one day while on the West Coast I drove from San Francisco to Redwood City and met Lori Maynard, a 109½-pound blonde who looked as though she could be kin to Otto: the same narrow lines and grace, the same vitality and good cheer. She had only recently returned from the National AAU Masters Meet in Atlanta, Georgia (open to athletes forty and over), where she had placed first in the twenty-kilometer (12.4 miles) race with a time of 2 hours, 9 minutes, 11 seconds. She was still grinning with the glow of her victory, and why not? She has only been race walking since early 1977. And furthermore, ". . . there were those hills!"

Lori had done some hill training, "but when I saw those hills in Atlanta, I realized it'd been only token training. My chief competition was a woman from Seattle and she had trained on hills. I thought, *Oh boy!* We had a five-mile loop course and there were two miles of it up and down those hills. Well, this other woman and I walked together and we'd converse a little— more like thinking out loud, like, 'Well, here come the hills!' We stayed together for the first five miles. I didn't leave her for seven miles and I thought surely she'd accelerate and come after me, but she never did. Finishing the first set of hills I was *so* tired. I thought, Oh, she can have it. And that's when something in my subconscious said: *Oh, no, she can't!*

Immediately I really started to work. I just figured she was going to have to take it from me. I wouldn't *give* it to her."

In the past, Lori Maynard says, she wasn't so competitive. "I used to think, Yes, I really want to win. But I really didn't feel the desire. The race in Atlanta was a turning point for me, and I wonder now if everyone experiences a moment like that."

• She says she never felt so competitive before, not even during her time as a runner. "I'd always finished in the middle of the pack. Then when I started race walking and began to catch the other girls or pass them—that was such an incentive that I stayed with the sport to see what I could do with it." Her husband, who had been a pole-vaulter at college, had always counseled her that when running, if she passed someone on the track, to act authoritative. But not until her win in Atlanta did she finally understand what that meant. "This whole sport is so much mental, and the nicest part for me is the self-confidence that I've gained from it."

During her peak training season, Lori Maynard walks at least six days a week, sometimes seven. And since she wants eventually to compete in the 20,000-meter races, it's essential that she develop endurance. "Proper breathing has always been the most difficult part for me, running or walking. I've had to learn to pace my rhythm of breathing the same way I pace my physical activity. It's not a short, shallow breath; it's what I call *belly* breathing. I breathe with my mouth open and I figure about five steps per half breath, or five strides per exchange of breath. Now I'm at a point where I don't have to think about my breathing. Except, of course, if I'm doing something wrong I know it, because I start to get a stitch in my side and I know either I'm in the wrong posture or I'm too tense . . . or my breathing is too shallow. Some days I go out on a workout and I don't know until I get started how I'm going to feel. But some days the rhythm is there, the breathing is right, and the energy seems to feed itself. You've got the walker's 'high'! I don't think it's anything mystical. The whole thing is just together."

Lori Maynard is so enthusiastic about race walking that together with another walker, a Finn by the name of Harry Siitonen, she has started the Golden Gate Club, which meets on Saturdays in Golden Gate Park in San Francisco, about thirty miles north of her home. Ten people turned up for the club's first meeting, one of them a woman of seventy. Among them was a friend of hers, a jogger who could no longer stand the pounding of that sport. At that first meeting she and Harry Siitonen demonstrated the stretching exercises they consider essential before starting out on a brisk walk . . . explained the importance of proper breathing . . . and showed what Lori calls "the fundamentals of walking." In subsequent meetings, she and Harry have taken the members out on walks. "We walk around a track that's about two-thirds of a mile. After that we go out on the road, where we've marked off a quarter mile and a half mile. Those of us who've walked heel and toe are doing that, and others are just out there for the pleasure of it. Some of them swinging their arms like hikers do. And I think that's great if it gives them pleasure. After all, it's a fun walk. There's no pressure, no competition."

Anyway, there are a variety of different styles of walking, even among race-walkers. "It's just amazing to me that practically every walker I see has a style different from the next," Lori observes. "I have a short stride. I stand quite erect—I don't tend to lean forward or backward like some walkers do. And I use my arms properly, which is a big benefit. The arms should be carried bent at the elbows, but not tight. Fingers curled, but loose. And the arms in moving shouldn't cross the centerline of the body, because then you begin defeating your forward motion. At the extension of the arm towards the back, a kind of shove with the elbow tends to thrust the forward foot even more forward, so you're getting help. You want as much efficiency as you can get the entire time you're walking. My style has been praised by judges at different walks I've gone to, so I feel I'm able to help these newcomers by *showing* them."

She was concerned that from Otto Wenk's letter I had perhaps got the impression that it's possible for race-walkers to carry on conversation while competing. "A five-kilometer race is considered a sprint, and it's an all-out effort," she explained. "But in the longer race your pace is somewhat slower and it's sometimes comforting to have someone to chat with— occasionally. Sometimes it's a case of a walker who has had a bad experience with his laps being counted correctly, so he may say 'What lap is it?' Now, in the walk with Otto we were out on unpopulated areas of the road and sometimes a person needs a pickup and I could feel that Otto needed that. It was nice for me, too. We didn't actually carry on a conversation. For instance, he asked me, 'What are you going after?' I said that I'd be very happy to finish in sixty-two minutes—of course hoping that I'd do it faster. Otto was going after his age record and he said, 'I *know* I can break that record!' He stayed with me all the way and I'd try to keep his spirits up when he'd start to get down. He'd begin to tell me about a negative experience he'd had and I'd say, 'Save it, Otto! Not while we're walking. While walking you can only think positively.' I don't usually talk because it interferes with my breathing, but it's worth it when you're with someone like Otto."

Inevitably, the name of Ron Laird came up, as it did, I discovered, every time I talked with a race-walker. Laird has walked in four Olympics. He's in *The Guinness Book of World Records*. As Lori explained it, "The name Ron Laird is one of the first names any race-walker learns." She had seen him compete years ago when she was still running and the idea of race walking had never entered her thoughts. In fact, "You couldn't have convinced me that I'd be doing it myself one day." Laird fascinates her, just as he seems to fascinate every other race-walker I have met.

"He's like a yo-yo," Lori said. "He stops training between Olympic years. It's an up-and-down thing where he works himself into fine shape in order to try for the Olympics, and then when the Games are over he stops training. The Olympics are the ultimate; after that there's nothing left until the next Olympics. And Ron knows he can come back. I remember once asking him how he thought he would do now that he's a Master—forty years old. Can you still come back? He said, 'Oh, I know I can. I've done it throughout my life ever since I was a kid.' So he *knows* he can do it. And I'm sure it's no big, complicated thing. He just works very hard on his training. I would guess he's just now starting to get back into the swing of things preparing for the 1980 Olympics."

When I told her that I had been hoping to meet Ron Laird, Lori immediately got on the telephone and made inquiries as to his whereabouts. California, after all, is his home state now. The last she had heard, he was working as a house painter somewhere out around Pomona. I had just missed him some months earlier as he passed through New York on the way to visit his parents in Ashtabula, Ohio. I managed to reach his father by telephone only to discover that Ron had left that morning to go back to California. Now Lori learned that he had just left for Oregon.

Well, I still hope to meet him face to face one day, though I'm beginning to think that this is probably as likely as sidling up to Garbo and having a heart-to-heart talk as we stride down Fifth Avenue together. Like the actress, Laird is a cult figure, a legend in his own time—the star of a sport largely misunderstood and underrated until very recently.

"Race-walker Ron Laird has no regular job and no address—only plans to be a U.S. Olympian for the fifth time," read a lengthy article in *Sports Illustrated* (May 8, 1978). It went on to categorize him as a sports hippie. "Like Peter Pan, he will not grow up."

Laird has won sixty-nine national championships (he's in *The Guinness Book of World Records* for the most national championships won by a race walker), and established eighty-one records. He won a gold medal in the 1967 Pan-American Games, two bronze medals in world championships, and traveled with twenty-four international teams. He has been a top race-walker for twenty-three years, and lives below the poverty level on an annual income of around three thousand dollars earned mostly as handyman, grass cutter—you name it. "He's a sort of vagabond," says Ray Lumpp, the sports director of the New York Athletic Club, where he can stay while in the city, and which has been known to give him traveling expenses that will take him to his next meet.

Ron Laird readily admits that his family would like to see him get a regular job. To that idea he replies, "Quitting and getting a job? It would be the easiest way out, but I don't want to melt into the crowd and become the average guy." He was rather average once upon a time. In high school he wasn't much of an athlete, earning only one sports letter. Then he discovered race walking at a Madison Square meet in 1955, and within five months he had defeated Henry Laskau in a handicap race. And since then, as Elliott Denman, a sports columnist who has known Laird for years, puts it, "Nothing has mattered in the man's life other than race walking. . . . I can't think of any other athlete who has devoted himself the way he has. I guess he's reached maturity, but I don't think he really grew up."

"Just now Laird is not in superior competitive condition," the *Sports Illustrated* writer noted. "He is 15 pounds overweight because he treated 1977 as if it were a throwaway year, letting his training deteriorate. . . . It is easy to tell he is not in top condition now because his eyes do not have that glitter of emeralds set in deep, hollowed-out sockets. This ethereal appearance comes from pushing one's body several levels beyond what it was built for."

Meantime, Ron Laird has to face some tough competition if he wants to make the 1980 Olympic team: younger men like Todd Scully, Henry Laskau's protégé, and former distance runner Neal Pyke. Don't you wonder how he'll make out? I do.

> "This was a banner day in our life, full of exciting episodes, and a most enjoyable experience. We are very glad that we were one of the 106 walkers who entered this walking match."
>
> —ALONZO CHAMBERLAIN, November 1923

Mr. Chamberlain was seventy-seven years old at the time and walking an average of fifty miles each week. The "most enjoyable experience" he refers to was the occasion of the thirteenth annual Coney Island Walking Race held on Thanksgiving Day, November 29, 1923. The race, which in those days began at City Hall in lower Manhattan and ended on the boardwalk at Coney Island in Brooklyn—a distance of ten and a half miles— is still an annual event, making it the oldest American footrace of record. The following account of his participating in it appeared in a booklet (one of a series titled "The Pleasures of Pedestrianism" and free to subscribers of the weekly newspaper he published), and was given to me by Henry Laskau, current president of the Walkers' Club of America, sponsor of the Coney Island Walking Race since it started in 1911.

We went down to New York City in our car, with our most expert driver, Frank Koehler, of East Rutherford, for the reason we wanted some one to carry our coat to Coney Island, as we wished to walk with only our sweater on—perhaps without it. But we found it cool enough to wear our sweater, and we were surprised that not once during the ten and one-half mile walk did we have to wipe away any perspiration. Which also showed we were in good condition.

We arrived at the City Hall at 1 P.M., and saw already a squad of policemen getting ready to handle the throng of spectators. By 1:30 there was quite a gathering, and we had the pleasure of making the acquaintance of quite a number of notables among the walkers and officials present.

We were the oldest entrant at 77 years, and Pathfinder Hocking of the Walkers' Club of America was next at 69 years. He regretfully stated he had always before been the oldest entrant. He has a head of pure white hair and was clad in light racing costume—a most pleasant and jolly hiker, that at once made friendly with us, and filled us with

117

friendship for him. There was one other old contestant and us two had the honor of being the first ones to start the race promptly at 2 P.M. We each had a handicap of 30 minutes.

Before the start of the race, some newspaper photographers twice asked us three oldest entrants to line up for a photo to appear in the New York dailies. Then a young lady took a snap-shot of us three.

Our companion in this start at once took the lead, and before we crossed the Brooklyn Bridge the Pathfinder passed us, but we were glad to have someone ahead to show the right way, as we are utterly unacquainted with the Brooklyn streets. Then more and more of the faster walkers passed us at fast pace.

The streets along the route had crowds of spectators, and we got many a cheer and encouraging shout of "Go it, Pop!"

The policemen along the route were unusually obliging to point out the right course, or to hold back the autos for us, and the autoists also were generous to always give us the right of way, and one stopped his car and asked "Are you Weston?" *

It was all a most pleasant experience, for the throngs we passed seemed all so most friendly, with encouraging shouts and wishes of good luck. The *Daily News* states that 100,000 viewed this race.

Nearing the end, a young contestant came along at quite a good pace and passed us, but we quickened up some and passed him, and then we had it "nip and tuck" for the rest of the way to the finish, and got quite some cheers and hand-clapping from the large crowds. We were ahead, a few yards from the finish, and would have finished first, but an auto crossed right in front of us two which gave him an opportunity to get ahead and then one of his friends caught the lad in his arms and carried him proudly off—it was quite a poetic finish—the youngest entrant versus the oldest.

After getting our time of 2:23, we were told there were two ladies looking for us, who proved to be Mrs. Adam and Mrs. Orr of the Paterson Ramblers and pleasant greetings were exchanged.

We then went over to a restaurant on Surf Avenue, where the officials were holding a conference and giving data to the newspaper reporters.

Here we had the pleasure of making the acquaintance of a fellow Jerseyman—Mr. L. B. Hohmeyer of North Bergen, a crack runner, who told us of innumerable prizes he had won in races. He was in rather light apparel for participation in this race and was worried over the non-

* Edward Payson Weston, well-known long-distance walker.

appearance of his wife with his coat. So we invited him to ride home with us in our auto, and then going along Surf Avenue, luckily he met his wife and child waiting for him, so the three of them had a ride to their home, as we crossed the 42nd Street ferry to accommodate them.

Reached home by Williams Avenue route around 7:30, with such an extra good appetite for supper—My! but the food did taste good.

NOTES BY THE WAYSIDE

We were placed No. 99 in this race and had a large placard with this No. fastened on our breast and back with safety pins before starting.

Our Coney Island friend, Mr. Stein, met us at the City Hall, with his wife, who had come to carry his coat for him back to Coney Island, so we had the pleasure of offering Mrs. Stein the courtesy of going to Coney Island in our auto with our driver, and they had a good opportunity of seeing the race on the road down. We believe Mr. Stein done the distance in about two hours.

We saw some of the walkers leaping up the curbstones, when they should have stepped up.

Were told 10 or more entrants were disqualified for unfair walking— we saw lots that looked as though they were running.

We lost at least a minute or two through three autos that held us up at crossings. And nearing Coney Island, there were so many autos we had to desert the nice smooth road and walk on a rough cinder path.

As we done the ten and one-half miles in 143 minutes, this was at the rate of a mile every 14 minutes.

We learned quite a lot about walking in this race. The first lesson was that our style of walking was no good against the style of most of our competitors. We have always cultivated an easy style of walking, avoiding all extra exertion, so as to conserve our strength. This is all right for long distances—but for this short race, the other contestants just swept past us. They all seemed to be exerting every muscle in their body—swinging their shoulders and making all sorts of muscular contortions, so that some few of them looked real humorous, and we would not have been surprised to see some of them fall all apart they seemed to be so exerting themselves. We were told that some fainted dead away before reaching the finish. The winner's time was 1.22.23. Our time was 2.23. However, at the finish we were still feeling good for 10 miles more, if necessary.

We had a hearty laugh when we saw our rather humorous picture in the *Daily News* the next day, with the title "A. Chamberlain, 77, was the oldest entrant in race, but he still has spring of youth." The artist must have snapped us in full action somewhere on the route.

On the road down were held up at Secaucus by fireman for a contribution to apparatus fund.

All along the route in Jersey City, children celebrating Thanksgiving in humorous masquerade costumes.

For the first time crossed on those new ferry boats, all the lower part for teams—passengers upstairs—fare 51 cents for auto. (Why that 1 cent?)

Flocks of seagulls sailing in the Hudson.

Fifty-five years later, on a dazzlingly clear Sunday in late November, I attended the sixty-eighth annual Coney Island Walk. And some things, besides the name of the competition, had very obviously changed since Alonzo Chamberlain competed. First, it was no longer held on Thanksgiving Day; so many wives had complained that it interfered with their family's holiday that it was changed to the Sunday after Thanksgiving. Then at about the same time, it was decided that the walk should be confined to the boardwalk at Coney Island rather than begin at City Hall and end at Coney Island. The street traffic had proved too distracting and dangerous. Now, walking down the street to the boardwalk, I fell in step with one of the eleven females entered in the event: thirty-one-year-old Young Kim, a pretty Korean who had got up that morning at six-thirty and taken the train from Poughkeepsie, New York, in order to be on the boardwalk and ready to start the walk at ten. A jogger who has been having trouble with her knees, she popped a couple of aspirin in her mouth before hurrying inside the YWHA building, where the walkers had use of the locker facilities.

On the boardwalk, between two orange plastic cones which established the starting place, Henry Laskau stood, hatless, wearing a windbreaker and holding a clipboard that contained a list of the sixty-seven contestants, who ranged in age from a boy of seven to a man of eighty-three. The race is conducted on a handicap basis, thus making it possible for, say, a seven-year-old boy to compete with men who, in a few instances, have walked in the Olympic Games. Stanley McIntosh, a seven-year-old black boy, was given a handicap of forty-six minutes, and his eleven-year-old sister, Tanya, a handicap of thirty-four minutes, since she has already competed in several races this year and won a few. Ed Doran, an eighty-three-year-old dentist from Buffalo, New York, had a handicap of forty-seven minutes.

Promptly at ten, with the temperature at a cold twenty-seven degrees, the walkers were assembled on the boardwalk, some in shorts and others in track suits but all with the large white cards containing their entry numbers hung around their necks. A man bundled inside a heavy overcoat held a cap pistol in the air, said "On your mark . . . ready . . . set . . . GO!" and the event officially started with the contestants setting out in pairs. While awaiting her turn, Young Kim stood with her hands on the boardwalk railing and did stretching exercises. All the walkers headed for the Brighton Beach end of the boardwalk, which is perhaps a quarter of a mile away, and then turned around and started walking the two miles that would take them to the Coney Island end, while Henry Laskau stood in place and watched their form and shouted either encouragement ("Good! Good! That's what I call *walking!*"), or caution ("Watch your form . . . You're coming up too high").

The families of some of the walkers stood around in groups or sat on the boardwalk benches hugging their coats around them, as husbands or children, and in a few instances both, proceeded up the boardwalk under the watchful eyes of the judges stationed along the route. Carrie McIntosh, the mother of seven-year-old Stanley and eleven-year-old Tanya, stood with a long woolen scarf covering her neck and chin. A runner herself, she told me that her eight-year-old daughter had walked in the two-mile event held an hour earlier, and that her youngest child, a four-year-old boy, "loves to walk too, and I expect I'll start training him on a daily basis next February."

Tanya, she said, had started as a sprinter before switching to race walking, and just the past summer at the East Coast Conference Meet she had set a new record in her age group for the 880-yard event, finishing in four minutes flat. Today was Stanley's first race. She told me that Tanya's been training under her supervision six days a week for anywhere from one to two hours. One day it will be for distance, another day to build endurance. Sometimes she'll walk around an outdoor track, and the next time walk six miles along the city streets at "a normal race-walking pace," which usually means covering those six miles in about fifty-eight minutes. Four-year-old Nicholas, she said, can't wait to start training too. "I'll work on his form first and then build up his speed," she said. "All children have speed; it's form you have to teach them. It's important to feel your body, to get to know what it can do. Now Tanya's at that point. She knows what her body can do. And she also knows it's the daily training that's important, that tones up the body and builds endurance." Meanwhile, Mrs. McIntosh watches their diet and sees to it that they eat plenty of the vegetables growing in their garden at home in New Jersey. "They're not into junk food," she said. "Oh, sometimes they sneak in a cookie or some candy, but most of the time they snack on celery or a raw carrot." While we were standing there talking, Tanya walked by, a slender child in a blue track suit, her hair in pigtails, and her eyes focused straight ahead. "You're looking fine!" her mother called after her.

Onlookers who earlier had been taking a constitutional along the boardwalk had now begun to gather around, watching the walkers heel-and-toe by, some clearly showing strain. When little Stanley McIntosh came along, some of the women in fur coats and woolen hats smiled and applauded, as Henry Laskau said, "You're doing good. Watch your form." A man in a ski parka settled down on one of the nearby benches and proceeded to play "Santa Lucia" on a xylophone he had brought with him. He wasn't paying the slightest attention to the walking race, and one got the impression that probably this seemingly impromptu musicale was a regular Sunday event. Another man was on the beach feeding the sea gulls and pigeons who were flying around him, and farther up the beach some youths wearing bulky sweaters were tossing around a football. The sky was a vivid blue and the sun very bright, and I thought that if this whole scene was being filmed, somehow "Santa Lucia" played on a xylophone would be the perfect background music.

Approximately twenty minutes after twelve noon, the last of the walkers made it across the finish line, and Henry Laskau led the way into the YWHA building, where the respective times would be tabulated and the winner announced. About a half hour later, nine-year-old Diane Romansky, who only one year ago began race walking, was handed the Adolph Arnold Memorial Trophy. Her actual time for the ten-mile walk was 1:39:00, but she had been given a handicap of forty-four minutes. A sixteen-year-old boy finished second, a forty-eight-year-old man came in third, and fourth place was taken by an airline pilot who had walked in the 1968 Olympic Games in Mexico. Diane's fifteen-year-old sister finished far back, having tripped and fallen during the race. Their father, a mechanic from Pennsville, New Jersey, was interviewed along with his daughters by a reporter from *The New York Times,* and I heard him say that the family is hoping that the Olympics will soon introduce women's walking. Meantime, he's the girls' coach, and in this Coney Island race he had passed up competing himself in favor of checking his daughters' time. "I've been trying to bring them along slowly," he said. "The big thing I aim for is for them to improve a little each time they race." He pointed out that Diane's best time last year for the same distance was 1:59. Meanwhile, the eighteen-year-old boy from Niagara Falls who had actually come across the finish line first sat across the room looking rather noncommittal. He had been disqualified for running. The eighty-three-year-old dentist from Buffalo had finished the walk in 2:20:29, just slightly less than one minute after seven-year-old Stanley McIntosh. Tanya McIntosh had finished in two hours and seven seconds.

A member of the Walkers' Club of America got to his feet and announced that he was conducting race-walking clinics every Sunday morning in Central Park, and added that the Road Runners' Club was now sponsoring race walking in conjunction with the Walkers' Club, and that a ten-mile walking race was scheduled for the following month. "The runners really go bananas when you walk faster than they run," he said, and that got a round of hearty applause.

I was leaving—almost out of the room, in fact—before I realized just who the father of Diane Romansky was. *Dave Romansky*, the "blue-collar walker" from New Jersey. At least that's what some of the sportswriters called him back in 1970, when no athlete in the country had set as many records as he had: fifteen American and three world records. Like Ron Laird, he started as a runner and then switched to walking, and, according to an article in *Sports Illustrated*, "the effect was as if Mozart had been hacking around with, say, sculpture until somebody said, 'Hey, Wolfgang, did you ever think of giving the harpsichord a whirl?' " Only two years after he'd taken up race walking, Dave Romansky set his first American record and, because he was a hundred-and-fifty-dollar-a-week pipe insulator for Du Pont, earned himself the tag of "blue-collar walker." He got off to the 1968 Olympic Games courtesy of a Dave Romansky Olympic Fund established by his town's Chamber of Commerce, and when he returned home, the New Jersey Jaycees presented him with their Physical Fitness Leadership Award and Jaycees in his town named him the Outstanding Citizen of the Year. In 1970, when he was a member of the track-and-field team sent by the AAU on a European tour, he carried our flag in the opening ceremony in Germany—the first time for a walker. I remember reading about it at the time, and I recall his remark: "It was the proudest moment of my life." Now here he was, eight years later, the proud father of the nine-year-old girl who walked away with the Coney Island Walk trophy, being interviewed by *The New York Times*.

Finally on my way out, I overheard a group in a corner of the room discussing the *Sports Illustrated* article on Ron Laird, which had also contained a reference to Dave Romansky. They all agreed that while the article gave a clear picture of Laird, it presented a distorted picture of most other race-walkers.

"What did it mean race walking draws the eccentrics? Look around this room, will you? Have you ever seen a healthier, more normal-looking bunch of people?"

"And it said that race-walkers are wanderers . . . that Dave Romansky trudged door to door to raise money so he could get to the Olympics. Now, how does that make him a wanderer? He's a family man with a full-time job. Do you know he was twenty-six before he ever got to visit New York? So he goes door to door to get up the money to get to the Olympics—that's wandering?"

"And they give an example of a South American who went on a four-year walk. That's not race walking. That's long-distance walking. Don't they know the difference? It's clear that the person who wrote that article doesn't know or care much about race walking."

"But it was a good profile of Ron . . ."

"Yes, but people shouldn't assume that every race-walker is as offbeat as he is."

On my way out of the building, I fell in step again with Young Kim and a youth who had also walked in the Coney Island event for the first time. Like Kim, he was a runner, too, and having leg trouble. Both said that they found race walking more difficult than running because it's more disciplined. "You use more muscles," said Kim, "and I have to fight not to break out into a run." Still, your weight is more evenly distributed when walking than it is when running, the young fellow said, and he thought that that meant less chance of injury. Both of them appeared excited by their participation in the race, and I got the impression that before too long both might be devoting more, if not all, of their exercise time to race walking.

"Afoot and light-hearted I take to
the open road,
Healthy, free, the world before me."

—WALT WHITMAN, *The Open Road*

LONG-DISTANCE WALKING

Before man discovered he could ride a horse or burro, he walked out
of necessity. But even after the invention of the wheel, some men continued to walk for the sheer joy of it and a smaller minority walked long
distances—sometimes hundreds and even thousands of miles—again for
the joy of it, although almost always for other reasons too.

Most long-distance walkers, if their walks have been of heroic proportions, have attracted public attention, and a few have won the public's
affections as well. But no one has ever managed to do both for so long a
period of time as Edward Payson Weston, who first walked into promi-
nence in 1861, when he walked from Boston to Washington, D.C., to see
Abraham Lincoln inaugurated, and then continued to walk and talk his
way into the consciousness of the public until as late as 1922.

Weston, who weighed four pounds at birth and was a sickly child,
credited the serious walking he began at eighteen with developing him
into the lithe and wiry young man who, to quote from his journal of the
1861 Boston-Washington, D.C., walk, had made "a wager with Mr.
George B. Eddy, of Worcester, Mass., to this effect: that, if Abraham
Lincoln were elected by the people, President of these United States, I
would agree to walk from Boston State House to the Capitol at Washington, D.C. (a distance of four hundred and seventy-eight miles), inside
of *ten consecutive days*. It was simply a banter between ourselves while
dining together one day, and I do not suppose that either of us at that
time had the remotest idea of ever attempting such a task. For my own
part, I was not aware, at the time, that I possessed any great locomotive
powers; and Mr. Eddy has frequently said to me, that, if he had been
the unfortunate victim, he would 'most decidedly have preferred to get
excused.' "

But Weston, who would soon be labeled in the press "a snappy little
kid," chose not to be excused, and no sooner had Lincoln been elected
than he was making plans to live up to his wager. On the morning of the

day he started his walk, he stood on the steps of the Boston statehouse, made a short speech to the crowd assembled there, and then made his way down to Beacon Street with his two companions following after him in a light carriage that contained his baggage and the advertisements and circulars he would be distributing en route for two companies that had chosen to underwrite his walk: a sewing-machine manufacturer and a photographic studio.

Weston walked the first five miles out of Boston in just forty-seven minutes, and for the rest of the way his progress was faithfully reported by *The New York Times*. In Stamford, Connecticut, "A gentleman mounted a platform and proposed three cheers for the 'pedestrian,' and it is needless to say that the pedestrian received the cheers." In Newark, New Jersey, "A large crowd received him, and he was obliged to call the assistance of several policemen to keep the crowd off his heels." The following day, as he made his way toward Rahway, New Jersey, his companions who were following him in the carriage, and taking notes as well, wrote, "He encounters a great deal of mud, which was quite deep, and consequently very difficult to travel through; he lunches upon sandwiches, and soon after became exceedingly exhausted and sleepy; complained of a severe pain in the chest, and attributed it to the eating of mustard on sandwiches. He stopped every quarter of a mile and sat down to sleep, was exceedingly irritable, which caused the whole party to have the blues, of the darkest kind. Mr. Weston concludes to go back half a mile to a public house and sleep (we having just passed the village of Rahway). He returns a few steps when, suddenly throwing off his blanket, he exclaims: *'No, I won't go back!'* and, wheeling around, strikes into a four-mile gait."

Weston arrived at the Capitol after ten days, four hours, and twelve minutes of walking. As he saw it, he was four hours and twelve minutes late. Still, he did attend the Inaugural Ball, and the next day, after a good night's sleep, he visited the Capitol, met Congressman Stephen A. Douglas, and a few nights later, at the Lincolns' first levee in the White House, Douglas introduced him to the President and Mrs. Lincoln. Lincoln offered to pay his fare back to Boston, but Weston politely declined the offer, explaining that since he had failed in the first attempt, he felt obliged to try it again and so would walk back to Boston. He didn't, however—at least not then. For while he was in Washington, "the Southern Rebellion broke out and I thought it proper to forego that task for some future occasion, and to use my pedestrian abilities in serving our government." There was rioting in Baltimore and communication between it, Washington, and the eastern cities was interrupted. So Weston walked into Baltimore with 117 letters for the New York and Massachusetts regiments stationed there sewn into the lining of his coat. After he'd walked seventy miles in less than twenty-four hours, he was nabbed by the Sixty-ninth Regiment of New York, put under arrest as a spy for the rebels, and thrown into a guardhouse. But soon afterward he was recognized by someone who had seen him on his Boston-Washington, D.C., walk and was released. The following year he made good his promise and walked from the Capitol to Boston in eight consecutive days, excluding Sunday. He had promised his mother that he would never walk on the Sabbath, and he never did.

By now the American public was fascinated by Edward Payson Weston. And, fiercely articulate, he enjoyed giving interviews to the press. "Nature," he told reporters, "has provided us with precisely the equipment that furnishes to *every one* the possibility of having the right kind of exercise— the *daily* use of the great external muscular system of the body, particularly of the lower extremities—in other words, *walking*." It was, he said, the only proper exercise for a lifetime. And he said he fully intended to live to be a hundred.

In 1867, when he was twenty-eight, Weston walked from Portland, Maine, to Chicago—a distance of 1,326 miles—in twenty-six days. According to *Harper's Weekly,* "This walk makes Weston's name a household word, and really gives the impetus to the pedestrian mania which has become so general." The next year he walked one hundred miles through New York's Westchester County in twenty-two hours, nineteen minutes, and in 1870 walked two hundred miles in St. Louis (including two miles of it *backward*) in forty-one hours. That same year five doctors connected with the Bellevue Hospital Medical College in New York City had him—with his permission, of course—under observation for one month while making a study of the physiological effect of such severe and protracted muscular exercise. Weston was then thirty-one years old and weighed 120½ pounds. By the time he left the hospital, the press had already started referring to the feisty Weston as "a walking machine."

He spent the period 1876–1884 abroad. He walked through England at the rate of fifty miles per day for one hundred days, and each night along the route he delivered a lecture on temperance. In 1879, Weston became an international celebrity when he won the Astley Belt, the then acknowledged emblem of championship in long-distance walking. The British nobleman he had bested was the first to congratulate "the nervy little bugger of a Yankee."

Back in the States after the turn of the century, the "wee Weston," as some members of the press had dubbed him, really hit his stride. In 1906, at the invitation of thirty doctors of the two cities, he walked from Philadelphia's City Hall to New York's Fifth Avenue Hotel, a distance of one hundred miles in twenty-three hours, fifty-four minutes, stopping just once for a thirty-minute sleep at New Brunswick, New Jersey. The following year he repeated his Portland-Chicago walk of 1867, and now, at sixty-eight, he did it in twenty-four days, ten hours, besting his previous record by twenty-nine hours. In 1909 he walked, with riding crop in hand, from New York to San Francisco, and the next year from Los Angeles to New York. By now the white-haired Edward Payson Weston had become a bona fide folk hero regarded by *The New York Times* as "the best known pedestrian in the world . . . still displaying the sprightly step of a youth."

His "ocean to ocean tramp" was financed by a millionaire who refused to be identified, but it was revealed that for each day he arrived in New York City ahead of his scheduled ninety days, he would receive a bonus of five hundred dollars. Reporters from all over the country reported on his daily progress, and not a day passed that *The New York Times* didn't carry some mention of the seventy-one-year-old walker who said that he would celebrate his seventy-second birthday en route by walking seventy-two miles that day.

A crowd of three thousand welcomed him when he arrived in Albuquerque, New Mexico, on February 28, with a riding crop—by now his trademark—in one hand, the other fisted, and wearing a high-crowned felt hat and high boots. He was averaging sixty miles a day and was four days ahead of schedule. On his seventy-second birthday, March 15, he walked his promised seventy-two miles through Kansas. "He came in at a fast gait and didn't appear at all fatigued," noted the reporter from the *Times*. "I must change my shirt and cap before I enter Emporia," Weston told him. "These are soiled. I'm not too old to forget my appearance, and never shall be. You may think that's funny, but there are two principles I adhere to: one is to look good when I can; another is to never discourage a person who tries to be a friend merely because he is a stranger. It braces me wonderfully to have these people, old men and old women, and the school girls and boys walk with me."

By March 28 he was ten days ahead of schedule. On April 15 he entered Erie, Pennsylvania, and the schools there were dismissed so that the children might see him walk by. Two days later he was in Fredonia, New York—sixteen days ahead of schedule. The next day he made it to

Buffalo and was met at the city line by crowds and squads of mounted police. But one week later it was reported that "a 30-mile-an-hour gale retards aged pedestrian near end of his trip." The next day, however, in Amsterdam, New York, he met "the merriest reception accorded him at any place during his walk." When he reached the city limits, all church bells rang, skyrockets were set off, and hundreds of cars honked their horns. An estimated ten thousand people were massed on both sides of the street. "Amsterdam has not seen a crowd to compare with the one of this evening since the last Presidential campaign."

The next day found Weston lying in a farmhouse outside Albany with a badly swollen ankle. He'd fallen, knocked over by the impact of a boy standing nearby who had been hit by a passing car. A day later, however, the *Times* reported:

> Weston pluckily resumes walking . . . stiff and bruised by his fall on the road . . . it was only by the exercise of his adamantine will that he was able to keep on his way at all. Mr. Weston was particularly irritated over automobiles to-day, and he said that if he had a revolver he certainly would have taken a shot at a touring car party which passed him near a bridge.
>
> A boy riding a bicycle also disconcerted the old man to-day, because he insisted on riding close to Weston after he had been warned away. The boy was so intent on watching the pedestrian that he did not notice a stone in his path, and when he struck it and fell off his wheel he rolled against Weston's left foot. Weston whacked the boy well with his walking stick. Fortunately the boy struck his strong foot and did Weston no harm.

The spunky septuagenarian entered metropolitan New York on May 2, having covered 3,500 miles ocean to ocean in seventy-eight days—twelve days ahead of schedule and, as a result, six thousand dollars richer. Ringed by reporters, Mayor Gaynor, an avid walker himself, greeted him at City Hall while a crowd of twenty-five thousand watched. "My old friend, I am mighty proud of you for what you have done," he told him. "The whole world is proud of you. Weston, you are a benefactor to the human race for you have shown people what can be done by a man who lives simply and healthfully in the open air. You have caused people to go out into the open and taught them how to live. Now if they will only follow your example and precepts they ought to live to be a hundred years old instead of the proverbial three score and ten."

Gaynor handed Weston a purse containing four hundred dollars in gold. The old man tried to thank him, "but his voice broke and tears trickled down his sunburnt cheeks." But he finally did manage to say, "This is the happiest and proudest day of my life. What a nation! It's worth all the hardships." And then, the man from *The New York Times* reported, "The crowd kept on yelling itself hoarse."

Interest in walking had never been so high, thanks to the example set by Weston, and the year of his walk across America an uncommonly large number of people were walking "the Weston way." A young English couple, married one month, left New York's City Hall, dressed in identical khaki walking suits, for a walk around the world, only weeks after the arrival there of a middle-aged couple who, with their dog and a little bay mare named Dolly, had walked the two thousand miles from Kansas City, Missouri. In December of that same year, a ninety-eight-year-old man from Mobile, Alabama, walked 2,800 miles from New Orleans to San Francisco. *The New York Times* published a stream of letters from readers regarding Weston and Walking. One suggested "a permanent department of pedestrian instruction, either by private beneficence or public donations of a national character, and veteran pedestrian Weston be appointed director general of the department for the balance of his life." Many readers wondered why there weren't pedestrian clubs similar to those found in England and Germany. "Let us hear from a 'Moses' with a 'club,'" wrote one reader. To which a young matron from New Jersey replied, "May I qualify as a 'Moses with a club'? It's only an embryo club, and consists of my three babies, but I'm training them. At three years they are able to walk about three miles without showing fatigue. The youngest learned to walk eight months ago, and now, belongs to the club. Who knows this may be the foundation of a big and energetic club, but I hope I shall not be called upon to supply all the members." And a reader in Chicago wrote that she had belonged to a walking club now for the past three years and "Saturdays, winter and summer, we tramp about the surrounding countryside." There was, she wrote, "something surprisingly refreshing about being with people who have come together because they love the 'open.' The truly undesirable person never comes."

Noting the growing interest in walking, *The New York Times* published an editorial on June 30, 1910, titled "The Charm of Walking" and made this point: "We have started the campaign; we trust that our readers will keep it up." The following year the Walkers' Club of America was founded in New York City for the purpose of physical exercise and competitive racing, and it is still active today.

The American public apparently couldn't get enough of Edward Payson Weston. For the next three years after his Los Angeles–New York walk, he toured the country delivering his lecture "The Vicissitudes of a Walker." A correspondent for the *Pittsburgh Christian Advocate* reviewed it as follows:

What a Monday morning that was when the famous Edward Payson Weston appeared upon our platform! What a record as a pedestrian this man has! As he described his famous feats in all lands, it is enough to make a trolley car blush for shame, and to turn an automobile green with envy. Mr. Weston is 73 years old, but shows no surface symptoms of this advanced age. It is true that his hair is touched with silver, but it is not the sheen of feebleness; it has the glitter of good, hard, enduring silver. He has a ruddy, wholesome face, a twinkling blue eye, and his body is compact and straight and well built. He tells his story in a straightforward, direct and forceful manner. It is done in the style of a businessman, and has none of the arts and tricks of the professional lecturer. He is all the time a Yankee, and the twang and colloquialisms of New England are constantly falling from his lips, all unconscious to him. He is really a fluent and fascinating speaker. He has a sharp and accurate knowledge of human nature, and unique and amusing incidents play lightly and easily upon the shining surface of his story as it sweeps steadily on. His sense of humor is unique and personal and always shows that shrewd Yankee flavor. If any of your churches want to have a charming morning's entertainment, be sure to send for our young friend Weston.

By 1913 Weston was ready for another long-distance walk, this time the thousand miles from New York to Minneapolis in sixty days. It was referred to in the press as "the crowning effort of his pedestrian career. He has the same buoyant step, the alert eye and quick nervous muscularity which he has possessed for a generation. He is a doer, not a boaster, clean cut and exact in all his business relations. He has given a dignity to a very simple exercise. He believes in his work and walks for the very love of it, and with a firm conviction, confirmed by a life-long experience, that he can but spread the gospel of walking and lead others to follow in his footsteps, he will have conferred a boon on humanity." Weston told reporters that he took on this, his final challenge, to prove "that the individual who walks, eats moderately, and leads a simple life, can accomplish a greater task in his 75th year than the ordinary man at 50 years can do."

For this walk Weston had commercial sponsors. Among them was a sock manufacturer who advertised:

On his walk from New York to Minneapolis Mr. Weston is wearing the same kind of sox he wore in his wonderful walk from Los Angeles to New York City. By his permission we have called them the Weston Heel & Toe Walking Sox.

And the Erie Railroad also ran an ad that read:

Mr. Weston in walking from New York to Minneapolis is following the lines of the Erie Railroad to Chicago . . .
    The Scenery is magnificent
    The Dining car service, excellent
    The Road bed, superbly rock-ballasted
    The Block signals, automatic
    The Service, tip-top

En route to Minneapolis, Weston delivered his now much quoted lecture every evening. Meanwhile, the Minneapolis Athletic Club which had invited him to lay the cornerstone of its new four-hundred-thousand-dollar building when he arrived in the city, promised him that "a royal welcome awaits you. You will be escorted by the Governor and staff, the National Guard, U.S. troops, 2,000 members of the Athletic Club, mounted and on foot, representatives of other clubs and civic organizations, and 500 decorated automobiles. A grand reception typical of Western hospitality will be given at the Athletic baseball park, a fitting tribute to an achievement. So come on, Weston!"

After that walk scarcely a month passed without his being quoted in the press. It was estimated that during the past forty-seven years he had walked in public a distance of more than three times the circumference of the earth. He told the *New York World*:

Walking is almost a sure cure for rheumatism. I got it good and plenty in 1898. I had to suffer all right. When I saw my doctor he said, "Why don't you take some of your own medicine?" I started in. The first day I was able to walk one block. I sweated like a young bullock. Next day I was just able to do it again. I took the salt foot baths. Hard work fixed me up for two blocks and then three. When I was cured I walked 34 miles every day. I left my rheumatism on the road and it's there yet.

Walk naturally for the best results. Carry a short stick like a riding crop and put it behind your back between your elbows, and you feel as if you were sitting down all the way.

Walking for women is the best thing in the world for them. In Kansas City a whole club of women walked with me for 13 miles. One young woman stayed with me on the road from 8 P.M. to 2 A.M. and did 18 miles. Such walking makes a woman natural—it's the best thing in the world there is. If our city women walked 10 miles a day it would make the next generation superior to ours. They want to learn the secret of what I have learned that the second or third mile is the hardest to pass. There they are introducing themselves to the unknown muscles in the legs and they must get acquainted. It's just this difficulty of acquaintance which keeps more women from walking. Why, after the fifth mile you want to keep on walking.

You ought to have the right kind of shoes when you walk. Sore feet would take the heart out of any one. The shoe should be loose enough to allow you to turn your toe under when you have your shoes on. This lets the air in about your feet and keeps them cool.

I wish I could impress upon everybody that there is no exercise more dignified or less expensive or more conducive to health than walking.

In 1922, at the age of eighty-four, Edward Payson Weston walked a distance of five hundred miles in thirty days—excluding Sundays, as always. He passed away in 1929, just weeks before his ninety-first birthday, still a daily walker and still maintaining that walking is the one perfect exercise.

In 1912, Minta Beach, a well-to-do New Yorker, decided to walk from New York to Chicago. A pretty brunette somewhere in her mid-thirties, Mrs. Beach was accompanied on her 1,071-mile walk by Jerome G. Beatty, a staff correspondent of the *New York Globe* and *Chicago Daily News*, who rode in her motorcar with her chauffeur, her maid, and the baggage. Mrs. Beach later wrote her account of the walk in a book titled *My Walk from New York to Chicago*, which was privately printed. A vegetarian, she dedicated her book "To all who find within the realms of Nature, their foods (without the shedding of blood), their inspiration (without the aid of human presence), their knowledge (which leads in time to perfect understanding), this book is joyfully dedicated by the writer."

In the preface, reporter Beatty wrote:

This book is the story of one of the more remarkable feats of endurance ever accomplished by a woman. It is the true tale of a sincere, unselfish effort to aid humanity.

The pace that Mrs. Beach set over the bad roads (sometimes hub deep with mud) and through rain and sleet, would have tested the nerve of any strong man, would have made the bravest want to turn back. But Mrs. Beach never faltered, never weakened. She laughed at the mud and made up songs about the rain.

Her object was to prove conclusively that hard labor can be performed on the most radical non-meat diet. She wanted everyone to have health, she wanted to cut the cost of living. She didn't theorize; she went out and proved that the meatless diet was the best diet.

When queried by a reporter about the walk that was to begin from his City Hall, New York's Mayor William J. Gaynor replied, "Do I suppose this big walk of Mrs. Beach will start all the women walking? I hope it will start them to walking to the market or to the grocery store, at least, so that they may pick out their meats and groceries and not have them pitched into the basement door by telephone orders any more. That is the sort of thing that is making the high cost of living." As for Mrs. Beach, who was following a strict raw, no-meat diet, His Honor feared that she would die before she got to Albany, unless she "drank something." Later, when she had completed her walk and was writing her book, Gaynor died, and Mrs. Beach noted, "In view of his attitude toward the walk, it may be well to state that had Mayor Gaynor known the severe effect of certain foods upon the heart action, and had he been willing to give up such foods, also stimulants of all kinds, he could have lengthened his life many years."

When Mrs. Beach set out from City Hall on the first day of her walk to Chicago, the park "was black with people. The police cleared the way for me up Broadway," and she took the center of the street, and walked between mounted policemen, talking to the crowds as she passed.

"I tried to impress upon their minds that the right food makes good blood; that exercise sends this red blood galloping through the system, fairly pushing out the impurities. Bounding vitality, bright faces, and healthy bodies are the inevitable results. Happiness follows."

Mrs. Beach averaged twenty-five miles a day and, as Beatty noted, she reveled in the rain. "Did you ever try walking in the rain?" she wrote. "If you ever think the world is against you, that nothing will ever go right again, put on an old pair of heavy shoes, a slicker and rubber hat, and go out and splash along a country road. I'll guarantee that all your troubles will be gone before you've walked a mile."

A doctor told the *Globe*, "She has a wonderful physique, and will power and determination. I have no doubt that she will reach Chicago, but the milk she drinks is all that will keep her going. Milk and eggs contain almost the same body-building properties that are in meat. I believe that on a strictly vegetable diet she could not make the trip." When his remark was repeated to her, Mrs. Beach replied, "It doesn't discourage me. In fact, I am rather pleased, because the greater number of persons who doubt my ability to make the trip, the greater my triumph will be." Meanwhile, she gave up milk and eggs for the remainder of her walk.

When a woman she conversed with while walking on her eighteenth day said to her, "In your own heart, I bet you don't have any hopes of getting there," Mrs. Beach replied, "Nothing in the world can prevent me from reaching Chicago. I know I can do it, because I love to walk, and since I know the right foods to eat and how to live, I can do almost anything I set my mind upon."

She had made up her mind to walk to Chicago and so she did, arriving there after 42½ days—four days ahead of schedule. On going down Michigan Avenue, she noticed a boy standing on a porch waving a handkerchief. She waved back, and minutes later discovered that it was the home of Ogden Armour, the meat packer. "I looked carefully around the corner expecting to see twelve-inch guns trained upon me from the home of this man whose business I was doing my level best to destroy, but there were none, only the little boy waving his good cheer."

Interviewed by reporters in Chicago, Mrs. Beach declared that she felt so improved in health that she could have continued her walk on a raw non-meat diet indefinitely, perhaps averaging even more than the twenty-three miles a day that she made going to Chicago.

The New York Times hailed her "really considerable achievement" while editorially it said that "her theory remains fallacious . . . meat-eating comes with progress. That man has attained the power of eating practically anything that any animal finds edible is not the least among his marks of superiority to all the others. That one fact gives him the freedom of the whole earth, and voluntarily to restrict his diet would be suicidal folly." To which Mrs. Beach replied, "This editorial proves beyond a doubt that the one who wrote it has no knowledge of foods best suited to the needs of the human being in accordance with age, temperament, climate and occupation."

In Chapter 20 of her book, Mrs. Beach wrote that after her walk was successfully completed, she had "learned more about walking than I ever had expected to know, and I had proved to myself my earlier contention that there is no better exercise, and certainly none cheaper.

Any form of exercise taken in the open air improves the health; in fact, fresh air exercise is absolutely necessary to acquire a strong body. Some say swimming is better than walking, as aquatic sports bring every muscle of the body into play. But not every one has the time or the place to swim. One can walk any time, but swimming necessitates an hour or so spent in preparation, and only women know the discomforts which follow a swim in which the water has gotten under the bathing cap. One can enjoy a four-mile tramp in the time required for preparing for a swim and for dressing afterward.

I wish some philanthropist would offer, say, fifty dollars to every person who walks five miles every day for two months. By that time the contestants would have formed a habit they would never care to break.

Walking quickens the circulation, thus aiding the system in its work. It helps the brain, too, because in walking one comes in contact with nature, and thinks new thoughts, conceives new plans, is inspired for better things.

It preserves the beauty of face and figure, providing one understands how to walk correctly.

The office-worker, particularly, should take long walks whenever possible. He or she is in a sitting position most of the day. They ride to and from work, and if the evening is spent at home, they invariably spend it sitting.

After a few years the walking muscles become almost useless, and we cannot walk any distance without so much fatigue that there is no pleasure in the exercise. We succumb to the surrounding conditions of habit, and each year finds us more and more disinclined toward this delightful exercise, until finally we are really not able to indulge in it at all.

I have in mind several persons, more than sixty years old. Some of them have taken daily walks most of their lives. Others are on their feet only a few minutes each day, and the difference in their appearance is marked. Those who walk have preserved an erect figure, bright eyes and clear skin. The others look continually tired.

I know a man seventy years old who has never eaten meat, and who has a greater knowledge of the intricate mechanism of the human body than any other person before the public. I refer to Dr. Hanish, the celebrated lecturer from the Orient. He walks thirty miles as easily as most of us walk ten, and does not appear to be more than forty or forty-five years old.

Actors and actresses, who try to keep their youth as long as possible, pay careful attention to their foods and to their exercising. We should all follow their example, and spend some time every day, even if it is not more than thirty minutes, in walking. While we exercise we also must breathe carefully, inhaling and exhaling vigorously, but evenly.

The business-girl, the one who does not work on her feet, should make it a point to walk at least two miles every day. She will so enjoy her exercise that soon she will add a mile or two or more without any extra exertion.

Take your walks thoughtfully; that is, use all your muscles to the best advantage. Keep the body erect, but not tense. The arms should hang easily at the sides; do not swing them. The muscles of the waist and back should do their part so that with each indrawn breath the walker is conscious of their existence: Comfortably broad shoes—they need not look ridiculous—with medium-weight soles and not too low heels, should be worn. Some require a higher heel than others, owing to a more arched instep. The rest of the costume may be arranged to suit one's convenience. The best stays to wear are those that are low-cut and lace in front; they can be adjusted so easily to fit the figure. They should not be laced too tightly. They can be pulled low before being laced, and provide splendid support to the abdomen, which is a great help in walking, and relieves all strain and pressure on that part of the body.

Any time is a good time to walk, though early in the morning is better in summer, and in winter the noon time is most suitable. I frequently put on heavy boots and a sweater whenever I feel the impulse to walk, and take a jaunt of five miles in my house gown, rather than lose the time required in donning correct walking togs.

As you walk, make it a point to get the best good from each step, and you will be surprised at the results. It is hard to tell you just how to walk, and it is not necessary, really, for you will teach yourself very quickly if you are observing.

Don't plead that you haven't time to walk. Take time. You have time to sleep and to eat, haven't you? Exercise is just as important as sleeping and eating, and the person who realizes this grows stronger and brighter each year instead of more feeble and more helpless.

If you live in a city, make a bee line for the nearest park. If in the country, take the most secluded road, if you don't mind the unevenness of the path. Get out and see what nature can do for you. You'll never regret it.

Minnie Hill Wood decided in 1916 to walk from Washington, D.C., to San Francisco to prove that "a woman, alone, can safely walk every step of the way across the United States." The influence of Edward Payson Weston was still very great, and Mrs. Wood grew tired of getting so much advice about practicing "Weston's step" as she went along. "People don't see that a walk that might be easiest and quickest for Weston might be almost impossible for someone else."

A petite, gentle person, she was an odd mixture of adventure and extreme caution, and each evening she wrote an account of her day that eventually became a book titled *Afoot and Alone*.

Stories of rabid coyotes concerned her. "It's said that one ran into the round-house at Imlay, and attacked a man sitting there; they killed it. They tell me if the coyotes are not running I may know they are not mad. I wish people would keep the stories to themselves."

In Burlington, Colorado, she decided, "The people here never walk the roads outside of the towns. They either ride, or drive. For several days I haven't seen a person on foot.

"I may be foolish about the cattle, but when there isn't a fence or tree in sight (seldom is there a house) and a bunch of cattle are near the road, I do what I did this morning—go looking for a railroad. The railroad is always well fenced—so far, at least. If people walked their roads, it would be different. But a person on foot is a curiosity to the cattle."

A woman walking the open road was a curiosity in some other quarters, too. A small-town postmaster apparently regarded her with suspicion. "He is a tall, gray-bearded man," she wrote, "and I got the impression from his manner, that he disapproved of a woman person who would walk across the country. (Why is it only men are supposed to have the privilege of wanting to see the country at close range?) When I went back later to buy a few things, he deigned a wintry smile—perhaps because I bought cold cream, and he may have thought that, after all, a woman's a woman for a' that, even if she tramps the roads."

Mrs. Wood thought that most of the country people she encountered in Indiana and Illinois "can't seem to understand my taking this walk. The burden of their ideas in regard to such a walk is the question 'What do you get out of it?' I say I am learning lots, seeing the country and the people, and they pipe up, 'But why do you want to if you don't get something out of it?' I say I'll get lots of beautiful scenery in Colorado and farther west. 'But what's the good if you don't get something out of it?' Daily the same formula is coming through. The women don't understand."

In Colorado, she stumbled into a camp of convicts repairing a road and had dinner with them. "I told them about my walk, trying to avoid having any pauses, for I didn't want them to feel that I might be thinking of them being convicts. Everything was good, and well cooked; even the apple pie was fine,—I don't generally eat apple pie, but I ate this."

She walked into San Francisco 140 days after starting her hike. "San Francisco is no longer a dot on the map, with mountains and deserts stretching endlessly between me and the dot," she wrote. "It is really a city—the busy Exposition city, wonderfully improved since 'the fire.' "

Her mirror reflection puzzled her. "I don't belong to the black, the brown, the yellow, or the white race," she decided. "I am a deep red bronze, the left (south) side of my face several shades deeper and bronzer than the right side. I can't imagine ever being white again."

It was November 11, 1916. The little woman had proved that a woman, alone, could safely walk across the United States—and she'd done it nearly seven weeks ahead of schedule.

Eleanora Sears, a Boston socialite, walked for the sheer love of walking; she had no cause to espouse, no product to sell. And the thought of this very proper Bostonian out there on the open road proved enormously titillating. Not since the "wee Weston" had a walker so captured the public fancy.

Miss Sears began her long-distance walking career in 1912, with a 109-mile walk from Burlingame to Del Monte, California. But thereafter she confined her feats of endurance to New England. In 1925 she walked from Providence, Rhode Island, to Boston—a distance of forty-seven miles—in 10½ hours. The next year she repeated the walk, clipping forty-three minutes from her previous time and then celebrated that evening with a dinner dance in her Back Bay home. Two years later she set a new hiking record by walking the seventy-four miles between Newport, Rhode Island, and Boston in seventeen hours.

"It would seem to stand as the longest sporting hike ever achieved by a woman," * reported *The New York Times*. "During this walk she averaged practically 4.4 miles an hour, an average that few men walkers, pros or amateurs, have ever equaled." She was accompanied by three Harvard seniors, alternately serving as pacers. She started from in front of the Casino in Newport at 4 A.M., and ended seventeen hours later "amid a downpour of cold, drenching rain at 122 Beacon Street. She took only tea along the route and at a five-minute stop she ate an orange."

* Apparently the *Times* considered the earlier walks of Minta Beach and Minnie Hill Wood feats of endurance, and Miss Sears's "sporting hike" a record of time.

* * *

In the ranks of long-distance walkers, men have always far outnumbered women, but it is the women who have almost always received the most attention from the press. And for good reason. They have been extraordinarily colorful copy, and none more so than Dr. Barbara Moore, a fiftyish Russian-born Englishwoman who, after walking the length of Britain in twenty-three days, arrived on these shores in 1960 determined to walk across America "to prove we women can do all that men can do." Like Minta Beach, she was a vegetarian, but with this difference: Dr. Moore also ate grass "and quite a lot of air, especially air in the mountains." A large glass of grass juice was said to be her favorite six-course meal in one. The blond five-foot-three doctor was also a pilot and a racing motorcyclist, and as feisty and charmingly imperious as Edward Payson Weston. *Life* magazine credited her with "starting the long-distance walking craze in England."

She arrived here on the *Queen Elizabeth*, around whose decks she'd paced six to eight miles a day to keep in condition for her marathon walk. "I expect to live to be 150," she told the reporters who came to meet her, adding that she considered herself "a walking laboratory in which the virtues of strict vegetarianism are being proved. I'm always using my body as a guinea pig. What futility to experiment on animals! There is no reason for a human being to deteriorate and die. It's people's bodies that muck it all up."

Dr. Moore flew to San Francisco, from where she planned to walk the 3,387 miles to Times Square in New York City.

Eighty-five days later, wearing a faded bandanna and the rubber-soled brogues that were specially made for her hike, Dr. Moore limped briskly into Times Square. And less than twenty-four hours later, with reporters huffing to keep up with her, she hiked five miles through Central Park to make up for a ride in a New Jersey patrol car she'd accepted the previous day in order to arrive in New York City before dark.

Her coast-to-coast walk had been a symphony of mishaps and celebrations. In Utah she had twisted her ankle. In Indiana she had been hit by a car and spent three days in a hospital, fuming at U.S. women motorists. Still, she had managed forty miles a day, despite dust storms, a tornado, and roaring truck traffic. Her most enthusiastic reception had come in Denver, where she was greeted by a crowd of a hundred and fifty thousand and where the governor, chief of police, and assorted civic officials awaited her on a speaker's stand. "Your Colorado is the most beautiful place I've ever seen!" she said enthusiastically. "Even your grass is very good," she added, holding her grass squeezer aloft. "It tastes the greenest."

The New York press lionized "Britain's Walking Woman" with "the constitution of Atlas and the stubbornness of Noah," marveling at her energy ("a handshake like Jack Dempsey's"), and noting that "she moves with the lithe grace of a teen-aged athlete."

Later that year, when U.S. customs officials confiscated her fruits and vegetables, Dr. Moore, declaring, "I've had enough of American officialdom!" took a polar flight back home to England. And except for a short visit here the following year, during which she hiked from Key West, Florida, to Boston, Massachusetts, she never came to America again. She died in England in 1977.

Early in 1970, thirty-five-year-old David Kunst left his small town in Minnesota to walk around the world. A little more than four years later he ended his thirteen-country, fifteen-thousand-mile odyssey. He had been greeted by Princess Grace of Monaco . . . stoned by anti-Americans in Iran and Turkey . . . and refused permission to cross China. Five thousand of his hometown's population of 6,700 were on hand as he strode up to what had been his starting place in 1970. The United States, he told them, was "the best damn country I've ever been in."

And most of America's long-distance walkers agree. A year ago young Peter Jenkins, confused by the turbulence of his times, set out with his dog, Cooper, to discover his country—to "give the country another chance." He says now that he started out searching for his country and himself and found both. In his book, *A Walk Across America*, he writes, "I had started out with a sense of bitterness about what my country appeared to be. But with every step I had learned otherwise. I had been turned on by America and its people in a thousand fantastic ways."

That same year Garry Moore, a young California writer, walked from Boston to San Diego, and during those eight months on the road he found that "the whole nation turned out to be amazingly, gratifyingly friendly . . . some rather extraordinary people do exist out there."

And walking is the best way to discover that. There is something about the presence of a walker that smooths out other people's souls.

ORIENTEERING

This is currently being referred to in some circles as America's newest cross-country sport, which may be a bit premature. Although orienteering is little known in this county, abroad there are estimated to be more than one million orienteers. At last count there were some 2,350 clubs in thirty-six countries. The O'Ringen, Sweden's annual orienteering meet, is said to be the largest single sports event on earth.

Briefly, here is what orienteering—sometimes described as a hike with a purpose—is all about. Using a map and compass, the orienteer must locate certain predetermined spots in a forest, a park (in Japan they even go orienteering in downtown Tokyo). Each participant is timed as he or she checks in at each checkpoint. The fastest in each category is the winner, and most meets are divided into beginner, intermediate, and advanced classes.

Sounds easy? It isn't. Which is why the orienteer needs a compass as well as a map; the course in a forest, for example, may be dotted with everything from hills and fields to swamp. Which is also why, despite the importance of speed (the orienteer can run or walk), it's often the walker, who combines strategy with common sense, who wins. After all, it's up to each one to decide which direction will take him to all contact points in the least amount of time. And once again, women, even intelligent children where the course is not too strenuous, are not at a disadvantage. Mental and physical agility count more than muscle.

Originally a military exercise, orienteering didn't get its start as a sport until 1918 when, in Sweden, a scout leader gave his boys maps and compasses and turned a cross-country race into a game. Although tremendously popular in Europe by the 1930's, orienteering didn't come to this country until 1946, when a celebrated Swedish orienteer set up a course in the Indiana Dunes State Park. Now, it may be the next way for a walkaholic to extend the pleasure of walking, or combine it with a little safe running.

If what I've told you about orienteering interests you, you can obtain more information by contacting the U.S. Orienteering Federation, P.O. Box 1039, Ballwin, Missouri 63011.

PART II

THE
ART
OF
WALKING

CHAPTER

6

WALKING TALL

"Walking is the easiest exercise for most individuals, one that can be done without equipment except good shoes, in almost any terrain and weather, and into very old age."

—Dr. Paul Dudley White, cardiologist

YOU'VE BEEN WALKING FOR AS LONG AS YOU CAN REMEMBER—AND BE-
fore then. None of us actually remember taking our first steps. But perhaps you recall someone telling you how proud, indeed how startled you were the day you discovered that you could, under your own power, take off and explore the world. So if walking is our first independent act, and if man is the only true walker among God's creations—where does the *art* come in? Walking with proper posture. Head erect, chin level; abdomen flat and hips tucked under; feet parallel and pointing forward. In short, walking tall.

Once you have that under control, then you hit your stride depending on how leggy, how heavy, how energetic you are; that is, the step that's the right length for your height, and the speed that's right for your weight and muscular strength. And once you have all that, you're off and walking with long, fluid strides, swinging the leg from the hip and both arms swinging easily, naturally, in opposition to your leg swing. No huffing. No puffing. No exertion. In fact, you don't seem to be carrying your weight at all. You're aware only of rhythm. That is when you've mastered the art of walking—joyous, effortless self-locomotion.

But first some of us have to unlearn some bad habits so far as posture and body mechanics go. For what we are at any stage of maturity depends in large part upon what has happened to our bodies since we were born, especially during the period of rapid growth and physical development up to the time of puberty. Each of us is, in a sense, the sculptor of his body.

Regrettably, proper posture, which is essential if you're to reap the full benefits of walking, isn't as common as it should be. It's estimated that up to 70 percent of American youth show imperfect body mechanics. It's not age but poor posture that leads to poor body mechanics that, in turn, contribute to runaway waistlines, sagging chins, and aching backs. And the damage doesn't stop there. Slouch, and blood circulation is poorer too, thus putting even more strain on the heart.

Why is it so difficult to stand erect? Why does it often require concentration and special effort before good posture and graceful movement take hold and become a good habit? Because we are, each of us, a work of extraordinarily complicated architecture composed of some two hundred bones and seven hundred muscles of varying sizes and shapes, which wasn't originally designed to stand upright. The spine, the foundation of good posture, is a series of curves itself, and yet it has to carry the weight of the upper half of our bodies.

Evelyn Loewendahl, a former professor of physical rehabilitation and consultant to the U.S. Department of Health, Education, and Welfare, says, "Why man ever stood up remains a mystery. Four-legged creatures move more efficiently." So we can't afford to take good posture and fluid, effortless movement—in short, good body mechanics—for granted.

Happily, as long as we're alive our bodies are subject to change. As long as there's life, there is pliability of the cells. Anyone's anatomy will "give" regardless of age. So you don't have to settle for poor body mechanics and the low energy level that inevitably accompanies them. You don't have to let them squeeze the joy out of walking. Not when it's so easy to unlearn those bad habits.

HOW TO PUT YOUR BODY IN ALIGNMENT

Evelyn Loewendahl suggests you stand with your back, head, and shoulders against a wall, with your heels about one inch away from the wall and toes pointing straight ahead. At that point, she says, you're in perfect alignment. "Your head is where it belongs. Your hips are swung under your spine. Your knees and ankles are directly in line with your hips." Close your eyes and concentrate on what perfect posture feels like, and then walk away from the wall imagining that the wall is behind you.

Dr. Charles Leroy Lowman, founder of the Los Angeles Orthopedic Hospital, was named "Doctor of the Century" by the Los Angeles Medical Society when he was well into his nineties. He wrote then, "Make a conscious effort at first, and soon good posture habits will come automatically."

Once you grow accustomed to standing and walking properly, your body will let you know when you're slouching. Stand tall and walk tall, and you feel lighter, more energetic. When your body is in alignment, you actually save energy. Slouch, and you feel heavier, and everything you do, including walking, seems to require more effort. So make a conscious effort at first and avoid the occasional backache, the feeling of tiredness that come when you slip in and out of good posture. Periodically, take inventory of your body parts. Remind yourself of how one part relates to the other, and feel how—when you're walking tall—all the parts assume their proper place:

> Stand with feet a few inches apart, toes pointing straight ahead. Slowly draw the buttocks tightly together. Then distribute your weight evenly on both legs by pressing on the ball of each foot. Tighten the muscles in the front of your thighs. Then slowly stretch the spine. Imagine that you are trying to touch the ceiling with the crown of your head. Don't tilt your chin in the process, however. Don't raise your shoulders, but draw your shoulder blades together, and allow both arms to hang loosely at your sides.

It actually takes longer to read the above than it does to do it. Repeat this body-inventory exercise several times during the day and, as Dr. Lowman promised, "soon good posture habits will come automatically."

STRETCHING EXERCISES BEFORE WALKING

Dr. Lowman believed it was necessary to stretch before improved body alignment could be obtained, adding that "limbering-up exercises improve all metabolic processes."

Effortless self-locomotion is not a rigid, stiff-armed, stiff-backed military stance, but one that's comfortably erect and free-flowing. Which is why stretching exercises do so much to prepare you for a walk. The hips, knees, and ankles, in particular, must be loose and flexible. If they're not, your walk becomes jarring and tiring. S-t-r-e-t-c-h for elasticity. S-t-r-e-t-c-h for greater mobility.

1. Swing both arms overhead and, as you do, stand on your toes and stretch as though reaching for the ceiling, and *inhale*. Exhale, relax, and return to starting position.

2. Standing with feet about ten inches apart, swing both arms up from the right side of your waist—up as high as you can go. Bring both arms down and over to the left side of your waist, then up again as high as you can go. Keep your feet in place and let your arms and waist do all the stretching.

3. Standing again with feet about ten inches apart, swing both arms straight overhead. Stretch from your waist as though trying to touch the

ceiling with your fingertips. Then, in one clean, fluid motion, bend forward (without bending your knees) and let your arms swing through between your legs.

4. Sit on the end of a table or desk, with one leg planted firmly on the floor and the other extended across the length of the flat surface. The toes of the extended leg should be pointing upward, and the knee as straight as possible. Now, using your toes as a kind of pulley, try to stretch that leg while keeping the knee straight and toes pointing upward. Chances are that the first few times you try this, your knee will raise. But keep at it, and when your knee remains straight, you'll know that you have good flexibility in your hip, knee, and lower leg.

5. Facing the back of a straight chair, position yourself about an arm's length away and, keeping both arms straight, take hold of the chair for balance. Raise your left leg to waist level and then, keeping it straight, swing it behind you, stretching it out as far as it will go while keeping it as straight as possible. Repeat, using your right leg.

RHYTHMIC BREATHING

When you're walking, the thing to concentrate on, once you have the proper posture, is *rhythm*. By controlling your breathing as you count steps, you'll discover the rhythm that is best for you. And once you've learned to coordinate your breathing with the steps you take, you will have the natural, effortless motion that makes walking a veritable breeze.

Inhale as you take, say, four to six steps, and then *exhale*, as you take your next four to six steps. How many steps you take is up to you. For as your lung capacity increases and develops, you'll quicken your pace, and take a longer arm swing. That's when you will begin to achieve respiratory fitness, when the miles will begin to slip by and your walks become longer and increasingly more enjoyable. You see, the faster your pace, the longer your stride and the less weight you put on your feet. When you're walking properly, all the component parts of you are working together toward a common goal: a brisk, invigorating walk.

HOW TO BUILD YOUR PERSONAL WALKING PROGRAM

The goal: fifteen miles for men; ten miles for women. Why the difference? A woman's bones are smaller, she's less muscular, and since she's more likely to be shorter, so is her stride. This is a generality, of course, and there are plenty of women who can outwalk most of the men they know. In any event, the goal doesn't mean that that distance must be your daily walk. Rather, it's the distance that, once attained, will prove to you beyond any doubt that you're in excellent physical condition. After that, four miles a day, every day—a continuous, uninterrupted walk—won't be excessive.

The following suggested program is geared to the abilities of someone who has been rather sedentary. You can, if you wish, begin with a longer walk and increase your time as you see fit. But remember, you're not competing with anyone, so don't try to exceed your ability. Walk to your capacity.

After completing your stretching exercises, walk for ten minutes each day, and then gradually work up to a half hour's walk. If you feel tired, winded, don't push yourself. During this period, go slowly for the first three to five minutes in order to gradually stretch your muscles and tendons. Then step up your pace each week thereafter, until you're covering a distance of 3½ miles per hour, which is a fairly brisk pace. If you're long-legged, it may be entirely possible for you to comfortably walk four miles per hour (120 strides per minute), but for most people this is a very fast walk and close to being a jog. But keep experimenting. The more efficiently you walk, the *faster* you'll be able to walk. There are many walkers, male and female, who can comfortably manage 130 strides per minute, which add up to 4½ miles per hour—more than a mile every fifteen minutes.

Twenty city blocks are said to constitute a mile, but on a long walk the blocks usually vary in length. Furthermore, you may be walking in a rural setting where there are no street signs with which you can measure your distance. I suggest that you invest in a pedometer, set it to your length of stride, and that way register your distance while measuring the time by your watch. Result: You will know *exactly* how far you've walked and in what time. Once you've hit your stride, however, and know your capabilities, I suggest you retire the pedometer. For as I wrote at the start of this book, walking is far too pleasurable to bother keeping track of the distance covered.

Now, undoubtedly you will experience some fatigue as you start adding distance to your walking program, but I promise you it will be a pleasurable kind of fatigue. In a special report to the American Medical Association, Dr. Paul Dudley White termed it "remarkably enjoyable" and thought that if the walker didn't experience it, he was missing something "invaluable," something that gives mental repose, peaceful sleep—a feeling of immense well-being.

FEET FIRST

"Feet are the most important thing in the world," said a young British Army sergeant back in the 1960s, just after completing a walk from San Francisco to New York. "It doesn't matter how fit you are or how strong. If you haven't got a good pair of feet you haven't got a thing." And how right he is. For when you walk, one foot at a time has to support *all* your body weight while the other is swinging forward through the air.

Each foot is a masterpiece of structural engineering: twenty-six bones intricately linked by thirty-three joints and tied together with two hundred ligaments. And since feet are so important, you can't walk well if (1) you're not placing them properly, and (2) you're not wearing the proper shoes.

When walking, make sure your whole foot is placed on the ground; heels first, then toes—with toes pointed straight ahead. Neither pointed in nor turned out. Never walk on your toes; this puts a strain on calves and ankles. Furthermore, during the physical act of walking the forward part of your foot is constantly changing shape, with your toes alternately spreading and contracting, bending and straightening. They're far too busy to stand up under the pressure of being asked to do more than they're meant to do.

If your feet—even one foot—is in a turned-out position, you don't walk so much as waddle. Your body is thrown off balance, and you're prone to fallen arches and lower back pain, all of which makes walking any distance fatiguing.

Toes pointed in—pigeon-toed style—puts a strain on ankle and knee joints, and the very introverted position of the feet makes a long, free stride impossible.

It isn't all that comfortable to try to change the placement of your feet, or even one foot. But daily exercise will help. I refer you back to exercise No. 4 of the stretching exercises in this chapter. Do it faithfully every day, and when walking do your very best to point feet straight ahead. The better you're able to walk in a straight line—both feet pointing forward— the more natural and beneficial will be your stride and the more pleasurable your walk. In fact, the longer your stride becomes, the more you'll discover the placement of your feet improving, until, without any conscious effort on your part, you'll be literally walking away from your waddle or pigeon-toed walk.

Exercises to strengthen feet.

1. *For ankles and arches.*   Stand with feet pointing straight ahead, anywhere from six to eight inches apart, and rise up on your toes, and then, slowly, to the count of ten, return to starting position. Do 10 repetitions. This very simple exercise is excellent for improving the elasticity of ankles and the long arch.

2. *For arches.* Start out as you did in the previous exercise and rise up on your toes, but this time roll your feet outward and back onto the heel 20 times so that your full weight comes on the outside border of your feet. You'll know when you're doing this exercise properly—both the *inner* and *under* parts of your feet will be lifting clear off the floor. Do 6 repetitions.

3. *For ankles.* Sit erect on a straight-backed chair with a leg crossed over the knee of the opposite leg. Now bend that crossed leg down, in toward the ankle, and then up. Repeat this motion 10 times, and again another 10 times reversing the direction of the circle. Then repeat this exercise all over again with your other leg.

4. *For calf to heel.* Sit on the floor with both legs straight ahead. Bend your feet upward as far as you can. Repeat 10 times.

5. *For arch and leg muscles.* Sit on the floor with legs straight ahead and, without bending your knees, turn the soles of your feet closely together. Repeat 10 times.

6. *For toes and feet.* Stand with feet parallel and curl toes upward as far as possible and then return to the floor slowly. Do 10 repetitions.

Footwear.   Dr. Robb Roy McGregor, medical adviser to the Footwear Council, says, "When people wear unsupportive flat shoes, they tend to shuffle. The posture assumed is one of a tottering forward lean. The arms are held in an outward, bent elbow, wobbly position—a picture of precarious balance. Conversely, when appropriate shoes are worn, a heel to toe gait is sponsored. The trunk will be held erect and the arms will swing backward and forward in their normal motion."

Regarding footwear, the council advises:

1. Look for cushioned heels and soles—for bounce on hard surfaces and traction on slippery ones.

2. Make sure there is at least a quarter inch of room in the front of the shoe.

3. Watch that the "toe box" is high enough so there is no rubbing.

4. Avoid high platforms, extremely high heels, and flat sneakers.

5. For support, feel for a rigid shank between the heel and the ball of the shoe or wear a solid wedge.

6. For long walks wear comfortable shoes that tie, whenever possible. Not only will they not fall off when walking heel to toe, but the simple act of tying is in itself a fitness exercise that will help develop flexibility of the lower back and legs.

Foot Care.   Dr. Richard Gibbs is a clinical professor of dermatology at New York University Medical School and runs a foot clinic there. He has taught dermatology to podiatrists for the past ten years. To Gibbs, feet are more exciting than hands, and a hallway of his office is lined with his own paintings of feet. While bone surgery is required for some foot problems—and that is the province of the podiatrist or orthopedic surgeon—many of the problems walkers face have to do with the skin of the feet, and that is the province of the dermatologist. I spent the major part of one afternoon discussing with Dr. Gibbs the proper care of feet.

Blisters are perhaps a walker's most common complaint. Caused by constant friction, they are actually an accumulation of fluid in or just under the skin, elevating the skin and causing a dome-shaped, often translucent fluid-filled sac. To treat a blister yourself, Dr. Gibbs recommends that you cleanse it first with alcohol or witch hazel, and then soak it for ten to fifteen minutes in salted water—that is, a teaspoon of table salt added to a pint of warm water. Do that a couple of times a day, and the blister will probably disappear. If not, you can open it with a needle. Sterilize the needle by heating it, and then rub both the needle and the blister with alcohol before puncturing the blister. It requires only very gentle pressure to extract most of the fluid. When this is done, apply bacitracin ointment or a triple antibiotic cream and continue doing so for the next couple of days.

Calluses, too, are caused by constant friction and are characterized by a thickening of the outer layers of the skin. Assuming that the foot is essentially normal and the shoe is at fault, there are over-the-counter products (Pretty Feet, Johnson's Foot Soap) that will soften the callus. And since one's skin is constantly shedding, a softened callus will usually fall off. For most persistent calluses, dermatologists use pomade or an ointment with salicylic or other acids, or skin-peeling agents.

Corns, like calluses, start out as a thickening of the skin owing to constant friction, but if the pressure is increased and persistent at the central point, a hard core develops that is what we know as a *corn.* Some corns, however, are due to a bony abnormality which makes proper walking difficult, and these, of course, are not treated by a dermatologist.

A corn is more difficult to treat because the affected skin is wedged between the shoe and an underlying bone. To alleviate the discomfort of the corn and to prevent any further rubbing against the shoe, you must separate that area from contact with the shoe. This you can do by the use of either a doughnut-shaped piece of felt or a piece of foam rubber. In short, use a physical barrier to prevent further rubbing against the shoe, and eventually most corns will disappear. Sometimes a larger shoe is necessary. Soaking in salted water will also help. Dr. Gibbs does not recommend over-the-counter corn removers.

When you walk, almost all of the sole of your foot bears some weight, but the major pressure points are at the heel, metatarsal area, and especially the first and fifth toes. So if a corn or callus is along this pathway, you'll experience some pain. The idea then is to try to thin the thickened skin with one of the over-the-counter "soaks" already mentioned, and then very *carefully* try to remove some of it with a pumice stone.

Walking on a soft surface (grass, sand, carpet) is much less likely to lead to foot problems than walking on a hard surface. Walking along a saltwater shoreline acts like a salt bath for the feet, and walking in sand acts like an extraordinarily gentle pumice for the soles.

Buy new shoes at the end of the day, when feet are their maximum size— sometimes as much as a size larger.

Use a talcum powder daily. Sprinkle it between toes and on soles of the feet. Dry powder allows "slip," and so the foot glides more easily and helps prevent the friction that causes blisters. Furthermore, feet are always a trifle damp, and this dampness, trapped between the toes, predisposes some individuals to fungal and bacterial infections. Dr. Gibbs considers the use of powder year round "the single most important bit of advice that I can give a walker."

That, and walk every chance you get. He deems walking the perfect exercise for healthy feet and legs.

WALKING CLOTHES

Clothing should be comfortable and free, no matter what the season. Tight clothes interfere with your ability to walk correctly. Dress warmly in cold weather, but don't pile on layers of clothing. During a brisk walk your body generates its own heat, and if your extremities are warm, your whole body stays warm. Protect your head, neck, hands, and feet, and the rest of you will stay warm without being blanketed with extra-heavy clothing.

On a really cold day, I suggest a simple wool hat that, if necessary, can be pulled down over the ears. Wool socks or stockings are also recommended, since they're not only warmer but fit better than cotton, and are softer and less apt to rub and cause a blister. Actually, two pairs of socks or stockings are better than one. Why not wool on the outside, and something thinner next to the skin? Woolen gloves are warmer than leather ones, unless the leather is lined with fur or fabric clear down to the fingertips.

In summer, do what people who live in tropical climates do: Protect yourself from the sun's rays by wearing loose-fitting, sheer clothing. A gossamer-thin blouse or sports shirt is infinitely more cooling than, say, a tank top, just as light-colored clothes are cooler than dark ones. White and light colors deflect the heat waves; dark colors absorb them. On a sunny day, a thin scarf worn around the neck, a shirt with a collar that can be turned up, or a hat with a brim is also a good idea. Otherwise a walker can't help but end his walk with a burn on the back of the neck.

Now, in some quarters you may be advised always to cover your head when doing any extensive walking during the summer months, while in others you'll be reminded that since about 40 percent of body heat escapes through the head, why cover it? I opt for coverage, but then my hair is unfortunately thin on top and the summer sun bakes my scalp. Still, trying to be as objective as possible, I suggest that women tie a filmy scarf around their heads, and men wear anything from a thin cotton cap to a lightweight, high-crowned planter-type straw with brim. And whether your head is covered or not, it's just plain common sense to choose the shady side of the street when walking on a hot, sunny day.

THE WALKING STICK

"There is something quite satisfying in the feel of a firm stick in the hand," a kilt-clad Scotsman said to me one summer as I poked through his cache of walking sticks, many of which he had made himself. "It's a great solace," he told me, "to walk with one or the other of my sticks along the hills above my house." His favorite was his toughest stick, made of ash. He said he had once had another exactly like it, and thereby hung a tale.

It seems that once when he was mountaineering, a boulder was dislodged and came hurtling down. He thrust his stick out in front of him to deflect the rock and save himself. The sturdy stick was "snapped clear through by the force of the boulder."

As I continued to inspect his collection, he recommended that I see

Sir Winston Churchill's stick collection at Chartwell, and when I picked up one stick shaped like a shepherd's crook, he told me that it was particularly British, and there was still another story to tell . . .

"I had an Irish aunt whose recipe for a long life was 'A walking stick, six deep breaths a day, and a lovely view,' " he said. It seems that when this maiden lady reached the age of fifty-five, the family doctor told her that it was highly unlikely that she would reach sixty. So she retired to the ancestral home in Donegal in Ireland, and there went to see the local doctor. "Rubbish!" he said, upon hearing the opinion of the other doctor. "You must walk up into the hills every day, and mind you take a walking stick. When you're up there take six deep breaths and drink in the view—and you'll live to be ninety." My Scottish friend said his aunt did what the doctor advised, and that very day bought a stick shaped like a shepherd's crook and took some local children along with her on her walk. "And she stood them in a row at the top of the hill, with the blackthorns they'd cut for themselves in their hands, and they all took six deep breaths, and enjoyed the view. My aunt," he concluded, running a hand lovingly down the length of one of his sticks, "lived till eighty-nine."

There are basically two kinds of walking stick: the *cane*, and the *staff*. The cane is about hip high and most commonly used by the city walker. The staff is taller, often coming up as high as just below the shoulder, and sometimes it has a leather strap attached that can be looped over the wrist. Unlike the cane, which has a fashion connotation, the staff is strictly utilitarian and is used most often by the country or wilderness hiker.

Paula Strain, a past president of the Potomac Appalachian Trail Club, carries a staff that she bought from a mail-order house. She says she uses it "because I'm awkward. I have weak ankles and I tend to trip. A stick helps me keep my balance. When I'm hiking, my stick touches the ground about every three steps, and it's particularly nice when I'm crossing a stream and hopping from stone to stone. There are many things you can do with a walking stick. For example, if you're carrying a pack, you can use the stick to balance the pack, and when you're sitting on the ground resting, you have something to lean against. The height requirement depends on the individual—it's whatever you feel comfortable with."

Most of the "2,000 Milers" who've walked the Appalachian Trail have carried sticks. Fred Leuhring did when he walked the entire two thousand miles at the age of eighty-two. "Sticks are especially valuable after seventy," he told a reporter on the occasion of his ninety-sixth birthday. "Going downhill, or when it's slippery out, sticks are a must for older folks. As your legs get tired, you can use your arms to push and take some of the load off your legs."

The legendary Grandma Gatewood also carried a walking stick when she walked the trail, flourishing it at hostile dogs and using it as a third leg when crossing streams.

Dr. John Prutting, mentioned earlier in this book, often walks with a cane, not for support but for style. "Walking is more fun when one adds a little style to it," he says. When the doctor, a tall, debonair fellow, walks with his brass-knobbed stick, it gives his walk "bounciness . . . a lift . . . and it puts a smile on my face. I take it with me as part of the art of walking. It looks attractive. It feels attractive. It's part of the costume, something to augment my style of walking."

Which is exactly why, at the turn of this century, no gentleman of quality out for a walk would have been seen without his cane any more than he would without his hat or stickpin. The man who could afford it had a wardrobe of canes. Then came the automobile, men walked less, and that signaled the demise of the cane as an important fashion accessory. Still, its popularity waned gradually. As late as 1926, a reporter noted 248 canes hanging from the hat shelf at a fashionable resort, and commented, "The man who decides to carry a stick automatically decides that he will not wear a battered old hat, down-at-the-heel shoes, a questionable suit or overcoat, badly soiled or worn gloves, or the kind of furnishings favored in the five-and-ten-cent stores."

Yet despite its undeniable style, the walking stick continued to slip further into obscurity. Then, in the 1970s, as we grew more and more health-conscious and began to walk more, the stick began a comeback. Taking cognizance of the fact, syndicated newspaper columnist George F. Will wrote, "The spirit of civilization was beyond saving when, early in this century, men quit carrying walking sticks." He confided that he treasured an antique walking stick he owned that was topped by a small silver bust of William McKinley, and the bust was inscribed, in flowing script, "Hon. William McKinley—Our Next President."

About that same time Bianca Jagger, wife of rock star Mick Jagger and a trend setter in her own right, made the walking stick even more news-worthy when she carried one both here and in England, prompting some fashion reporters to recall the days when the stick was "as necessary to the lady of fashion as her fan."

A Connecticut Yankee whose hobby once was collecting canes is now making and selling walking sticks at the rate of several thousand a week.

His firm, the E. J. Marshall Corporation, operating out of Collinsville, a quaint New England town in central Connecticut, produces canes of sturdy northern white ash—the wood that baseball bats are made of, and that also deflected the boulder that otherwise would have squashed my Scottish friend. Tied to each stick is a quite handsomely produced booklet titled *The Walking Stick . . . For Good Health and a Secure Feeling* that contains a plethora of facts about both walking sticks and *walking*.

"Walking is the universal exercise. Walking briskly will really get you into shape. Walking is a fine overall conditioning exercise . . . especially if you get a rhythm going and swing your arms freely." And it goes without saying, I suppose, that a stick really gets a rhythm going.

Furthermore, "Down through history, the walking stick in its various manifestations has remained the mark of strength and authority, and the hallmark of men of distinction." Voltaire owned eighty. Napoleon had one with a music box attached. And King Louis XIV needed his to keep his balance on the high heels that gentlemen of that period wore. Financier J. P. Morgan had a walking stick with a built-in battery-powered flashlight. Obviously, the walking stick can be both practical and ornamental, and sometimes downright whimsical. I remember that a friend of my family had a souvenir walking stick that contained a rolled-up map of the 1939 World's Fair.

Why walk with a walking stick? My friends who do tell me that it helps you develop a good sense of pace and rhythm, so that you get the most out of your walk. And some orthopedic surgeons recommend their use as a way to prevent fatigue when on long walks.

"The older you get, the stiffer the tissues are—
the less elasticity, the less responsivness."

—Dr. Charles Leroy Lowman, orthopedic surgeon

STRETCHING EXERCISES AFTER WALKING

Dr. Lowman believed we should all continue exercising all our lives.
When he was past ninety, he was still walking miles every day. And Harry
Kaufman, an attorney and chairman of Maryland's Physical Fitness Commission, was just as passionately devoted to walking. I don't believe the
two men ever met, and that's a pity. Because they were in total agreement
on the value of walking as a daily exercise, and the need of every person
to exercise regularly regardless of calendar age.

In 1965, Harry Kaufman was cited by President Lyndon Johnson as
one of the twelve persons who had contributed most to physical fitness in
the United States. And in 1967 he developed a walking program he called
"Swedish Walking" that, over a twelve-week period, was designed to gradually build up the walker's endurance. Kaufman, a marvelously energetic
and enthusiastic man, had an undeniable flair for promotion as well as a
keen awareness of Sweden's reputation as a nation of walkers, which is
why he hit upon the name "Swedish Walking." He figured it gave his fitness
program a touch of glamour and would entice people to give it a try. And
of course he was right.

I suspect "Swedish Walking" was primarily aimed at people over sixty
and they were largely the ones who joined it at first, but soon it was also
attracting men and women of all ages who, together with the senior citizens,
were walking briskly around the all-weather, quarter-mile track of the
Gilman School in Baltimore. Among them was Brigitta Eden, a nineteen-
year-old visitor from Gothenburg, Sweden. Soon members of the local
press were joining them on their 7 A.M., three-times-a-week walks.

"If you take care of your body, your body will take care of you," Harry
Kaufman told a reporter from the *Baltimore Sun*, who, in an article head-
lined "Walk, Don't Run, to Fitness," wrote that "he has the physique of a
nineteen-year-old long-distance runner." Harry Kaufman was past sixty-five
at the time.

The first week of "Swedish Walking" began with instruction on deep

159

breathing and proper body posture, followed by a slow three-quarter-mile walk with deep-breathing exercises every 220 yards, and concluded twelve weeks later with what Harry Kaufman called the "Graduation Ceremony," a brisk 2½-mile walk around the track. It wasn't long before "Swedish Walking" fitness programs were mushrooming all across the country. In Pasadena, California, for example, eight housewives who read about it started their own "Swedish Walking" program in their housing development. Then Harry Kaufman's Maryland Fitness Commission and the Maryland Office on Aging, together with the Travelers Insurance Companies' PEP ("Physical Exercise Pays") program, went on to design a Senior Citizen's Exercise Program consisting of twelve stretching and twisting exercises specially recommended for after a brisk walk, to allow one to continue to enjoy the feeling of elasticity that the walk gave. And although these dozen aerobic exercises have been created for men and women over sixty, I strongly recommend them—all twelve or any group of them—for anyone of any age who wants to prolong the lift you get after a good walk.

1

Deep breathing. Take a
deep breath, rise on toes
with arms extended over
head, exhale slowly.
Repeat 3 times.

2

Walk in place. Lift left knee
up, lower knee; lift right
knee up, lower knee.
Repeat 10 times.

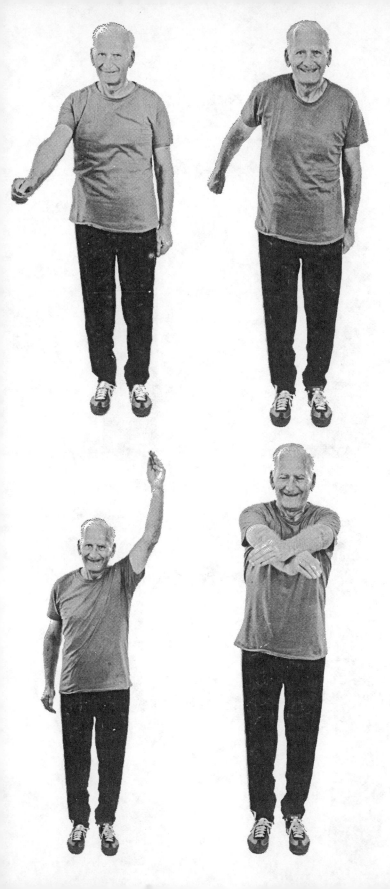

3

Arm swings. Swing right arm rotating forward 5 times; reverse motion, rotating backward 5 times. Repeat with left arm. With both arms together in a windmill fashion swing forward 5 times; reverse 5 times.

4

Finger squeeze. Extend arms shoulder high in front, palms down; squeeze fingers slowly, release. Repeat 5 times. Turn palms up, squeeze fingers 5 times. Extend arms again in front and shake fingers 5 times.

5

Arm turns. Extend arms to side, palms up, cup hands, turn arms down in a circular movement, and return to starting position. Repeat 5 times. Extend arms, cup hands, facing down, turn arms in opposite direction 5 times.

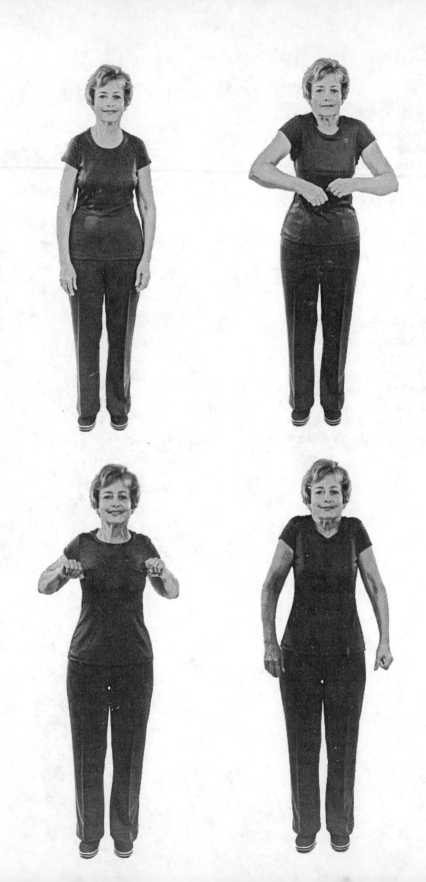

← 6

Shoulder rolls. Beginning with arms at side, roll shoulders forward in full circle, slowly, 5 times; reverse by rolling shoulders backward in a circle, slowly, 5 times. Then shrug shoulders up and down 5 times.

7 →

Body stretch. Extend right foot forward as far as it will go, leaving left foot firmly planted; bend body forward with arms extended, stretch forward 5 counts, stretching farther forward on each count. Reverse procedure. Lift up on your toes, stretch overhead to count of five.

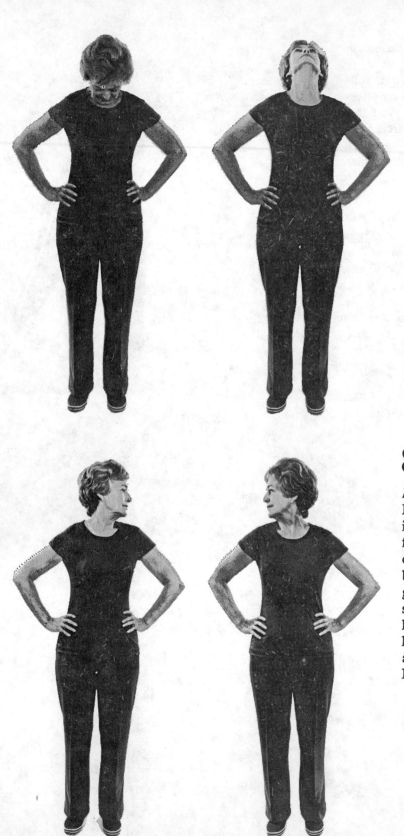

8

Head and neck exercises. Place hands on hips. Keeping eyes open, bend head forward so that chin touches chest, then bend head backward as far as it will go, then bend head to starting position and turn head to left, then return head to starting position and turn head to right. Repeat 5 times.

9

Body bends and turns. Bend body slowly forward as far as it will go, then bend body back. Return body to starting position, then turn body to left, return to starting position, turn body to right. Repeat 5 times.

10

Body side stretch. Extend right arm over head, bend to left side toward the ground, to the count of two. Return to starting position, place right hand on right hip with left arm extended upward over head, and bend to right, to the count of two.

11

Posture exercise. Stand erect with feet about six inches apart. Tighten leg muscles, tighten stomach by drawing it in, extend chest, bring arms up with clenched fists chest high, take deep breath, let it out slowly (keeping muscles taut and rigid), vibrate arms back for a count of three.

12

Arm thrusts. With feet
about six inches apart, make
fists, bend elbows, then
thrust arms forward, bring
back; thrust sidewards,
bring back; then thrust
arms upward and down.
Repeat 3 times.

CHAPTER

7

THE ART OF WALKING WITH A PACK ON YOUR BACK

"You know as much of the art of walking as I do. It consists of walking in rain, fog, or snow, as well as on clear days by moonlight. Some of its most beautiful moments are in storm."

—Dr. M. Beckett Howorth, *Consumer Bulletin,* April 1973

Not surprisingly, I suppose, this does take some know-how. For instance, you walk with a *bent* knee when climbing. On steep terrain, you do well to follow the relaxed technique of those Swiss hikers who outwalked Henry Laskau: breathe deeply and climb slowly with a shortened stride Rest five to ten minutes of every hour even when you're not tired. And as for speed, I refer you to what Dr. Howorth had to say about it in an article he wrote:

> Speed may be acquired by tilting the body forward, thrusting harder with the legs, and even a slight crouch, with a longer arm swing. The length of stride should not be too great, as the effort of forcing the body to reach that forward leg becomes excessive, or too short, and energy is wasted in swinging the legs too many times.
>
> Uphill speed may be increased by leaning forward and in a crouch, and forcing the body well forward on a high step. Breathing should be deeper rather than faster, and in rhythm with the other movements. There should be no tenseness of the muscles, for this results in quick fatigue. Nor should there be any disturbance in rhythm or smoothness, as one will quickly lose rather than gain in accomplishment.

And when it comes to downhill walking—something that presents a challenge to many a novice—Dr. Howorth says:

> Downhill walking also requires a forward lean and slight crouch, to reduce the shock of each step, as well as the chance of a slip. On a very steep slope, a slight turning to the side, or zigzag traversing, will help. Relaxation is most important in downhill walking, especially "loose knees." The movement then becomes almost a dance, with light quick steps, or a series of slides, similar to skiing. Small jumps may often be used. The knees are usually kept close together in this technique. The

174

crouch brings one closer to the ground, with the muscles and joints acting as springs, minimizing the possibility and danger of a fall. Most falls are backward, with the body extended, in a blind direction, the weight coming hard on the coccyx or wrists. These falls can be avoided by the method mentioned.

And while normally the whole foot should be placed on the ground, Dr. Howorth notes that walking on the toes is suitable for short distances steeply uphill on narrow trails, "but usually it is better to turn the feet to the side, together or in herringbone fashion, and use the whole foot."

EQUIPMENT

Here the key words are *quality* and *weight*. The best quality. The lightest weight. And whether you're choosing a day pack (sometimes called a *knapsack*), or a backpack for longer hikes where you'll camp out, waterproofed nylon is your fabric. Look for a nylon pack with these features: padded adjustable shoulder straps, nylon (instead of metal) zippers, and outside pockets for holding small and often used items.

The backpack can either be made with a padded back, or constructed to fit onto a frame. The frameless, or "soft," pack is usually somewhat smaller and lighter, but when a pack load weighs in the vicinity of, say, 40 pounds, a frame is called for. Furthermore, a frame keeps the pack from direct contact with your back, thus reducing perspiration. Still, for the average weekend hiker the best choice seems to be the frameless pack that is fitted with a hip or waist belt. In fact, no load of over 15 pounds should ever be carried without a padded hip or waist belt. Look for one with a quick-release buckle so that the pack can be shed fast in case of emergency, such as slipping when crossing a stream. Furthermore, use of a padded hip or waist belt transfers the weight of the pack from the shoulders down to the pelvic region, the strongest weight-bearing part of the body. Worn very tight, it allows you to walk without bending forward.

Pack frame. The lightest is made of hollow aluminum. While sturdy and rigid, the frame should also be contoured to your body with movable crossbars, and should also feature well-padded shoulder straps that can be adjusted to your weight and your shoulder width.

Tent. A tube tent— a cylinder of plastic strung between two trees— is the very lightest, weighing no more than four to eight pounds. More expensive but also more protective is a crawl-in nylon tent with telescoping aluminum poles and zippered netting at the entry.

Sleeping bag.   The key word here is *down*: 100 percent goose-down filling is best, although some very good bags contain white duck down. Beware of any bag that's described as being "down and feather mixture" or, worst of all, makes no mention of down at all.

Down comes from the undercoat of geese and ducks, and it's the most efficient insulator because it can be compressed over and over again into a tiny space, and then, when released, it fluffs up to its original shape, creating thousands of tiny air spaces that insulate the sleeping body. One drawback: Wet down loses most of its insulating ability. So take care to protect your sleeping bag from dampness and moisture.

The cut of the bag is important. There mustn't be any spare space in it; the snugger the fit, the more efficient the insulation and the more comfortable you'll be.

The washing of a soiled sleeping bag requires very special care. Careless handling can ruin it. A bag with down filling can't be washed in a machine. You must put it in a tub and wash it with pure soap flakes (regular detergent laundry powders will strip down of its oil). Rinse the bag *thoroughly*, treading the excess water out of the bag by walking the length of it until the rinse water looks as clear as when it first poured out of the faucet. Then, holding the bag along its length, gently lift it out of the tub and let it dry out in natural heat for the next several days, now and then massaging any down lumps that may have formed. Never store a damp sleeping bag; the down will rot.

Mattress.   Think in terms of a two-inch foam-rubber pad in waterproof sheath, or a nylon air mattress. Length can be anywhere from half the length of your sleeping bag to its full length; the full length one can double as a ground cover. (Contact cement is by far the best leak stopper should your air mattress spring a leak.)

PACKING THE PACK

Think light (every ounce of weight is crucial, and it's estimated that one-fifth of your body weight is the maximum you can expect to carry comfortably), but don't skimp on essentials. Be sure to include a small flashlight (one for each hiker) and a supply of batteries; waterproof matches; lighter; whistle for each hiker; trail map and compass; toilet paper; wide-mouthed water and food bottles; extra plastic bags; safety pins; masking tape; pen, pencil, and paper; extra bootlaces; and a pair of small needle-nose pliers (for lifting hot cooking pots).

First-aid kit.   Your kit should contain: Band-Aids; moleskin (for possible blisters); adhesive tape; gauze squares; talcum powder; burn ointment; razor blade; plastic bottle or tube of antibiotic ointment; aspirin; salt tablets; insect repellent; snake-bite kit; medication for diarrhea, poison ivy; needle; fever thermometer; rubbing alcohol; eyedrops; sunscreen lip protector; suntan lotion (if called for).

Maps.   Before your hike, collect all the literature you can on the area you'll be walking. Get a trail guide that suggests routes and gives mileages. And by all means get a topographical map of the area that shows the *contours* of the terrain (otherwise it's all but impossible to tell where a trail gains or loses elevation), where streams are, and where to go if you and the trail separate at some point during your hike. Order your "topo" map by writing:

For areas west of the Mississippi River: U.S. Geological Survey, Distribution Section, Federal Center, Denver, Colorado 80225.

For areas east of the Mississippi River: U.S. Geological Survey Distribution Section, Washington, D.C. 20242.

Wind and rain are tough on maps. Dry them flat, fold carefully, and use strong masking tape to hold torn parts together.

FOOD

Light is right again. Pack a butane stove plus a nest of three cooking pots whose covers can do double duty as plates or frying pans, a spatula, and a stirring spoon. In the case of food, light means a dehydrated, freeze-dried diet of proteins, carbohydrates, fats, minerals, and vitamins. Be sure to include a supply of nuts, raisins, seeds, and honey; hikers tend to eat several light meals during the day, rather than the conventional three big ones, and these are excellent "fillers" that are also generally regarded as energy foods. And it probably goes without saying that the flavor of dehydrated foods improves immeasurably when you add things like onions, celery flakes, and assorted dried herbs. Water should be taken in *small* quantities—sips rather than gulps—and as often as you feel you need it.

Of course you'll have a supply of water in your pack (small streams can be dry by, say, late August, so don't necessarily rely on water shown on your map), but nothing is as refreshing as water freshly dipped from a cold mountain stream.

CLOTHING

When hiking in warm weather, wear loose clothing that's light and airy, shorts with wide leg openings and pockets, and since you don't want to be overexposed to the sun, a brimmed hat or large cotton bandanna. A long-sleeved shirt is a good bet, since the sleeves can be rolled down if you're walking through an area thick with mosquitoes and flies. In other than warm weather, wear several thin layers of clothing rather than one thick one; this way you can peel off or pile on as the weather changes. It's important to stay warm but not get overheated.

The thickness of your socks and their material depend, of course, on the weather conditions. Wool socks are more widely preferred since they're softer and less apt to rub and cause blisters. They dry more slowly, however. Most hikers I know wear two pairs of socks. A popular choice is to wear a smooth, thinner sock—nylon or a thin cotton—next to the skin, and a thick sock of absorbent wool over it. It's recommended that you wash your socks each night you're on the trail. Clean, dry socks make for clean, dry feet, which are their own protection against blisters and frostbite. Never, by the way, darn your socks; a darn invites a blister.

Rain gear is essential for any season of the year, and the most practical is a full-length hooded poncho of plastic or Gore-tex.

SHOES

They are the single most important piece of equipment a hiker can take when he or she hits the trail. Now, there are some hikers who recommend wearing boots whenever and wherever you go hiking. Others maintain that the type of footwear varies with the weather and the terrain. In any event, on the assumption that at some point a serious walker will need hiking shoes, I am reprinting here what I believe is the most complete, most comprehensive article I have ever read on what you should look for when buying a hiking shoe. It expresses the opinions of one person, of course, so it's offered to you simply as a guide to give you an idea of the choices you

have. The article was written by Len Wheat and illustrated by Patty Zu-
kerowski, members of the Potomac Appalachian Trail Club, which published it in booklet form.

Twice recently I read articles giving advice on hiking shoes. The gist
of both was the same: buy the lug soled, padded, lined types sold as
"hiking shoes" and priced above $40. A PATC equipment guide par-
tially endorses this advice by recommending Vibram lug soles. My own
opinion favors a different type of shoe. The so-called hiking shoes sometimes sell for two or three times the price of different shoes having better
qualities. To recognize these qualities and find the right shoe, we must
look at a shoe's parts, choose what is best, then assemble the best features and see what we have. The views that follow reflect 18 years of
extensive hiking and bushwhacking in this area (mainly Shenandoah
Park) and in national parks elsewhere in the United States and Canada.
During this time I have tried at least ten pairs of hiking shoes and pre-
maturely discarded six. I've learned a lot.

The parts to consider—but not necessarily seek—in a hiking shoe are
(1) the sole, both its material and its shape, (2) any midsole, (3) the
insole, (4) the upper, (5) any padding and lining, (6) stiffening pieces,
(7) the tongue and lacing, and (8) any padded collar.

The Sole: Material

Soles should offer traction, comfort, and durability. In general, the
softer and rougher textured a material is, the better its traction. Soft
materials yield to conform to irregularities in the ground, letting sharp
edges and abrasive surfaces bite into the sole; rough materials give
added friction on smooth surfaces. Softness also spells comfort: it lets
the sole cushion the foot against all-day pounding on the trail and swal-
low the stones you step on. But soft materials also wear out faster. Keep
these characteristics in mind when choosing among alternative materials: leather, PVC, hard rubber, gum crepe, cushion crepe, high-carbon
SBR, neoprene, and cork (including neoprene cork).

(a) **Leather.**   You won't find any leather-soled hiking shoes. But if
you're new at hiking and are tempted to try leather-soled street shoes,
don't. Leather soles are not just bad on trails, they're dangerous. Leather
gives no traction; it is quite slippery going up and down hill, especially

on rock. If used on moist ground, leather absorbs water, giving you wet socks—which can lead to blisters by causing friction.

(b) **PVC.**   The next worst thing to leather is PVC (polyvinyl chloride). PVC is a clear amber plastic; advertising claims for it give the impression that it wears like steel and, in truth, is about as comfortable. The problem is a combination of hardness and flexibility. Because it is hard, PVC neither cushions your step nor absorbs small stones; because it is flexible, it bends around those stones, letting them push into your feet. PVC's traction is usually passable on dry surfaces. But PVC is slippery when wet and in cold weather, when it gets very hard (sometimes cracking). Not acceptable.

(c) **Hard rubber.**   The hard, black rubber found in the soles of some of the cheapest work shoes is another poor choice. The black color is from carbon black, which is added for increased strength; durability is no problem. But comfort is. Although I've never actually worn black rubber shoes, except in shoestores, they are too hard and (usually) thin to protect your feet.

(d) **Gum crepe.**   Crepes—true crepes, are varieties of unvulcanized rubber. Gum crepe (plantation crepe) is a yellowish material resembling art gum. It is soft and affords good traction on dry surfaces. On wet surfaces, however, it adheres poorly, and it lacks durability for the weekly hiker.

(e) **Cushion crepe.**   Cushion crepe (blown crepe) is not a true crepe but microcellular rubber—rubber containing millions of tiny air cells (bubbles). You see it in gray and brown on many casual shoes and on those ubiquitous white wedge soles. The air cells provide softness, lightness, and traction. But they also cause it to wear out faster. Some grades of cushion crepe wear extremely rapidly: I have bought inexpensive canvas shoes with blown crepe soles that wore out in one summer of part-time use. The crepe on white wedge soles usually has better quality rubber—it is sometimes 50 to 100 percent neoprene—and has acceptable durability.

(f) **High-carbon SBR.**   SBR, or styrene-butadiene rubber, is a synthetic rubber used in automobile tires—and in some popular lug soles.

When highly loaded with carbon black, SBR is extremely abrasion resistant but also very hard. Most mountaineering style hiking shoes use lug soles, the best grades (yellow label) of which use high-carbon SBR. The high carbon is used mainly to reduce rapid wear caused by the lugs (but it is also used in nonlug styles). Secondarily, SBR helps keep the lugs from tearing and provides the stiffness that mountain climbers—but not hikers—need for quarter-inch toe holds and for crampons. The cost of these virtues is hardness and poor traction. SBR won't cushion your steps. And, despite the claim that some lug soles provide "the best traction under most circumstances," they are best only when compared to leather. SBR is particularly bad where traction is vital: on sloping rock, stepping stones, logs, and wet surfaces. It simply won't grab like softer rubber. The lugs don't compensate: they are not designed for firm surfaces. After slipping many times while using SBR on rock slopes, I consider it too risky for bushwhacking.

(g) **Neoprene.** Neoprene—a compound, not a trade name—is the synthetic rubber closest to natural rubber in its properties. It is recognizable by the word "neoprene" embossed on the sole. Neoprene is oil resistant (a quality appreciated by gas station attendants) and has high tensile strength, which makes it durable. Softer than SBR, it offers comfort and traction.

(h) **Cork.** Cork soles consist of granular cork suspended in rubber, usually neoprene. Cork's surface is packed with minute hemispherical voids. These act like suction cups, providing outstanding traction on wet or dry surfaces. (Cork's high coefficient of friction explains its use for catwalk flooring, nonslip handles, etc.) Secondarily, the cork particles wear faster than the surrounding rubber, leaving a pitted surface (additional gripping power) that never wears smooth. Cork soles are lightweight and cushiony. And they wear surprisingly well, though not as well as straight neoprene.

The Sole: Shape

Broadening the concept of the sole to include the heel, we can choose from four shapes: wedges, modified wedges, lug soles, and conventional soles with separate heels.

*Wedge sole,
six-inch shoe*

(a) **Wedges.** Wedge soles are one-piece types that are thicker in back; the extra thickness substitutes for a distinct heel. Wedges are okay but have three shortcomings. First, they can't economically be reheeled. Many shoe repair shops won't touch them; others charge $7 for the necessary surgery—or $16 for a whole new sole. (Work shoes with wedge soles usually sell for $18 to $25.) On any shoe, the heel wears out first, and if you can't conveniently and economically replace it, you've lost much of your investment. Second, wedges throw you off balance when you step crosswise on fallen logs or cross a stream log-and-pole style or on rounded stepping stones. Conventional heels grip the log or rock with the crotch formed by the heel; wedges rock back and forth.

The third shortcoming concerns snow. In snow, particularly the hard granular kind found above timberline in the Rockies, wedges provide no heel for digging in. I can't forget the time in the Canadian Rockies when I had to cross a snow-covered slope above a cliff. I was wearing wedge-soled shoes and was unable to jam my heels in. Though I survived, the experience was unnerving.

*Modified
wedge sole*

(b) **Modified wedges.** Modified wedges are wedges with a rounded indentation under the arch. Or, in what might more aptly be called modified conventional soles, you get low molded-on heels with a 45-degree slant (rather than square corners) at the arch. Modified wedges are slightly better on logs and stepping stones. But they too involve searching and expense to reheel, and the low, unsquared heel is less than ideal for snow.

(c) **Lug soles.** Lug soles have molded cleats (lugs) on sole and heel. Lugs are supposed to provide better traction. But that advantage applies only on snow, where the lugs can sink in. (Lugs theoretically could help on muddy slopes too, but mud practically always occurs in flat areas—no traction problem—and can usually be skirted; if not, count on the lugs to pick it up and carry it along.) Lug soles are like snow tires. Snow tires are no better on solid surfaces than regular tires. Ditto for lug soles. In fact, on solid ground lugs actually perform worse than ordinary soles. (Speedway and drag racers don't use lug tires.) This is partly because traction tends to increase as the contact area increases: a larger area offers more chances for interaction between sole and ground—for example, the sole pressing into tiny pits in rock. At the same time, lugs require hard (strong) materials, which are less slip resistant. French studies show that hard soles with pronounced sculpturing, such as cleats, are the least slip resistant; soft soles with shallow tread designs give the best traction.

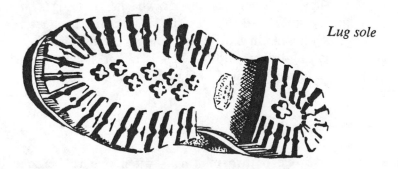

Lug sole

And lugs have other problems. They wear out faster, just like snow tires. The lugs cut the area of the wearing surface roughly in half. By concentrating your weight and the sliding friction on half the area, lugs more or less double the rate of wear. (This is partly—but only partly—offset by the toughness of the high-carbon SBR rubber in lug soles.) The lugs soon become rounded, then shallow, and before you know it, your soles have had it.

Reheeling and resoling are again drawbacks. If you can find a nearby place that reheels lug soles, you can get new heels for about $7 (almost twice what you pay for ordinary heels). Some shops replace sole and midsole (usually frayed) for $18 to $22, but if they are too inconvenient you can expect to pay up to $30 at a neighborhood shoe repair shop— if you can find one that handles lug soles.

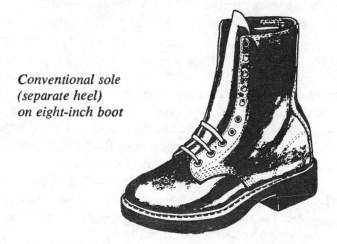

Conventional sole
(separate heel)
on eight-inch boot

(d) **Conventional soles.** Conventional soles with separate heels are what I prefer. They have none of the drawbacks of wedges and lug soles. Although lug soles are better for snow (until the lugs get worn), that advantage is limited. In hard snow you dig in by jamming down with your heels; a dug-in heel without lugs is about as effective as one with lugs. Besides, in most snow situations it is winter: you are wearing winter boots.

The Midsole

Some shoes have one or two midsoles—often one rubber and one leather. These are additional soles above the wearing sole (outsole) that offer stiffness, warmth, and a base to glue lug soles onto. You can spot a midsole by looking at the edge of the sole: the midsole is a layer anywhere from 1/16 to 3/16 inches thick. It should not be confused with the welt, a thin band of material used to help stitch the sole to the upper.

Midsoles are not necessarily something to seek. Lug holes are molded too thin—1/4 to 3/8 inches, not counting the lugs—for strength and comfort without a midsole. Also, lug and crepe soles can't be stitched, so they must be cemented to a midsole.

If you're buying shoes with lug soles, make sure you get adequate midsoles. Cheap midsoles are too thin for comfort: you can feel stones through the sole. A second midsole is all right if both midsoles are thin, but two may be gilding the lily. The marginal benefit of a second midsole might not justify the extra weight and price—unless you plan to carry an extremely heavy pack whose weight might help stones push in against a thinner sole.

*Mountaineering boot
with lug sole,
two midsoles*

Avoid the monsters with two thick midsoles, always accompanied by stiff, thick uppers. Thick soles and thick uppers are designed to protect your feet from the cold surface above snowline and to stiffen the sole for crampons. But for your purposes they are too hot, too heavy, too stiff, and too expensive. Don't buy a space suit for a plane ride.

The Insole

A good insole is perhaps the hardest requirement to satisfy. The insole is inside the shoe under your sock. It may be made of plastic, cellulose, leatherboard, covered foam, or leather.

Plastic (usually vinyl) is a cheap material used to cut costs. Because it won't absorb perspiration, it does not belong inside a shoe: it encourages clammy feet and wet socks, hence blisters and athlete's foot. Cellulose insoles, like paper and cardboard, are made from cellulose fibers. The insoles are whitish, often wrinkled, and cardboardlike in appearance. Cellulose will absorb perspiration, though not as well as leather (the cellulose fibers are rubber-treated), and it is supposedly quite durable in the better grades. But you can't be sure what grade you're getting, and once a cellulose insole bunches up inside your shoe you'll want to rip it out.

Leatherboard is made from ground leather scraps and cellulose fibers bonded together. It is better than cellulose, since it not only absorbs perspiration but is stiff enough to act as secondary armor against stones that push in on the sole. The binder, of course, limits moisture absorption.

Sport shoe with terry-cloth insole

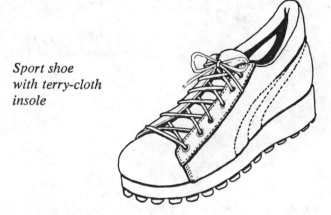

Foam insoles are too soft to be of much value for absorbing shocks. Foam also fails to absorb perspiration, though the thin leather covering (plastic is out!) helps some. Even worse, foam doesn't stand up under pounding and the corrosive effects of sweat: it soon crumbles under your heel, leaving a depression and causing blisters. This happened to me first on a pair of oxfords and then on some hiking shoes. I even experimented with a third set of foam insoles (purchased when I couldn't find leather). These were torn up by a pebble that sneaked into one shoe. Efforts to install replacement leather insoles don't seem to work. The old glue can't be cleaned off well enough for the new glue to hold. Foam dooms your shoes to an early death.

The only really satisfactory insole is leather. It is tough and durable. It absorbs perspiration. And it is firm enough to help the sole ward off sharp stones. This assumes, however, that the leather is firm. Suede and glove leather insoles look fancy but give less protection; avoid them.

The Upper

The upper is the main part of the shoe—what your foot fits into. A 5½-inch or 6-inch upper—one that combines with the heel to make a shoe about 6 inches high—is best. A 6-inch upper (a) keeps out most twigs, pebbles, and trail dust, (b) keeps out water and snow when you accidentally step in shallow water or cross patches of snow, (c) keeps the shoe from pulling off—and keeps mud out—when you step in mud, and (d) protects the ankle, particularly the protruding ankle bones, from being cut and jabbed by rocks and broken sticks you occasionally brush against.

Some would say a 6-inch upper offers a fifth benefit: ankle support. But that depends partly on whether you choose a stiff design. I prefer a flexible design that allows your ankle to bend according to irregularities in the terrain—a real help for bushwhacking and a source of comfort in any situation. Few people need ankle support; but if you want it, buy a stiff upper and be prepared to keep it laced uncomfortably tight at the top.

Avoid 7-inch and 8-inch uppers. Eight inches—even seven—is overkill; six does the job. Tall uppers are hotter, because they cover more skin. They are heavier. They are uncomfortable where the top rubs against the back calf (so friends tell me). They are harder to get on and off. And for all these drawbacks you must pay substantially more.

The upper can use full-grain leather or splits. When hides are made into leather, the hide is split into two or more layers. The outer layer (hair side) becomes "full-grain" leather, unless the grain is buffed into a nap—a suede finish. The inside layer (flesh side) is called a "split." Full-grain and outer-suede leather has tighter fibers, hence better water repellency, shape retention, and abrasion resistance; insist on it. Splits are buffed to make suede. Split suedes, because of their more open fibers, tend to absorb water, and they give less protection against sharp objects.

Full-grain leather has a rough side (where separation took place) and a smooth side (grain side). Either can go on the outside of the shoe; both sides repel water. I prefer smooth-side-out—you can slap on a little shoe polish to restore water repellency after the shoes get soaked —but you might like the rugged appearance and scuff resistance of rough-side-out.

Full-grain leather can be split to varying thicknesses. Stiff, extra-thick leather should be reserved for mountaineering and maybe heavy backpacking, where the extra warmth, stiffness (ankle support), and protection justify the expense, weight, and discomfort.

Combination smooth and roughout upper

Padding and Lining

Those fancy hiking boots with the lug soles come with foam padding covered by a smooth leather lining inside the rear half of the upper. Some other outdoor shoes have the lining but no padding. Soft glove-leather linings really seem nice, especially when padded; they give the shoe a look and feel of style and quality. But think twice before you buy.

Ask yourself: Why do I want padding and a lining? Is it to protect my ankle from scrapes and jabs? That's another case of overkill: in years of bushwhacking under ankle-menacing conditions, I've never found unlined full-grain uppers to give inadequate protection. I did, however, own one pair of shoes where I needed protection from the upper itself. It was too stiff and bruised me on the inside ankle bones. A little oil and some kneading licked that problem. But padding sure would have helped on the first hike.

This points to the true role of padding. Mountaineering shoes, which are designed for snow conditions and technical use, need stiff uppers of thick leather; they also need warmth. Padding and linings protect the ankles from that stiff leather and provide warmth. They, and the lugs (for snow), also give mountaineering shoes their distinctive style.

Padding on hiking shoes is a blatant and largely inappropriate attempt to imitate the styling of mountaineering shoes. The fashionable look of mountaineering-style hiking shoes unquestionably helps to sell shoes; it appeals to one's sense of the outdoors and conforms to what is expected in a shoe for mountain trails. But, alas, padding is insulation, and foam is a vapor barrier. That's the rub. One can get hot when hiking, and I for one can do quite well without insulation. I can also do without anything that impedes evaporation of the moisture in my shoe when I'm sweating.

Split suede
chukka

Stiffening Pieces

Hiking shoes have heel counters and, sometimes, back stays. A counter is a piece of stiff material, such as leatherboard or plastic, that fits around the heel inside the shoe. It helps the shoe keep its shape, ensures a good fit, keeps you from walking on the side of the shoe, and protects you when you kick yourself in the heel. The counter goes behind the lining of a lined shoe, or, usually, behind a leather "counter pocket" (cut to fit the counter) in an unlined shoe. Sometimes the pocket uses smooth leather, but other times it is rough to a degree. A little roughness is all right. But if the pocket is very rough or of suede, reject the shoe. My sad experience with rough pockets was that my socks wore out at a fantastic rate and were constantly getting pulled down into my shoes.

A back stay is a vertical strip of leather that runs top to bottom over the Achilles tendon on the outside of the shoe; it stiffens the ankle area. After two bad experiences that led to early retirement of relatively new shoes, I avoid shoes with back stays. Back stays provide a double thickness of leather in the ankle area, where the leather needs to bend. When your rear foot pushes off, your ankle bends backwards. As your new shoe breaks in, it develops horizontal folds around the hamstring to accommodate this bending. In my case at least, the double thickness caused too heavy a fold. The fold dug into my tendon with each step, raising a painful bruise and causing me to limp. When this happened with a second pair of shoes some years after the first experience, I realized that the earlier situation was no freak event. Everyone won't have this problem, but why take a chance?

Tongue and Lacing

The tongue should have expansion pleats ("bellows" construction) attaching it securely to the sides of the laced opening. Usually the pleating stops two or three eyes short of the top, but if it goes all the way up, so much the better. Pleating helps three ways. First, it keeps out twigs, pebbles, and dirt that sneak in between the laces. Second, it keeps out water when your foot invades a stream or puddle. Third, it keeps the long tongue from falling to one side and making a nuisance of itself.

Some shoes have two overlapping "ski flaps" that fold over the tongue from opposite sides and, held down by the laces, seal the tongue. This is primarily an insulating feature of heavyweight mountaineering shoes. But I have seen flaps used on "hiking shoes" too, as a substitute for pleating. This I can't buy: flaps will keep out foreign objects, but they might not always work with water and they won't hold the tongue in place.

Back stay,
ski flaps, hooks,
and speed laces

Lacings involve two considerations. One is your choice of hooks, eyes, or loops (speed laces). Hooks are nice for the top three anchorages: you can quickly unlace three notches, spread the sides to instantly loosen the lower notches, and remove the shoes. However, hooks do tend to snag on cuff hems inside pants. Below third position, eyes and loops are best. These notches don't need to be unlaced; loosening is sufficient. Loosening is easier with eyes and loops: laces don't slide easily through hooks. Moreover, hooks in the lower positions can come unlaced while you walk; eyes and loops can't. Loops have a minor advantage over eyes for tightening (but not loosening) laces.

The other aspect of lacings is whether they go all the way to the toe. Some people rave about to-the-toe lacings, though it's hard to see why. Toe lacings certainly don't help you get the shoe off and on. They do allow you to lace tightly for a snug fit in the toe, but snug toes are useful only in rock climbing and technical mountaineering. For normal hiking, tight fitting shoes are uncomfortable and encourage blisters. You need some roominess.

Padded Collars

The stylized hiking shoes come with padded collars around the ankle opening for snugness and "comfort." Collars have definite value on heavy mountaineering shoes, where they can seal out snow and scree. They are also useful if you want a high degree of ankle support, which requires stiff leather, laced tightly at the top. Here the collar will keep the shoe top from cutting into your ankle. However, some collars, particularly those that are not cut lower in back, have a way of digging in at the rear and causing the sort of discomfort they are supposed to prevent. Before buying shoes with padded collars, put on both shoes, lace them up tightly, and walk around the store to see if you like the feel.

Personally, I dislike stiff uppers and padded collars. A loose, flexible top is more comfortable and helps the shoe ventilate. Like some other hikers, I even leave the last notch unlaced in hot weather. For my tastes, soft leather is far better than a padded collar.

PUTTING IT ALL TOGETHER

Your choice of a hiking shoe involves four main alternatives: (1) men's 6-inch work shoes, (2) women's soft-soled oxfords, (3) men's

and women's 7-inch or 8-inch boots, and (4) men's and women's mountaineering-style "hiking shoes."

Neoprene cork-soled
work shoe with
separate heel

Work shoes.   For men, a good pair of work shoes gives the best combination of parts at the lowest price. My present shoes, which have
neoprene-cork soles, leather insoles, and 6-inch full-grain leather uppers,
now sell for $35. (Models with cheaper insoles sell for $18 to $25.)
In contrast, leather-insoled 7-inch and 8-inch boots and 6-inch "hiking
shoes" range in price from $41 to $85—not counting higher priced
mountaineering shoes.

For the money you save, here's what you get: The traction, durability,
and softness of neoprene or cork soles. Economically replaceable heels.
Six-inch, full-grain leather uppers. The relative coolness and better
ventilation of unpadded, unlined, uncollared shoes. Steel shanks under
the arch. And—but only if you are extremely patient and persistent—
leather insoles.

The insoles are admittedly the fly in the oinment. Until about ten
years ago, you could buy work shoes with leather insoles almost anywhere. Then just about everyone adopted cheaper insoles—foam and
cellulose. Foam deteriorates rapidly and won't absorb perspiration; cellulose is flimsy.

Soft-soled
oxfords

Oxfords.   They don't make 6-inch work shoes for women. Women should therefore consider soft-soled oxfords. "Soft-soled" means crepe or any other soft rubber sole and includes wedges. The upper should be sturdy full-grain leather; thin-skinned suedes and canvas are poor substitutes.

Oxfords don't provide the benefits of 6-inch uppers. And they are quite unsuitable for days when large patches of unmelted snow lie in ambush and cannot entirely be avoided. Yet soft-soled oxfords do have advantages. Compared to "hiking shoes" with lug soles, they give superior traction and comfort; they are far safer for crossing streams. Compared to both "hiking shoes" and 7-inch boots, they are lighter and cooler—great for hot weather.

Oxfords are certainly acceptable for women who hike infrequently, only on snowless days, and on good trails. They are also acceptable— not necessarily best—for frequent use by women who own snow boots and are willing to suffer the boots on warm days when the ground has light, patchy snow. But if you can't justify snow boots and want a single pair of fairly versatile shoes (still unsuitable for heavy snow), get something with 6-inch or 7-inch top.

High top boots.   Boots with 7-inch and 8-inch tops are often picked by such users as hikers, hunters, and lumberjacks; they give extra protection against deep snow and mud. Some styles have leather lining around the foot; otherwise the only lined models are insulated ones intended for winter.

A major drawback is cost. These boots often use special, oil-tanned leather for extra water repellence and softness; softness helps offset the discomfort of high tops. For this you pay two or three times the price of work shoes. One widely sold brand of hunter-hiker boots with lug soles sells for $85.

The soles, in turn, are another drawback. The best soles—neoprene and neoprene-cork with conventional square heels—rarely come on these boots. What you get is crepe wedges (reheeling problems, bad for snow), dark crepe modified wedges (fast wearing), and lug (slippery, fast wearing).

Finally, 7-inch and 8-inch tops are not what the doctor ordered for warm weather. Make no mistake: they fight the body's efforts to cool off.

*Mountaineering-style
"hiking shoe"*

Hiking shoes.   Mountaineering style "hiking shoes" should be considered if (a) having stylish footwear means a lot to you or (b) you
can't find a work shoe with a leather insole. But before you buy, give
careful thought to those two distinctive mountaineering shoe features:
lug soles and padding.

Lug soles are grand for snow. But on solid surfaces they are
treacherous when traction really counts—on sloping rock, stepping
stones, moist logs, and so on. Even when dry, lugs are too hard and
smooth to adhere to difficult surfaces; wet is downright dangerous.
Hardness also deprives a lug of the cushioning effect found with other
soles.

*Hybrid work-
mountaineering styling*

Like lugs, padding is fine for snow country. Mountaineering shoes
need it because their thick, stiff leather can bruise the ankle. And above
snowline, padding is an asset, not a liability. But for ordinary hiking

you don't need padding; you want shoes that are cool and well ventilated.

At least one "hiking shoe" avoids these drawbacks. It is unlined (except for a padded ankle cuff) and has dark crepe modified wedge soles, special silicone impregnated leather, and hybrid work-mountaineering style. But at $56 it is not a strong challenger to a comparably soled work shoe.

SUMMING UP

Men's 6-inch shoes with leather insoles and, preferably, neoprene-cork soles are the best buy. But finding leather insoles is a real problem, the styling won't help your King of the Trail image, and work shoes aren't made for ladies.* So whatever you buy, it will probably be a compromise.

━━━━━━━━━━━━━━━━━━━━━━━━━━
━━━━━━━━━━━━━━━━━━━━━━━━━━

HOW TO SOFTEN NEW BOOTS IN A HURRY

Ideally, you should wear them about the house and wherever else you can, and that way give them a chance to adjust to the shape of your feet. All of which takes time. British marathon walker John Merrill has been quoted as saying that it takes five hundred miles to break in a pair of really sturdy, heavy hiking boots. The stiffer the boot, the longer it takes. Lighter, more flexible boots can usually be broken in after about fifty miles. But there is a way to break in a pair of boots in a hurry . . .

Fill a deep bowl with enough lukewarm water to cover the boots, then put them on, lacing them tightly over a pair of thick socks. Pull up a chair, sit down, and soak your booted feet for about a half hour. By that time the soaked leather will have formed itself to the shape of your feet. Lift both feet out of the water, unlace the boots as much as you can, and then take them off, doing your level best not to spoil the newly molded shape. Wipe off surplus water and leave the boots on their sides to dry out. Do NOT place them before a fireplace or under a radiator. Then just before they're fully dry, apply a wax polish to them, rubbing it in well but in no way disturbing the molded shape as you rub. When that's done to your satisfaction, put the boots on the floor in an upright position and leave them to dry fully.

* Dorothy Laker, who has hiked the entire length of the Appalachian Trail three times, wore a pair of men's work shoes with 6-inch tops and rippled crepe soles.

"Hiking is a perfect way to communicate your values to your children. It is a good way to teach them about flowers and bugs and berries, and the more they know about these things, the more they will respect and protect them."

—MICHELE BREMER, *Prevention*, May 1977

BACKPACKING WITH CHILDREN

How successfully it works depends not so much on the child as the parents. A two- or three-month-old infant can enjoy a hike, provided its parents can relax and enjoy having the baby along. But if that causes concern, better that the first hike for the child be delayed until it is old enough to be self-propelled. Ideally, I think, the earlier a child is exposed to the wonders of nature the better. If the civilizing effects of walking in the wilderness have such impact on adults, think of the effect on the developing personality of a child. So if you can relax and not regard a hike with a really small child as a grit-your-teeth experiment, I say carry your infant on your back and hit the trail.

How does an infant who can't sit up yet enjoy a hike? Through his senses. The sounds of birds, the flutter of leaves, the feel of sun and breeze on his skin, the scent of wild flowers. And let's not forget the motion and body warmth of the adult who's carrying him.

There are, of course, special carriers for small children. For the infant who can't sit up yet, there's a soft fabric frame that can be worn on your front or back, and supports baby's head and body. Later, when the baby can sit up, there is a kiddie carrier with a lightweight aluminum frame covered with a fabric sling seat; some even have pillows attached to the front bar of the frame. By the time the child is two and able to walk, there are all-nylon backpacks designed for him that weigh only a few ounces. At age four or five, he can graduate to an all-nylon pack with an adjustable frame that will "grow" as he grows.

Susan and Siegfried Othmer took their two sons hiking when they were still infants. When each child reached age two, he was put down onto his own two feet and taught that "a hike is a round trip—to and from. Chil-

196

dren aren't exactly familiar with the idea, and it takes a little while for most of them to accept it. So for the first few hikes, we brought the carrier along just in case it was needed on the way back." By three, each boy had his own hiking boots, and that, Susan says, is important psychologically. "When a child has his own boots, he really accepts the fact that now he's responsible to carry himself."

When he's older, the child should share in preparations for the hike. He should be permitted to pore over the maps with his parents, and go with them when they buy equipment. For it's important that a family hike be fun and enjoyable for everyone. Certainly that doesn't mean that it must revolve around the child, but neither should the child be made to feel that a sacrifice is being made in order to include him. Actually, it's more of a compromise. Parents will not be able to walk quite so fast, at least not at first. Soon, however, the child who likes hiking will be out in front, leading the way. Until then the little child who's managing on his own two legs must be permitted the pleasure of exploration. Siegfried Othmer says, "With children one has to be more relaxed. What keeps them interested in hiking is what they encounter along the way. A bone. A feather. A rock. Insects, squirrels, gophers." Ten-year-old Brian, by now a veteran hiker, has a shoe box full of bones he's soaked in bleach. They're his "bone collection" and he's fiercely proud of it.

Susan Othmer says that parents have to be "flexible. Sometimes we see people with small children and they're knocking themselves out trying to maintain the same standards they have at home. Like trying to keep the children from getting dirty. That's all so unimportant. Children just naturally love to be outdoors, so long as their parents will relax and let them explore and climb trees and get dirty. It all washes off when they get home. I say to parents: Relax and let yourself enjoy it!"

Siegfried agrees. "That's really the secret. Children pick up their parents' fears. I think it's so important for parents to rein in their fears. For example, when Brian climbs trees he's doing something that I can't do, but I don't tell him that he can't just because I can't. Now obviously, not being able to do it does leave me at a disadvantage in trying to assess the danger that's involved. But simply by paying attention to him a number of times when he does this, I can begin to assess whether he's cautious, whether he can handle what he's doing. And I try to be in a position to help out if help is needed. Or if he falls, I'll try to be underneath to break his fall. But I won't admit to him the fact that I fear for him. The point being that we do allow Brian to do things—to take risks—beyond what we ourselves would take. And that, we think, has helped make Brian the kind of boy he is: He's very proud of how hard he can hike, how much he can carry, and how far he can swim."

Personally, I wish it were possible for every child in America to attend a school like the one Siegfried Othmer attended as a small child living abroad. His school placed emphasis on a child's relationship to nature, and often took the students out into the local forest. Siegfried recalls, "I asked the teacher if gnomes existed—after all, they were in the stories we read and I had some doubts, you see. But no one at the school ever discouraged you, never removed those doubts, because they didn't want to stifle imagination. If I wanted to believe that gnomes existed, they weren't going to deny me that . . . the richness of that belief. And I remember going out at night and feeding the gnomes in likely places. I'd walk for miles on my own into the mountains. I had a mushroom garden that was a couple of miles from the school, nestled in the Westphalian mountains. All of us children were very oriented toward nature, and hiking was very much a part of that. We might go to a cave—this was a limestone area. Or another time we might go on a long hike to see where a river disappeared into the ground, and another time on another hike to see where it had reappeared."

Michele Bremer, who says that her son, Max, said his "first clear and unmistakable word, 'backpack,' at the age of nine months," maintains that her children are her favorite hiking companions. "Children," she says, "come equipped with an insatiable curiosity about all they observe. Mine have asked why the ripe berries are black and the unripe ones are green, why the watercress likes to live with its feet in the stream, why the skunk cabbage smells funny, where the sun goes at night, and who belongs to the stars. When I'm feeling very removed from God and nature, I can find both by packing up my children and spending the afternoon hiking through the woods and meadows near my home. As an extra attraction, I can sometimes bring home some wild asparagus or blackberries for supper."

. . . As well as children who cannot help but grow up with a healthy respect for every living thing in this world. And what a loving gift that is for a parent to give a child!

"Winter is the season of silence. To be outdoors in the hush of a twilight snowfall is to
open the doors of your mind to a natural tran-
quillity that is at once restful and enlivening."
—BILL GOTTLIEB, *Prevention*, Novem-
ber 1977

WINTER BACKPACKING

Midwinter backpacking isn't for the novice, but it isn't all that difficult
either. And the advantages are obvious: the purity of the landscape, the
tingling cold, the incredible peace and quiet. Nowadays winter backpacking is being touted as "the hot new winter sport."

The main difference between hiking in winter and hiking any other time
of year is that when there's snow, you use cross-country skis or snowshoes
on the trail. Snowshoes are favored above skis, since they're considered
safer unless you're a really competent skier. Long, slim-model snowshoes
are recommended, because their narrow design puts less strain on leg muscles; furthermore, carrying a backpack on snowshoes is actually easier
than carrying it on foot. And whether you use skis or snowshoes, ski poles
will come in handy as balancers and they can also do double duty as tent
poles and save space in your pack.

You won't have a lot of daylight; in midwinter it can get dark by 4
P.M.—even earlier if weather is bad. So make certain you arrive at your
campsite before 4 P.M.

As for clothing, it's not all that complicated either. Again, it's the layer
system of shirts and sweaters so you can adjust your clothing to changes
in temperature. Wear thermal underwear, two pairs of wool socks, two
pairs of mitts (heavy wool underneath thick cowhide), and I recommend
one of those wool knit caps that turn into a face mask if you pull it down.
To your year-round first-aid kit add a pair of dark goggles (sun on snow
can be fairly blinding) and a bottle of vitamin C tablets.

"Vitamin C has been shown to increase . . . skin temperatures in the
cold as well as to decrease the sensation of discomfort resulting from cold
exposure." That's an excerpt from a report published by the Canadian
Defence and Civil Institute of Environmental Medicine. In one experiment, four people were exposed to extreme cold and their skin temperatures

199

measured. After that and for every day thereafter for one month, the four were given 2,000 mg. of vitamin C. Then they were exposed to cold again, and it was found that all four had higher skin temperatures.

With the proper preparation and equipment (a collapsible shovel, for example), winter backpacking can be an exhilarating experience. As Bill Gottlieb wrote, "After a few minutes outside you'll wonder—not only at the beauty of snow and ice and cold, clear air—but how you ever managed to stay indoors for so long."

I started this chapter with a quote from Dr. Howorth, and now I'll end it with more from this veteran hiker for whom the art of walking consists of many parts:

It consists of knowing what to eat and drink, and how to prepare and consume it, alone or with others; how to make or erect a shelter; how to find comfort in a sleeping bag; the names of flowers, their structure, their odors, and how they grow. The names of birds, their flight, their songs, their eggs and young, their virtues and their vices. How the earth is made, its hills and valleys, its rocks and soil. Streams, a trickle on a rock face high on a cliff, or a Valley of a Thousand Falls; a cool drink from a spring, a hot face washed in a tiny brook, or a tingling bath in a mountain stream or glacial pool. Fire, for a cup of tea, or a full meal at the end of day, a fire for warming, or a big campfire with tales and song, and even the dread forest fire. Scenes, big, little, at all angles and all distances, with snow, or the greens of spring climbing uphill, the great flower beds of summer, evergreen forests, glaciers, ice in chimneys, the colors of fall; and clouds, all kinds, never two alike, never a sky the same; and pictures, with their memories. Last, and most important, companionship, all sorts, cheerful or glum, bright or dull, active or lazy, skillful or clumsy, bold or timid. Of all such is the art and pleasure of walking.

CHAPTER

8

FOODS FOR ENERGY AND ENDURANCE

"There is no good reason why people should
tire more easily as they grow older."

—GAYELORD HAUSER, *Look Younger,
Live Longer*

I HAD AN AUNT WHO, INSTEAD OF LISTENING TO SOAP OPERAS ON THE radio, used to tune in a man by the name of Alfred McCann, who devoted an entire program five days a week to the subject of nutrition. She became a disciple, a believer in such things as whole-wheat bread, vegetable juices, and using honey as a sugar substitute. And although she was far from affluent and this was during the days of the so-called Great Depression, my aunt saw to it that her family's diet consisted solely of those foods Mr. McCann deemed worthy, and consequently, I think, some of her friends considered her lovingly eccentric. But I also recall that when one of her three sons had his picture published in the Sunday rotogravure section of one of the metropolitan dailies in the act of throwing a discus and looking like a Greek god, a few of them began to wonder if perhaps she hadn't stumbled upon something worthwhile after all.

And a decade later even some of them were talking knowingly of the nutritive value of such things as whole-grain cereals, yogurt, and black-strap molasses in the wake of the phenomenal success of Gayelord Hauser's book *Look Younger, Live Longer,* published in 1950. In a chapter titled "Refuse to Be Tired" Hauser wrote:

> If you want to experience a quick pickup in energy (at any age) make your diet extremely rich in the B vitamins. You can do this by taking (daily) 3 or more heaping tablespoons of powdered brewer's yeast in milk, or in fruit and vegetable juices.
>
> Twenty years ago, I learned, through my studies and experiments in nutrition, that people who ate natural foods such as whole wheat breads, whole grain cereals, whole sugar (brown), and blackstrap molasses were less likely to be plagued by fatigue. The tired ones were those who ate white breads, denatured and over-refined cereals, and white sugar.

202

Yet, despite the national attention Hauser's regimen of "wonder foods" attracted, most athletes, amateur and professional, were still stoking up on masses of protein before a competition. Lots of red meat was considered the ticket for energy and endurance. Today? We're being warned that red meat is high in fats and so contributes to heart disease. In fact, we've been informed that proteins play no part at all in the production of energy. Experiments undertaken in Sweden have indicated that meals high in protein eaten several days before a sports event tend to depress the storage of glycogen in muscles and, as a result, *decrease* endurance.

Ironically, today, when Americans are more health-conscious than ever before, there's probably more confusion about diet than ever before. Meanwhile, many are still thrashing around in search of the *super* diet that will keep them lithe and bubbling with energy.

A few years ago, a speaker at an Ohio State University symposium on sports said, "If your athlete feels tired or nervous and feels the need for aid to increase his efficiency, I suggest that you give him a cup of coffee." And *The New York Times* has quoted a Swiss chemist and former world-class sprinter who advocates caffeine laced with a little niacinamide, one of the B-complex vitamins. Yet there are many doctors who maintain that caffeine causes jangled nerves that masquerade as energy.

Several research papers have claimed that vitamin E has value in postponing fatigue, and that wheat-germ oil, in addition to vitamin E, may contain a factor that's important in the production of physical effort. Yet there are many doctors who counter that there is a paucity of controlled clinical experiments proving that E is of any real value.

Meantime, John Merrill, one of Great Britain's most famous long-distance walkers, who last year left his footprints along the entire coastline of Britain—a distance of more than seven thousand miles—considers chocolate bars his energy food. During his marathon walk, Merrill consumed approximately 60 pounds of cereal, 570 pints of milk, 123 pounds of sugar, and *1,700 bars of chocolate*.

Dr. John Prutting, one of the growing army of internists who have made a study of nutrition, believes that many Americans who are extremely vitamin-conscious neglect to take in enough minerals. Nuts, fruits, and vegetables contain a lot of minerals, while alcohol consumed in any but the most modest quantity deprives the body of magnesium and potassium, two of the minerals Dr. Prutting considers most valuable.

Walter Gregg, chairman of the Department of Health and Physical Education at Northwestern University, says, "Athletes are forever looking for more energy, but they are leaning toward carbohydrates to be sure of an energy supply." Which brings us back to what has become commonly known as *carbohydrate loading*, which we touched upon briefly in the first part of this book. The scientific terminology for it is *supercompensation*, and the concept is based on the belief that a diet of easily digested high-carbohydrate foods can give an athlete supernormal stores of energy. Actually, it is a careful balance of training schedule and diet stretched over a seven-day period, during which the athlete at first exercises strenuously while eating a diet heavy on protein but low on carbohydrates and fat, and then dramatically switches to a light training schedule and an almost total carbohydrate diet, which supposedly sends him into competition with a larger reserve of glycogen, which, once the body converts it into glucose, is oxidized and turned to energy—*quick* energy, because it requires about 10 percent less oxygen to metabolize a given unit of carbohydrate energy.

Not everyone agrees that carbohydrate loading is the answer, however. Even Eric Hultman, the Swedish physiologist who developed this "super-compensation diet," doesn't promise that it works the same for everyone. According to Dr. Ralph A. Nelson, assistant professor of nutrition at the Mayo Medical School in Rochester, Minnesota, "While carbohydrate-loading technically will improve athletic performance, an athlete should take care to eat approximately 15 percent of calories as protein, 35 percent of calories as fat, and 50 percent of calories as carbohydrates—48 hours before competition." This distribution is similar to the distribution of nutrients recommended for the general population by the American Heart Association.

Then, of course, there's the high-fat, low-carbohydrate diet advanced by Dr. Robert Atkins in his book *Diet Revolution*, during the early stages of which the dieter eliminates carbohydrates *entirely*.

If you're confused, you certainly have a right to be. Particularly when one reads that Dr. E. R. Buskirk of Penn State contends, "There is no evidence that superior performance results from taking more of a single nutrient than required."

Well, at least this much is still sacred: A calorie is still a calorie no matter what its source. Fat is still stored energy, and the only way to get rid of it is to expend more energy in physical activity than you take in as food calories. And, happily, you can burn up to approximately 300 calories in only thirty minutes of brisk walking. And the more you walk, the more calories you burn.

Personally, I'm not convinced there is a single quick-energy food or diet. Not that I haven't experimented. For some years I drank a glass of warm water laced with cider vinegar and fortified with a tablespoon of honey, the first thing in the morning. Then, for no reason I can think of, I stopped, and I don't feel any the less energetic. But about three times a week I fill an electric blender with skim milk, 3 tablespoons of wheat germ, 3 tablespoons of brewer's yeast, a whole banana, half a cup of commercial yogurt, and one raw egg—and drink the frothy potion. I believe those foods are good for me and that, I think, is perhaps half of it. Believe that what you eat will give you more energy and greater endurance and, unless it's a really inferior food, it will. You'll feel more energetic because you've programmed yourself to feel more energetic. And energy seems to feed on itself and produces still more energy. I go along with Dr. Prutting when he says, "I really feel that a person's health depends on what goes on above the ears as well as what goes into the stomach."

The only way I know to have more energy and endurance is to eat sensibly and exercise regularly. That is, if you choose an exercise you really enjoy and not one that you do out of a sense of duty to yourself. "Listlessness and fatigue give way to energy and excitement when you are doing what you really want to do," Marie Beynon Ray observed in her book *How Never to Be Tired*. And I think that makes as much sense today as it did when she wrote it over thirty years ago. Emotional energy generates physical energy.

Walking is my exercise and I love it. Every time I walk I feel a surge of fresh energy that lasts and lasts, making everything I do afterward seem so much easier. As for diet, most doctors still maintain that if you eat a well-balanced diet, you're getting all the nutrients your body needs. And what we need has been established by the Nutrition Board of the National Academy of Science and is known as RDA (Recommended Daily Allowances).

And since there is so much confusion and misinformation about diet nowadays, let me give you a list of vitamins and minerals, their RDA, and the foods in which they're found in abundance.

VITAMIN	RDA	SOURCES
A	5,000 IU *	Green and yellow fruits and vegetables, milk, dairy products, fish-liver oils. A cup of cooked spinach gives 8,000 IU; one raw carrot, 10,000 IU; one whole tomato, 1,250 IU.
B_1	1–1.5 mg †	Brewer's yeast, brown rice, blackstrap molasses, wheat germ, peanuts, poultry, nuts. 1¼ cups of peanuts provide 1 mg; 4 tablespoons of brewer's yeast, 2.25 mg.
B_2	1.3–1.7 mg	Blackstrap molasses, whole grains, nuts, organ meats. 2 slices of beef liver provide 2 mg. And the 3 tablespoons of brewer's yeast I pour into my blender give me 1 mg.
B_6	1.5–1.8 mg	Blackstrap molasses, brewer's yeast, leafy green vegetables, organ meats, wheat germ, egg yolk, milk. Would you believe that only one cup of peas provides 2 mg?
B_{12}	3 mcg ‡	Milk, dairy products, fish, organ meats. A single egg contains 1 mcg; a ½ lb. can of tuna, 5 mcg.
B_{15}	None given	Whole grains, brown rice, organ meats.
C	45 mg	Fresh citrus fruits, vegetable juices, cantaloupe, red and green peppers. One green pepper gives 120 mg; one orange, one grapefruit, 100 mg each.
D	400 IU	Sunshine, cod-liver oil, egg yolk, organ meats. A ¼ lb. can of tuna or salmon has 300 IU.
E	12–15 IU	Eggs, organ meats, wheat germ, vegetable oils, green lettuce, avocados. Two tomatoes, 3 IU; one tablespoon of safflower oil, 20 IU.

MINERAL	RDA	SOURCES
Calcium	800–1,400 mg	Milk, buttermilk, cheese, yogurt, powdered skim milk, molasses. One slice of American cheese provides 200 mg.
Iodine	100–130 mcg	Seafood, iodized salt, kelp tablets. One kelp tablet is purported to provide 150% of the RDA.
Iron	10–18 mg	Liver, apricots, oysters, organ meats, blackstrap molasses, eggs, wheat germ. A ¼-lb. serving of beef liver gives 200 mg.
Magnesium	300–350 mg	Honey, nuts, seafood, spinach, bran. One cup of roasted peanuts with skin intact provides 420 mg.
Phosphorus	800 mg	Meat, poultry, fish, egg yolk, peas, beans, grains, yogurt. A ¼-lb. serving of calf's liver, 600 mg.
Potassium	None given	Raisins, peanuts, seafood, dates, figs, peaches, blackstrap molasses, baked potato. One whole banana, 500 mg; one baked potato, 500 mg.
Zinc	15 mg	Brewer's yeast, spinach, liver, mushrooms, seafood.

* International Units
† Milligrams
‡ Micrograms

PART III

THE
ANATOMY
OF
WALKING

"It is not God, but people themselves who shorten their lives by not keeping physically fit."

—Carl Linnaeus, Swedish naturalist, 1763

Swedes believed it was true then, and still do more than two hundred years later. Exercise is part of their life-style, with the result that many sixty-year-old Swedes are in better physical shape than their thirty-year-old American counterparts. A Swedish male heart, for instance, is said to tick 5.3 years longer than its American counterpart.

Dr. Per Olaf Astrand, physician and exercise physiologist at Stockholm's College of Physical Education, says, "Physical activity improves the functional capacity of the oxygen-transport system. This increases the power of what one could call the human combustion engine. This decreases the heart rate at a given cardiac output. In other words, you improve the efficiency of the heart muscle. . . . Exercise strengthens the heart and circulation system, and in this way is part of preventive medicine. And the best exercise is the easiest exercise. . . . *Walk*. It's one of the best exercises going!"

CHAPTER

9

WALKING AND YOUR HEART

"Walking briskly—not just strolling—is the
simplest and also one of the best of exercises."

—American Heart Association

"THE MECHANIZATION OF AMERICA, PRINCIPALLY INVENTION OF THE elevator and the motor car, has reduced the majority of its population to a sedentary life-style," said Dr. Albert A. Kattus in 1974, when he was chairman of the Exercise Committee of the American Heart Association. "This life-style has a great deal to do with the development of atherosclerosis—the clogging up of arteries of the heart, brain and kidneys—the disease process that kills and cripples more people than all other disease entities combined. What an irony of our time that this scourge of the human race is self-inflicted!"

But we *can* do something about it. In his book *Heart Attack? Counterattack!*, Dr. Terence Kavanagh, medical director of the Toronto Rehabilitation Center in Canada, wrote, "Wherever pockets of primitive peoples are still to be found, they are relatively free from heart attack. The Australian aborigine, the Kenyan Masai tribesman, the Mexican Taranumara Indian, all rely mainly on their legs for locomotion." *Walking* can be preventive medicine.

Some years ago a study done in Great Britain showed that London letter carriers, whose work compelled them to walk a considerable distance every working day, had fewer heart attacks than postal workers who held desk jobs. Still another British study of the same period examined the relationship between simply walking to work and changes in the electrocardiogram because of poor circulation. Some 8,948 men, civil servants between the ages of forty and sixty-five, were studied. Even the men whose walk to work took less than twenty minutes averaged one-third fewer electrocardiographic changes than the men who didn't walk to work.

Dr. Meyer Friedman, director of the Harold Brunn Institute for Cardiovascular Research at Mount Zion Hospital and Medical Center in San Francisco, is "extraordinarily, fantastically enthusiastic" about moderate rhythmic exercise, but he has reservations about jogging, both medically ("a violent exercise") and aesthetically ("boring"). He himself takes morning and afternoon walks.

Dr. Kenneth Cooper, whose book *Aerobics* is credited with starting the whole jogging craze, has said, "I restrict many of my patients to walking." He feels that any exercise program of an aerobic type promotes cardio-vascular fitness.

In 1978, deaths owing to cardiovascular diseases totaled 1,003,300, according to statistics compiled by the American Heart Association, and over one-fourth of the victims were between forty-five and sixty-five years of age. The sedentary, middle-aged male is the most likely candidate for a coronary, although his female counterpart isn't immune, either. After menopause the female's partial immunity to heart attack disappears. "Pre-menopausal women have an extremely low rate of heart attack," says Dr. Ezra Amsterdam, director of the Coronary Care Unit at the Sacramento Medical Center in California, "but post-menopausal women catch up to men and, in their seventies, pass men in terms of incidence."

Dr. Amsterdam elaborated for me on the connection between walking and a healthy heart.

How does walking benefit the individual? The basic answer to that is how does aerobic exercise benefit the individual? Walking is an excellent example of aerobic exercise; the rhythmic tensing and relaxing of the large muscles aids the flow of blood and makes the exertion of the heart less. If the average sedentary individual walks up a flight of stairs, he may start, say, with a heart rate of 100 and may end at the top of the stairs with a heart rate of 120. His blood pressure may begin at 120 over 80 and end at 160 over 100. After a period of training, such as walking, he may make that trip from the bottom of the steps to the top and raise his heart rate from 80 to only 100 instead of 120. What's happening is that while the muscles that do the work need the same amount of energy, the heart, the primary organ that delivers that energy in the form of oxygen and nutrients through the blood, is able to do that now while beating less frequently, less forcefully. And blood pressure won't go up so much, because the trained muscles now can take oxygen out of the blood more efficiently.

Which is precisely why our leg muscles are sometimes referred to as a "second heart." Walking makes the muscles below the waist—the muscles in thighs, calves, buttocks, abdomen, feet—help the heart pump blood, a full-time, twenty-four-hour-a-day job for as long as we live.

"The heart has two very important auxiliary pumps. One is the leg. One is the diaphragm. The more important of these two is the leg."

—DR. PAUL DUDLEY WHITE, cardiologist

To make the sedentary individual get up and walk, Sweden's Dr. Per Astrand suggests, "Start walking upstairs—stairs are made for walking." . . . "Get off the bus a few blocks from your stop. If there's no bus in sight, walk to the next stop." . . . "Leave the car at home and walk to the shop." . . . "Go walk the dog—even if you don't have a dog." In other words, *Walk*. It's one of the best exercises going!"

There is no question that our bodies work better the more they're exercised. Or that heart disease can be significantly alleviated by a suitable exercise program. But all exercises do *not* improve cardiovascular fitness. Weight lifting, for example, builds muscles by causing them to tense up, but in the process this motion squeezes the blood vessels so that less blood passes to the heart muscle rather than more. There are other exercises that promote blood flow but that are so strenuous they can't be kept up long enough to keep a steady flow of oxygen to the heart muscle. Only aerobic exercise—rhythmic, repetitive exercise involving motion—both aids the flow of blood and supplies enough oxygen to the exercising muscles for a sufficiently long period of time. Walking, jogging, swimming, bicycling are all aerobic exercises, but none is so readily available, so easy to do, as walking. And that is vitally important, since once you achieve physical and cardiovascular fitness, you must maintain it. To do that, exercise must be part of your life-style. Which is why most doctors consider walking, the easiest of exercises, to be the *best* of all exercises.

Several years ago Michael L. Pollock, director of the Cardiac Rehabilitation Program and Human Performance Laboratory at Wake Forest University in Winston-Salem, North Carolina, undertook an investigation to determine if an individual could get as much benefit from walking as from running. "The energy cost of running is generally higher than walking, and yet many men and women would rather walk than run," he wrote in an article in the *Journal of Applied Psychology* that summarized this particular study. The question was, "When the intensity of walking is less than running, can one get similar training effects by the former if duration and frequency are increased?"

Pollock and his associates conducted a twenty-week fast-walking study with men forty to fifty-seven years of age, who walked for forty minutes four days per week. They reported that the improvement from the walking program equaled the improvement in a thirty-minute, three-day-per-week jogging program with similarly aged men. The lower intensity of the walking program (65 to 75 percent of maximum heart-rate range) was offset by the increased duration and frequency of training. In short, because walking is so easy and so pleasurable, this form of exercise makes it easier to stay fit.

For that reason alone, Dr. Amsterdam considers the potential of walking to be "fantastic. Jogging is very hard to adhere to . . . it's very stressful. But walking is easily 'do-able' by virtually every single person."

Which is why in *Fit for Fun: A Swedish Message*, created to introduce Americans to exercise and diet "the Swedish way," Berit Brattnäs wrote, "If Alfred Nobel were making up his list of prizes today, I am pretty certain that he would add a few subjects to be honored, along with the famous prizes for peace, literature, medicine, physics and chemistry. I have a feeling that one of those additional prize areas would be listed something like this: '. . . and a prize shall be awarded annually, with the winner or winners named by the Royal Karoline Institute, to the person or persons who have contributed most to mankind by encouraging modern man to walk.'"

The researchers at Wake Forest University concluded, "It is well established that improvement in aerobic capacity is directly related to intensity of training." And in a booklet she wrote for distribution by the American Heart Association, Lenore R. Zohman, M.D., a specialist in the field of cardiopulmonary rehabilitation, stated, "There is an amount (intensity or vigorousness) of exercise which is enough to condition the muscles and cardiovascular system leading to physical fitness, but is not overly strenuous. That is, there is a target zone in which there is enough activity to achieve fitness, but not too much to exceed safe limits. The name of the game is finding your target zone." That, according to Dr. Zohman, is between 60 and 80 percent of an individual's maximum aerobic power, which is approximately the same level as 70 to 85 percent of maximum attainable heart rate.

The middle-aged men who took part in the study at Wake Forest University found their target zone with the guidance of Michael Pollock and his team. Take a stress test and your doctor will be able to tell you yours.

And while aerobic power can't be measured easily, you can count your pulse rate, which is almost always the same as the number of heartbeats per minute. The following chart, reprinted from Dr. Zohman's booklet,

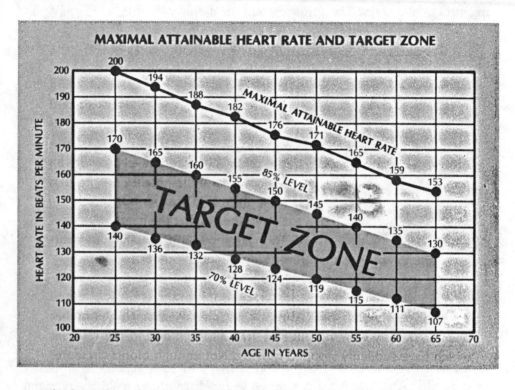

This figure shows that as we grow older, the highest heart rate which can be reached during all-out effort falls. These numerical values are "average" values for age. Note that one-third of the population may differ from these values. It is quite possible that a normal 50-year-old man may have a maximum heart rate of 195 or that a 30-year-old man might have a maximum of only 168. The same limitations apply to the 70 per cent and 85 per cent of maximum lines.

gives the heart rate in beats per minute based on a normal active individual of each age indicated. Your maximum attainable heart rate may be below the level for the so-called normal active individual of your age, since in addition to age it also depends on heredity as well as the state of your physical fitness and health.

As the chart shows, an average twenty-year-old man or woman has a maximum heart rate of 200. His or her target zone would be a heart rate of

140 (70 percent) to 170 (85 percent) beats per minute. However, a sixty-five-year-old with a maximum attainable heart rate of 153 beats per minute would have a target zone of 107 (70 percent) to 130 (85 percent) beats per minute.

Dr. Zohman advises that while experimenting to find your target zone, there should be a warm-up of five to ten minutes, and then a five- to ten-minute cool-down before starting your walk. (The stretching exercises in Chapter 6 are perfect here.) And she points out that it's very important that you count your pulse *immediately* upon stopping exercise, because the rate changes very quickly once exercise is slowed or stopped. You're instructed to find the beat within a second and count for ten seconds. Then multiply by six to obtain the count for a minute.

"By trial and error, develop an exercise pattern that seems easy for five to ten minutes," suggests Dr. Zohman, "and count your pulse immediately after this warm-up." It should be less than 70 percent of your age-related maximum attainable heart rate. Then exercise more vigorously to get to the target zone. Count again after three to five minutes at this level to check whether you are doing enough to be on target. If your heart rate is below 70 percent of your maximum, exercise more strenuously. Conversely, if it is above 85 percent of your maximum, exercise less vigorously either by exercising slower or less forcefully. . . . Repeat counting at five-minute intervals until you have determined just how much exercise is necessary to put you in the target zone.

Once you have thoroughly checked out your own responses to exercise, you will begin to recognize certain normal sensations you get when you are in the target zone such as an awareness of a certain amount of rapid heart action or breathlessness. You will recognize how much effort it takes to get you there and will no longer need to continue to count your heart rate during each exercise session. You will be able to perceive intuitively with reasonable accuracy just how high your heart rate is and whether you are in the target zone.

HOW TO COUNT YOUR PULSE

There are several pulses: inside the bend of the elbow toward the body side; the groin area; the side of the neck; and the outer side of the wrist. Take your pulse by using the first two or three fingers of the opposite hand. You'll feel a little thumping under your fingertips.

THE STRESS TEST

Since walking is the least strenuous of aerobic exercises, a stress test isn't necessarily recommended before starting a walking program unless you're over forty and have been extremely sedentary—or unless you're thinking in terms of competitive race walking or backpacking. In fact, Sweden's Dr. Astrand feels it's more important to have a medical checkup to determine if it will be safe for your heart if you *don't* exercise. Still, Dr. Amsterdam feels "it would be a valid generalization to advise any individual who has been sedentary and plans to increase his physical activity significantly to take a stress test. I think a stress test for anyone, forty or older, who is going to undertake increasing amounts of activity is very rational and reasonable."

The electrocardiogram (EKG) taken while the individual is walking a treadmill is an intrinsic part of a stress test. This is the way the attending physician can monitor the patient's heart rhythm during stress, noting any telltale clues that suggest there may be a coronary artery disease. The individual being tested walks the treadmill in a series of uninterrupted and increasing work stages with continuous monitoring of his heart rate. Each stage lasts three minutes and serves as a warm-up for the next stage, the idea being to carry through to the point of reaching 85 percent of the maximum heart rate predicted for the person's age. If the heart rate reaches the critical 85 percent of its original rate rapidly, it indicates an inability to cope with moderate demands; it's a good sign when it takes a while to reach the 85 percent mark. The treadmill stress test is generally regarded as the most effective way of detecting cardiovascular obstructions.

Walking is now accepted as an effective treatment for a damaged heart, but I can remember not so many years ago how startled I was when an acquaintance of mine who had suffered a heart attack told me of the long walks he was taking every day on orders from his doctor. At that time I was still wedded to the idea that any kind of coronary malfunction automatically turned one into what Sam Lutz says he used to be—a coronary coward.

At the time of his heart attack in 1964 while on a business trip around South America, Sam, a research scientist, was smoking three packs of cigarettes a day and was overweight and tense. After his attack, he was "a typical cardiac coward. Then one day I got the idea that what I needed was some moderate exercise. I'd gotten tired of being safe. Our laboratory was on a hill, and I decided I would walk up that hill from the back side where there was a good bit of underbrush. So I took along some pruning tools and I walked up that hill. Well, I made it and I felt better for it, and before I knew it I found that I'd gotten hooked on walking. I began fashioning walking sticks from the bloomstalk of the yucca, which is a desert plant. The bloomstalk comes when the plant goes to seed, and it's tough outside and pulpy inside so it's extra light but stiff, and it gave me a third leg when I walked."

With stick in hand, Sam began hiking in the area around his home in Southern California and eventually got a number of his friends interested in going with him on half-day hikes through the Santa Monica mountain range. In jest they christened themselves the Sierraitas Club—a diminutive for the Sierra Club, which Sam assumed was composed of gung-ho mountain climbers. Then one day he discovered he was dead wrong and he joined. "Anyway, by that time I was far from being a cardiac coward anymore. I'd just gotten back from a trip through south New Zealand, where I'd walked the thirty-three-mile Milford track across the McKinnon Pass in three days. I'd taken a stress test before I went."

Today Sam Lutz is a member of the Sierra Club's One Hundred Peak group of hikers, who qualify by making it up a total of twenty-five peaks that are over 11,000 feet high. Once you've done that, you get a patch for your backpack and you're eligible to go on from twenty-five peaks to a hundred peaks, and, says Sam, "when you make that final peak, you sign your name on a piece of paper, deposit it in a waterproof can, and when you come down it's champagne for everybody."

Retired now, he hikes with a group every Wednesday. One week it may be a nature hike, the next a peak hike, and the following week perhaps it's through a valley and on to a waterfall. In between hikes, Sam and his wife have a business working out of their garage—making earrings specially designed for pierced ears. "Crazy thing for a scientist to be doing," he says, laughing.

Joe Roland is a handsome, vigorous sixty-two-year-old man who, after open-heart surgery, was told by his doctor to start walking every day. "Start with one block . . . next day two blocks. Build gradually," he said. "Try to make it a mile if you can. Don't jog. *Walk*. I'll see you again in one month's time."

One month later Joe walked to his doctor's office. The doctor was amazed. It was, after all, a four-mile walk. He advised Joe to take the bus back.

"I sat in the park opposite the doctor's office and I thought about it, and then I got up and walked the four miles home." Since that day Joe has been walking three times a day, *every* day—a total of seven miles. "And I feel better than ever," he says. "I'm telling you that walking is number one! All I do now I'm retired is walk walk, *walk*. As long as I walk, I know I'll live. The only medicine I take nowadays is a walk. It's the best medicine I know for staying alive. Recently a man who lives here in my apartment building came up and introduced himself to me. Two heart attacks, and only four weeks ago he had four bypasses. Now my new friend walks with me sometimes, and yesterday he managed a three-and-a-quarter-mile round trip in one hour and ten minutes."

When it rains, Joe prefers to walk the lobby of his apartment building, a high-rise in Los Angeles, for at least a half hour nonstop. Meanwhile his doctor tells him, "Keep up the good work. Keep walking. You'll be your own doctor." Joe Roland weighs 175 pounds, which is exactly what he weighed when he was thirty. "Walking," he says, standing tall and patting his flat stomach, "is the number-one thing in my life."

And if walking can improve a sick heart, why wait for a heart attack before you start a walking program that will take care of your heart?

"Atherosclerosis is the condition that under-
lies most heart attacks."

—American Heart Association

FOOD AND THE HEALTHY HEART

Walking by itself can't guarantee a healthy heart. A combination of
proper exercise and diet is needed to stave off atherosclerosis; according to
the American Heart Association and cardiologists around the country, this
means a fat-controlled, low-cholesterol diet.

The low incidence of atherosclerosis among people who can't afford our
rich diet is a matter of record. I have yet to talk to a cardiologist who at
some point doesn't speak of the primitive Batu people in southern Africa,
who number some 50 million and yet have a heart-disease rate just this
side of zero. Their diet is only about 10 percent fat and they eat about a
fifth of the cholesterol we do.

The heart-disease rate in Japan is only a ninth of what it is in our country. The Japanese diet also contains about 10 percent fat and is very low
in cholesterol.

The Masai tribesmen in Kenya cover miles every day on foot and have
a diet some of us might consider Spartan. Heart disease is relatively unknown among the Masai.

There's no question but that the exercise you do or don't do and the
food you eat or don't eat can protect your heart or endanger it.

The so-called typical American diet is high in animal (saturated) fats
and foods that tend to raise the level of cholesterol in the blood, which, in
turn, contributes to the development of atherosclerosis.

Cholesterol, a waxy material, is manufactured by the body, and we all
need a certain amount of it, but if we take in too much, it becomes embedded in the lining of the artery walls, and over a period of time the
arteries narrow and eventually may close off completely. And if that occurs
in a major artery serving the heart muscle, a heart attack is the result.

Now, to control your intake of cholesterol-rich foods, the American
Heart Association recommends:

. . . Eat no more than three egg yolks a week, including eggs used in
cooking.

. . . Limit your use of shrimp and organ meats.

To control the amount and type of fat you eat:

. . . Use fish, chicken, turkey, and veal in most of your meat meals for the week; use moderate-sized portions of beef, lamb, pork, and ham less frequently.

. . . Choose lean cuts of meat, trim visible fat, and discard the fat that cooks out of the meat.

. . . Avoid deep-fat frying; use cooking methods that help to remove fat—baking, boiling, broiling, roasting, stewing.

. . . Restrict your use of fatty "luncheon" and "variety" meats like sausage and salami.

. . . Instead of butter and other cooking fats that are solid or completely hydrogenated, use liquid vegetable oils and margarines that are rich in polyunsaturated fats.

. . . Instead of whole milk and cheeses made from whole milk and cream use skimmed milk and skimmed milk cheeses.

On a more positive note, the American Heart Association recommends six basic food groups, the number and size of servings for each . . . and then what foods in these six groups to either avoid or use sparingly.

1	**Recommended**	**Avoid or Use Sparingly**
MEAT, POULTRY, FISH, DRIED BEANS and PEAS, NUTS, EGGS *1 serving:* *3–4 ounces of cooked meat or fish (not including bone or fat)* *or* *3–4 ounces of a vegetable listed here.* *Use 2 or more servings (a total of 6–8 ounces) daily.*	*Chicken, turkey, veal, or fish in most of your meat meals for the week.* Shellfish—clams, crab, lobster, oysters, scallops, and shrimp—are low in fat but high in cholesterol. Use a 4-ounce serving as a substitute for meat no more than twice a week. *Beef, lamb, pork, and ham less frequently.* Choose lean, ground meat and lean cuts of meat. Trim all visible fat before cooking. Bake, broil, roast, or stew so that you can discard the fat which cooks out of the meat. *Nuts and dried beans and peas:* Kidney beans, lima beans, baked beans, lentils, split peas and chick peas (garbanzos) are high in vegetable protein and may be used in place of meat occasionally. Egg whites as desired.	Duck and goose. Heavily marbled and fatty meats, spare ribs, mutton, frankfurters, sausages, fatty hamburgers, bacon, and luncheon meats. Organ meats—liver, kidney, heart, and sweetbreads—are very high in cholesterol. Since liver is very rich in vitamins and iron, it should not be eliminated from the diet completely. Use a 4-ounce serving in a meat meal no more than once a week. Egg yolks: limit to 3 per week, including eggs used in cooking. Cakes, batters, sauces, and other foods containing egg yolks.

2	**Recommended**	**Avoid or Use Sparingly**
BREAD and CEREALS (Whole grain, enriched or restored) *1 serving of bread:* *1 slice.* *1 serving of cereal:* *½ cup cooked;* *1 cup, cold, with skimmed milk.* *Use at least 4 servings daily.*	*Breads made with a minimum of saturated fat:* White enriched (including raisin bread), whole wheat, English muffins, French bread, Italian bread, oatmeal bread, pumpernickel, and rye bread. Biscuits, muffins, and griddle cakes made at home, using an allowed liquid oil as shortening. Cereal (hot and cold), rice, melba toast, matzo, pretzels. Pasta: macaroni, noodles (except egg noodles), and spaghetti.	Butter rolls, commercial biscuits, muffins, donuts, sweet rolls, cakes, crackers, egg bread, cheese bread, and commercial mixes containing dried eggs and whole milk.

3	**Recommended**	**Avoid or Use Sparingly**
VEGETABLES and FRUIT (Fresh, frozen or canned) *1 serving: ½ cup. Use at least 4 servings daily.*	*One serving should be a source of Vitamin C:* Broccoli, cabbage (raw), tomatoes. Berries, cantaloupe, grapefruit (or juice), mango, melon, orange (or juice), papaya, strawberries, tangerines. *One serving should be a source of Vitamin A— dark-green leafy or yellow vegetables, or yellow fruits:* Broccoli, carrots, chard, chicory, escarole, greens (beet, collard, dandelion, mustard, turnip), kale, peas, rutabagas, spinach, string beans, sweet potatoes and yams, watercress, winter squash, yellow corn. Apricots, cantaloupe, mango, papaya. Other vegetables and fruits are also very nutritious; they should be eaten in salads, main dishes, snacks and desserts, in addition to the recommended daily allowances of high Vitamin A and C vegetables and fruits.	If you must limit your calories, use vegetables such as potatoes, corn, or lima beans sparingly. To add variety to your diet, one serving (½ cup) of any of these may be substituted for one serving of bread or cereals.

4	Recommended	Avoid or Use Sparingly
MILK PRODUCTS	*Milk products that are low in dairy fats:*	*Whole milk and whole milk products:*
1 serving: 8 ounces (1 cup). Buy only skimmed milk that has been fortified with Vitamins A and D. *Daily servings: Children up to 12—3 or more cups; Teenagers—4 or more cups; Adults—2 or more cups.*	Fortified skimmed (non-fat) milk and fortified skimmed milk powder and low-fat milk. The label on the container should show that the milk is fortified with Vitamins A and D. The word "fortified" alone is not enough. Buttermilk made from skimmed milk, yogurt made from skimmed milk, canned evaporated skimmed milk, and cocoa made with low-fat milk.	Chocolate milk, canned whole milk, ice cream, all creams including sour, half and half, whipped, and whole milk yogurt. Non-dairy cream substitutes (usually contain coconut oil, which is very high in saturated fat).
	Cheeses made from skimmed milk or partially skimmed milk, such as cottage cheese, creamed or uncreamed (uncreamed, preferably), farmer's, baker's, or hoop cheese, mozarella and sapsago cheeses.	Cheeses made from cream or whole milk. Butter.

5	Recommended	Avoid or Use Sparingly

FATS and OILS (Polyunsaturated)

An individual allowance should include about 2–4 tablespoons daily (depending on how many calories you can afford) in the form of margarine, salad dressing, and shortening.

Margarines, liquid oil shortenings, salad dressings, and mayonnaise containing any of these polyunsaturated vegetable oils:

Corn oil, cottonseed oil, safflower oil, sesame seed oil, soybean oil, and sunflower seed oil.

Margarines and other products high in polyunsaturates can usually be identified by their label which lists a recommended liquid vegetable oil as the first ingredient, and one or more partially hydrogenated vegetable oils as additional ingredients.

Diet margarines are low in calories because they are low in fat. Therefore it takes twice as much diet margarine to supply the polyunsaturates contained in a recommended margarine.

Solid fats and shortenings:

Butter, lard, salt pork fat, meat fat, completely hydrogenated margarines and vegetable shortenings, and products containing coconut oil.

Peanut oil and olive oil may be used occasionally for flavor, but they are low in polyunsaturates and do not take the place of the recommended oils.

6	Acceptable	Avoid or Use Sparingly
DESSERTS, BEVERAGES, SNACKS, CONDIMENTS *The foods on this list are acceptable because they are low in saturated fat and cholesterol. If you have eaten your daily allowance from the first five lists, however, these foods will be in excess of your nutritional needs, and many of them also may exceed your calorie limits for maintaining a desirable weight. If you must limit your calories, limit your portions of the foods on this list as well.* *Moderation should be observed especially in the use of alcoholic drinks, ice milk, sherbet, sweets, and bottled drinks.*	*Low in calories or no calories:* Fresh fruit and fruit canned without sugar, tea, coffee (no cream), cocoa powder, water ices, gelatin, fruit whip, puddings made with non-fat milk, low calorie drinks, vinegar, mustard, ketchup, herbs, and spices. *High in calories:* Frozen or canned fruit with sugar added, jelly, jam, marmalade, honey, pure sugar candy such as gum drops, hard candy, mint patties (not chocolate), imitation ice cream made with safflower oil, cakes, pies, cookies, and puddings made with polyunsaturated fat in place of solid shortening, angel food cake, nuts, especially walnuts, peanut butter, bottled drinks, fruit drinks, ice milk, sherbet, wine, beer, and whiskey.	Coconut and coconut oil, commercial cakes, pies, cookies, and mixes, frozen cream pies, commercially fried foods such as potato chips and other deep-fried snacks, whole milk puddings, chocolate pudding (high in cocoa butter and therefore high in saturated fat) and ice cream.

"The program is simple. You eat all day of the permitted foods. You walk an hour a day."

—NATHAN PRITIKIN, director, Longevity Center

Gayelord Hauser, the nutritionist, was the first to tell me about the Longevity Center. I had read about it, of course; that there was a possibility that its program of low-fat diet plus exercise may be curing heart disease. Actually, by that time there were already two centers: the original one in Santa Barbara, California, and the other in Bal Harbour, a suburb of Miami, Florida. Hauser had recently been to the one in Santa Barbara and he was extremely enthusiastic. He had been, he said, the oldest (eighty-three), the tallest (six feet three), and the only person there who had never suffered a heart attack. "Some people are practically carried in there, but after two weeks they're walking along the beach with wings on their feet! You eat . . . walk . . . eat . . . walk. They make walking a religion—a *science*, I should say."

A few months later I visited the Longevity Center, which by that time had moved from Santa Barbara to more expansive oceanfront quarters in Santa Monica, in what had formerly been the home of the Del Mar Beach Club.

A marquee shades the entrance door leading to a short flight of stairs, with a ramp to one side for the guests who arrive in wheelchairs. On the day of my visit the front desk was manned by two young men attired in black jackets and striped gray trousers. To the far right of the lobby is a huge dining room commanding a spectacular view of the beach, and just ahead, up a flight of thickly carpeted stairs, the office of Nathan Pritikin, the center's founder-director. Everything looked expensive, and indeed it is. The program, which requires a stay of twenty-six days, costs $4,320. Gayelord Hauser had told me it was expensive, but he thought it was worth it. "It's better than dying," he had said. "Think what a bypass operation costs. Think what a room in a hospital costs. With that money you can buy a lot of fresh fruits."

At the center the concept of exercise and diet as a way of protecting a healthy heart and, in a sense, rejuvenating a damaged one is being packaged and presented in a way never seen before. And, not surprisingly, it has attracted believers and disbelievers. In some quarters it's referred to

229

as "The Lourdes of the West" for people suffering from medical problems ranging from angina and hypertension to arthritis and diabetes, and elsewhere as a "medical novelty, way-out, unscientific."

A 1977 article in *New West* magazine commented, "Any therapy that claims to actually reverse the heart and blood vessel diseases that afflict an estimated 29 million Americans and cause over 1 million deaths annually is bound to be the subject of great controversy in the medical profession."

Nathan Pritikin, the man at the center of the controversy, is not a physician and has had no formal medical education. He describes himself as a nutritional scientist, and before establishing the first Longevity Center, in January 1976, he served as adviser for nutritional research to the Ampex Bio-Research Institute, California College of Podiatric Medicine. His wife, Ilene, plays an active role at the center, where, in addition to helping direct diet research, she's in charge of food preparation demonstrations and lectures. The center stresses its program's intent: to provide participants (they refrain from using the words *guests* or *patients*) with all the knowledge they'll need to adopt a whole new life-style.

A slender, soft-spoken man who looks at least a decade younger than his sixty-four years, Nathan Pritikin is fired with a missionary zeal: he's out to eliminate fat from our food, from our blood, and from our arteries— to open up clogged arteries with diet and exercise—believing that it's usually the arteries, not the heart, that are diseased. And you don't have to be past forty to suffer clogged arteries. During the Korean war, autopsies performed on American soldiers revealed that an alarming number of youths in their teens and early twenties were already suffering from the early stages of atherosclerosis.

Pritikin claims that twelve years ago, through "self-experimentation," he cured himself of coronary insufficiency with a largely vegetarian diet similar to the one the people who enroll in the center's twenty-six-day program follow—a diet of eight mini-meals a day (interspersed with daily walks of increasing length) that has been termed Spartan by some and grim and unpalatable by others.

The diet formula is 5 to 10 percent fat, 10 to 15 percent protein, and 80 percent complex carbohydrates (grains, vegetables, fruits)—in contrast to the average American diet of 40 to 45 percent fat, 15 to 20 percent protein, and 40 to 45 percent carbohydrates. Most of the menus at the center are said to be drawn from standard recipes with appropriate substitutions made.

Ilene Pritikin maintains that meat and fish should be regarded as "tasty condiments rather than full-fledged entrees. Using them as flavoring in conjunction with grains and vegetables has been a common practice among different cultures throughout time. Once the majority of fat is eliminated from the diet, appreciation of vegetables, fruit, and grains is greatly enhanced." In response to criticism that the Pritikin Diet is so bland that it's virtually impossible to stay with it, she replies, "The diet certainly pleases the body. With a little creative cooking it can please the palate." (Which may explain why the food director at the center in Bal Harbour is a gourmet cook.)

Now here is the Pritikin Diet capsuled for you, a diet that Nathan Pritikin says provides all daily nutritional requirements. Being realistic, he also says, "It takes ten days to two weeks for tastes to change. The first to fourth days, you can't stand it. The second week, the food becomes palatable. The third week, you enjoy certain dishes. By the fourth week, you're saying 'Delicious!' " In short, you can count on your jaded taste buds to adjust.

THE PRITIKIN DIET

The Seven Commandments: *Thou shalt not smoke, nor eat fats, sugar, salt nor foods containing excess cholesterol; neither shalt thou drink coffee or tea.*

	YES	NO
Fats and oils		Butter, lard, meat fat, all oils and margarine.
Meats, poultry, fish, eggs, nuts	Chicken, turkey, fish (fresh, frozen or canned in water), veal, beef (lean), hamburgers (lean). Only three ounces of red meat (range-fed cattle) a day. Trim all fat off meats, and bake, broil, roast or stew them. Dried beans and peas; egg whites.	Lamb, pork, ham, duck, goose; all marbled and fatty meats: spareribs, mutton, fatty hamburgers, grain-fed beef, bacon, luncheon meats, frankfurters, sausages; organ meats: liver, kidney, sweetbreads; shellfish; fatty fish such as salmon; egg yolks and nuts of all kinds.
Vegetables and fruits	All fruits, but only four pieces a day; all vegetables, raw, baked or boiled; dried fruit: one ounce a day for raisins, two ounces for prunes and others.	Olives and avocados.

	YES	NO
Grains	Sourdough bread, any other sugarless breads without shortening; corn tortillas, pita, Scandinavian crackers, matzos; rice, pasta, noodles (not egg); oatmeal, shredded wheat, any cereal without shortening or sugar.	All foods baked with shortening and sugar, which means cakes, crackers, doughnuts, sweet rolls: commercial mixes containing dried eggs and whole milk.
Dairy foods	Skim milk (nonfat), powdered skim milk; cheese made from 100 percent skim milk, such as farmer's, baker's and hoop cheese.	Whole milk, chocolate milk, canned whole milk, powdered whole milk, cream, yogurt with butterfat and sugar, nondairy cream substitutes; all cheeses, except those made from skim milk.
Desserts, beverages, condiments	Canned fruit (not in syrup), only four pieces a day; decaffeinated beverages, herb teas, no more than one ounce of alcohol a day, vinegar and spices.	Coffee, tea, sugared drinks; puddings, ice cream, sherbets, canned fruit in syrup, gelatin desserts, fried desserts, candy; sugar and salt. Do not add salt to your plate or to your cooking.

The diet is also said to be slimming. Following it and exercising daily, some people have reported a weight loss of up to seven pounds a week.

As I've already written, the program consists of eight mini-meals interspersed with increasingly extensive walking. Nathan Pritikin reasons that you can't stay on a diet if you're hungry. The schedule that Gayelord Hauser summed up as eat . . . walk . . . eat . . . walk goes like this:

7:45 to 9 A.M.	*Cereal (whole grain)*
9:00 to 10:15	*Fruit*
10:15 to 11:45	*Salad*
11:45 to 1:30	*Soup I*
1:30 to 3:00	*Potato (baked)*
3:00 to 4:00	*Soup II*
5:50 to 6:45	*Entree*
8:15	*Dessert*

To date, well over two thousand people have participated in the program. An evaluation of data compiled on the first 893 participants (most were fifty to seventy years old, and two-thirds of them suffered from athero-sclerosis heart disease) was made by the Loma Linda University Survey Research Service, and the following are some of the highlights of that report:

. . . More than 85 percent of hypertensive patients who came to the Longevity Center on medication lowered their blood pressure and left drug free.

. . . For many angina patients, pain was greatly diminished and the use of drugs was reduced or sometimes eliminated.

. . . Overweight people lost an average of thirteen pounds during the twenty-six-day program, and some lost from twenty-five to thirty pounds.

. . . 85 percent of smokers stopped smoking by the end of the program.

. . . People who rarely enjoyed the outdoors and those physically unable to enjoy it were out walking every day; the mean distance was five miles a day.

Dr. J. Bernard of UCLA heads up the center's exercise program, which varies according to individual needs. While I was there, I visited an exercise room replete with treadmills, stationary bicycles, and a carpeted track running around the perimeter. Outside there is a raised walking deck fronting the beach, as well as a bicycle path running the five miles from Santa Monica to Venice. But walking is the only exercise that is mandatory. At least twice a day each day, a pedometer attached to his or her belt, every man and woman in the program is checked out and again when coming in from a walk. Two half-hour continuous (no stop and go) walks is the basic requirement.

The Aviation Insurance Company of Atlanta, Georgia, has sent airline pilots to the center for the twenty-six-day program—all of them heart patients on medicine that prevented them from flying. The insurance company had insured them as pilots to the tune of seventy-five thousand dollars each, and was committed to pay unless the men's hearts improved enough to pass the aviation physical. Of the dozen grounded pilots, all but two passed the physical after spending the required time at the Longevity Center. Which no doubt explains why the Grey Eagles (Retired Airline Pilots Association) has dubbed the center the "Institute of Miracles."

Dr. Wilber Currie, formerly on the staff of the Harvard Medical School, champions the program. "If everyone with heart disease in this nation went on the diet-exercise program tomorrow and stuck to it, most of the million or so Americans who will die of heart disease in the next year could be saved. And 80 percent could be mostly free of their symptoms."

Dr. Peter Wood, deputy director of the Heart Disease Prevention Program at Stanford University in Palo Alto, says, "I know Pritikin is cutting all corners and I think he is doing what has to be done, and I admire him for it. Furthermore, I wouldn't be the least surprised if all his claims turn out to be true."

Still, there are plenty of other distinguished medical men who are withholding opinion until there's a great deal more substantiated evidence. After all, they point out, the Longevity Center has been in existence all of three years.

The day I visited the center, I took a walk down to Palisades Park, high on a hill overlooking the beach. It's about a mile from the center, and some of the people from the center walk through it on at least one of the walks they take during the course of a day. The grass is lush, the palm trees tall and sturdy, and the view breathtaking. Among the people from the center was a married couple, barely forty and in perfect health, at the center now for the second year in a row. It was, they told me, the most enjoyable, most intelligent way they knew to spend a vacation. A man I walked with said he was about to wind up his twenty-six days. Suntanned and smiling, he told me that he'd arrived in a wheelchair recuperating from a heart attack, and now here he was walking seven miles.

The following Sunday I was in San Francisco, watching the CBS program "60 Minutes," which contained a segment devoted to the Longevity Center. Actually, it was a follow-up to a segment of the previous year, which had, said host Dan Rather, drawn much criticism from some doctors. Now the program was rechecking "our three patients," each of whom had originally gone to the center after suffering a heart attack: a fifty-eight-year-old travel agent from the Midwest, a fifty-four-year-old businessman from the Southwest, and a fifty-four-year-old electrical contractor from the eastern seaboard. Each of them had recently been flown by CBS-TV to the Miami Heart Institute for a thorough going-over.

Max Eisenberg, the travel agent, referred to himself as "a happier, more vigorous man" who was still observing the Pritikin Diet "fanatically." His wife said, "It's like living with a new person."

The man from Texas said that some days he walks as much as twenty miles. "I used to have to ride a buggy cart on the golf course. Now I make my friends walk."

The electrical contractor said it was the difference between feeling alive and feeling half dead.

"Would you say they were cured?" a doctor who had supervised their tests in Miami was asked. "A functional cure, yes," he replied. "Now we must see if it holds for forty people, a hundred people . . ."

It's this wait-and-see attitude on the part of some medical men that irks many of the center's "graduates," who take it as a kind of rejection of their return to vigorous living. Some of them went to the center in spite of their doctors' disapproval, sometimes after being scheduled for coronary bypass surgery.

Soon after returning to New York, I met Michael Nee, who'd gone to the center in 1976 suffering from angina. He had read about the Longevity Center in a magazine his wife had brought home from the supermarket. "If I hadn't gone there," he told me, "I'd be in a wheelchair now—or dead." He was curious about what any doctors of my acquaintance thought of Nathan Pritikin's work. "I have complete trust in the man's integrity," he said.

Nee, seventy and retired, walks every day, weather permitting. When the weather is bad, he uses a treadmill he's installed in the basement, walking at the rate of three miles an hour nonstop for a half hour. He said, "The first thing my doctor told me was walk. Walking's a big thing with the doctors today." But he feels the average doctor isn't knowledgeable enough about diet. The Pritikin Diet he considers "fantastic—as helpful as any ever put together." High praise coming from a man who was once addicted to prime ribs of beef with plenty of fat, and lobster tail dipped in shrimp sauce.

Nee treated me to a cup of soup made according to the Pritikin recipe. He told me that it contained mixed vegetables, lima beans, chopped onions, salt-free tomato juice, a half dozen stalks of celery, three or four green peppers, and a cup of brown rice. "It's quite tasty considering there's no salt in it," he said, and he was right. It was very tasty.

At the time of my visit, the center was developing an outpatient program for those who preferred to live outside the center. There is a waiting list for admission. Yet, in *Life Span*, a quarterly newsletter, Nathan Pritikin wrote, "The life and death of any organization depends on the amount of support it musters. . . . To this end we must achieve the highest level of credibility. All doubt must be consumed in a conflagration of fact."

Earlier, Senator George McGovern, head of the Committee on Nutrition and Human Needs, had visited the center for a couple of days at Pritikin's invitation. The senator later said, "I was very impressed with the people I met and talked to. I saw many individual case histories of former center guests that are quite impressive. People suffering from severe heart problems, people plagued with crippling diabetes, who were able to discontinue medication and function as normal human beings. I think these are the things we need to know about. I personally hope that we can get a study funded on the Pritikin method so that we can do some controlled studies and really collect the kind of scientific data that will be necessary to get public and medical profession acceptance of what the Pritikin people are doing."

Personally, I'm in total agreement with medical writer Benno Isaacs, who believes, "If Pritikin is only half right, Mr. Average—even Mr. Seemingly Fit—had better take a hard look at his diet, and cut out at least half of the fat he now eats. He'd also be doing himself a favor by at least taking long walks daily."

WALKING AND WEIGHT CONTROL

"The nation's Number One enemy is fat!"

—RICHARD KEELOR, director of program development, President's Council on Physical Fitness and Sports

CONTROLLING YOUR WEIGHT WILL NOT ONLY HELP KEEP YOU HEALTHY and looking good, but it also goes a long way toward keeping you alive. Research studies show a close relationship between weight and longevity. After age forty-five, it is indicated that there is an 8 percent increase in the death rate for people ten pounds overweight; twenty pounds overweight, 18 percent; thirty pounds overweight, 28 percent; and fifty pounds overweight, 56 percent. "The smaller your waistline, the longer your lifeline," is the way Gayelord Hauser puts it. Dr. Leslie S. Libow, chief of geriatric medicine at Mount Sinai Hospital Services in Elmhurst, New York, is more specific: "If you keep your weight normal, you'll not only look younger, but you may retard other aging symptoms such as diabetes, high blood pressure, or hardening of the arteries."

To slim down and stay that way, you don't have to go on a reducing diet; you don't have to do anything but walk. Walking is the most sensible way to lose weight—and stay slender for the rest of your life. In what has been called a nation of dieters, this is a revolutionary concept but one that is backed by a considerable amount of new research.

The food you eat is potential energy, and your body has this option: to burn up this energy or store it as fat. Inactivity is generally considered to be the most important factor explaining the frequency of overweight in our society today. Both fat adults and fat children are less physically active than people with normal body weight.

Consider this: In a pound of body fat there are approximately 3,500 calories. Eat 3,500 *more* calories than your body needs, and it stores up that pound. Burn up 3,500 *more* calories than your body needs to maintain its same weight, and you lose that pound of body fat.

Now, I won't tell you that a brisk walk burns up a great many calories, because it doesn't. What it does do, however, is stimulate your body's

238

metabolism—the rate at which energy is made available to your body—and that in turn lights a fire under those unwanted calories. Walk an hour more each day (beyond your usual routine) for one month, and you can lose three pounds. Remember, how quickly you lose weight isn't as important as keeping it off once you've lost it.

But will this exercise also stimulate your appetite? The answer is no. New research shows that if you're overweight, walking an extra hour or so a day won't increase your appetite and you will not eat more.

Besides often imposing a punishing regime, a reducing diet may have other disadvantages. Some researchers estimate that approximately 2,400 calories per day are needed to ensure adequate nutrition, and many low-calorie diets, because of their small quantity of food, may lack some nutrients. So treating overweight by diet alone isn't the answer.

In 1975 a study was done by Drs. W. B. Zuti and L. A. Golding, the purpose of which was to compare the effects of diet, exercise, and a combination of the two on the body composition of adult women. Twenty-five women between the ages of twenty-five and forty-two were chosen to take part in the sixteen-week study. Each of the women was anywhere from twenty to forty pounds overweight. For twenty-four days before the study began, they recorded all food and fluid intake in specially prepared booklets and were weighed three times a week. They were then assigned to one of three groups: a diet group, an exercise group, and what was called a "combination" group. One thing was constant, however: all the women undertook a 500-calorie deficit, but they did it in different ways according to the rules of the group to which they'd been assigned. The diet group did it by diet alone, the exercise group by walking alone, and the third group by a combination of diet and walking. When the sixteen weeks were up, the average weight loss for the three groups was: 11.7, 10.6, and 12 pounds, respectively. As you can see, all the women lost similar amounts of weight. Drs. Zuti and Golding concluded, "We recommend that those interested in losing weight combine a lowered caloric intake with a good physical fitness program." Yet, as their study proved, walk and you'll lose weight whether or not you change your eating habits.

Printed tables of ideal weight correlated to height to the contrary, there is no such thing as an ideal weight, for the good reason that no two people are built exactly alike. But each of us has a *best* weight. I stand six feet four and a half inches, and my best weight is about 190 pounds, yet I know men my height and approximate age but of a broader frame who weigh 220 pounds and there isn't an ounce of extra body fat on them. It's generally agreed that your best weight is what you weighed when you were between the ages of twenty and twenty-five, provided, of course, you weren't overweight or woefully underweight at the time.

A year before the Zuti-Golding study, Dr. Grant Gwinup, chairman of the Department of Metabolism and Endocrinology at the University of California in Irvine, was interested in finding out the effect of exercise alone on weight reduction. A total of thirty-four people (twenty-nine women and five men) were selected for his study; all of them had tried dieting with varying degrees of discouraging results. In the introduction to the report of his findings, Dr. Gwinup referred to the frustrations of treating overweight by diet alone and added, "Perhaps the reason that exercise is rarely emphasized is because there have been no systematic studies of the effect of exercise alone on human obesity. The present study, therefore, is undertaken to examine the influence of exercise on the body weight of obese subjects on an ad lib diet."

The thirty-four subjects he selected were from among patients who sought medical consultation for weight control. After a complete medical history, physical examination, and basic laboratory tests, only those found to have no major medical problems other than obesity were chosen for participation in the exercise program. All of them had by that time given up dieting and had shown no marked change in weight for three months prior to taking part in Dr. Gwinup's study.

Each was instructed to continue eating the same kinds of food in the same quantities as before. They were not to keep track of what they ate or to count calories. In short, they were to be as unconcerned as possible with their dietary intake. Each person selected a form of exercise to engage in on a regular daily basis, beginning with a short exercise period that was to be gradually lengthened until it lasted thirty minutes or more. All subjects were instructed to keep written records of each period spent exercising as well as a record of weekly weights, recorded on the same scale at the same time of day. Each time the subjects were examined by Dr. Gwinup, their exercise logs were reviewed in detail and their weight taken and compared with the most recent weight recorded at home.

Unlike the Zuti-Golding study, which ran for sixteen weeks, this study extended over a period of one year, during which time all but eleven of the thirty-four original participants dropped out, failing to meet the study's criterion of maintaining thirty minutes or more of exercise daily. And what exercise had the eleven women chosen who stayed with the program? *Walking*.

"It is interesting that all five of the men failed to continue exercising," noted Dr. Gwinup in his report to the American Medical Association.

They were all employed in full-time work and gave the excuse that they could not continue to devote the time required, although three of the five had achieved a marked weight loss when they dropped out of the study. It may be pertinent that the other two men as well as the four women whose data were not presented elected to take their exercise in the form of jogging. One of the men and two of the women were forced to discontinue this because they developed injuries, but the other man and two women could not tolerate jogging long enough to produce much of an effect on their weight. Three other women who elected to exercise with cycling and two who elected to exercise with swimming also failed to progress in their exercise programs for the length of time necessary to be included in the study. On the basis of this experience, walking would have to be recommended as the most practical form of exercise for obese subjects who wish to lose weight.

The eleven women who stayed with the study ranged in age from twenty-four to thirty-nine. They weighed from a low of 134 pounds (a five-foot-two housewife) to 218 pounds (a five-foot-eight receptionist). All except two would be considered relatively inactive: one housewife managed a twenty-minute walk to school five times a week, and another did light gardening. Some of the women had suffered obesity for only a few years, while for others it had been a lifelong problem. Dr. Gwinup found that there was some correlation between the degree of obesity and its duration. For example, the woman who weighed 218 pounds said that she had been overweight for twenty-three of her twenty-four years. The next heaviest, a thirty-nine-year-old housewife, claimed that she had been overweight for thirty-four years. And as already noted, all the women had previously tried dieting but with discouraging results; whenever a large amount of weight had been lost, it had always been promptly regained. So the eleven women were most amenable to an attempt to control weight with exercise alone.

No weight loss occurred until walking exceeded thirty minutes a day, except for the two women who were already getting some exercise before they entered the program. Generally, the weight loss paralleled the length of time spent walking. When a certain amount of walking was maintained and weight stabilized at a lower level, more weight loss occurred when walking was increased. Six of the women added two hours of walking to their total daily activity, and three women added three hours daily.

It's especially interesting that all the women lost weight in spite of the fact that during the year of the study they all ate even more than they had before the study began. Had their food intake been more stable, they would have lost weight even sooner than they did. Nevertheless, what is important is that the three women who were obese for the longest time were as successful in losing weight as the other eight women. The greatest weight loss was thirty-eight pounds, and the weight loss for the group averaged out to twenty-two pounds.

Dr. Gwinup concluded his report with the observation that the women were particularly pleased with their "general feeling of well-being. . . . They frequently commented that weight loss through exercise, unlike that previously achieved through dieting, was not accompanied by feelings of weakness and increased nervousness, but rather by feelings of increased strength and relaxation."

Jennifer Pader, a twenty-five-year-old working woman I met recently, has lost fifty pounds in a six-month period by following a diet-exercise program. Looking at her now, one finds it extremely difficult to believe that so short a time ago her five-foot-three frame carried as much as 187½ pounds. But she has a snapshot handy to prove it; it shows a round doll-like face atop a Buddha-like body.

Jennifer says she had been overweight since the age of five. Her mother was slender, and so was her older brother. Her father was slightly overweight, but not obese. "I'd see my brother eating a rich dessert and I'd want some, but my mother would refuse. 'No, you can't have it . . . you're too fat.' She was well-meaning. She was concerned, but it took the form of nagging. So I'd get even by eating twice as much behind her back, and each year I'd gain a couple more pounds. I'd eat until I felt that I was really going to throw up. Later, when I was earning a salary, I'd sometimes buy clothes a size too small. It was a little game I played with myself. I would imagine that one day the weight would magically melt away." Meanwhile, she made no effort at all to reduce.

"I was miserable, but fat was all I knew. I hated the very idea of exercise. At lunchtime I didn't even get up and go out to eat. Instead, I sat at my desk and stuffed myself." Then a combination of events started Jennifer Pader thinking about really trying to lose weight for the first time in her life.

Two women of about the same age and degree of experience started working in her office on the same day. One was attractively slender; the other was some eighty pounds overweight. The obese woman proved herself to be the far more capable one, but in a relatively short time the other woman was promoted. Jennifer liked her work and was interested in moving ahead. "I became aware then of how important appearance is. You have to package yourself a certain way if you want to move up and be treated with respect." And at about the same time Jennifer's husband started a new job, and as part of his company's insurance plan he and his wife had to take physical examinations. Jennifer hadn't been weighed in two years. "I stepped on the scale and discovered that I weighed a hundred and eighty-seven and a half pounds! That blew away all my illusions. I figured one-third of my body weight was excess fat. I was almost a hundred and ninety pounds, and that's only ten pounds away from the two hundred mark. I thought, '*This* is it.' "

Jennifer consulted a nutritionist. "She was very professional, very un-threatening. There was no moral lecture. She simply asked that for the next two weeks I write down what I ate, and not to worry about what she'd think about it." Two weeks later Jennifer returned, and the nutritionist gave her a low-calorie diet to try for two weeks, and again she asked her to keep a record of what she ate while following the diet—"so I can com-pare it with what you've been eating." Meantime, the nutritionist wanted her to walk every day, at least a mile a day. "Start with about ten blocks and gradually build until you're walking one mile—briskly." She suggested she make each walk an event. "Walk in the evening with your husband. Walk in the park on Sundays. Walk for pleasure."

Jennifer followed instructions, "and the surprising thing is that I dis-covered I really enjoyed walking." At the end of two weeks of diet and daily walking, she had lost six pounds. Her husband is a six-footer and a fast walker. "After two months I was walking faster than he."

As she began to shed weight, people in her office would ask her if she were exercising. Jennifer would say offhandedly, "Oh, I don't exercise. I just walk." But she soon discovered that other people, like her husband, "really believed in walking as a legitimate form of exercise. And I found the more you walk, the more you like it. Walking is very seductive."

Furthermore, she found that walking was also making her a much more physical person. Now when she and her husband plan a vacation, they choose some place that will provide them with plenty of physical activity. "Our next vacation we're going to a dude ranch where there's horseback riding and swimming. That would have been unheard-of before! Walking has provided me with a gentle introduction to other kinds of exercise. I was afraid of sports before, afraid that I couldn't measure up. But when you walk, you don't have to compete with anyone. Nobody's judging you on the quality of your walk. That gave me confidence. And as I lost weight, the walking was making me more and more aware of my body. It made me feel in control of the new me. Now if for some reason I don't walk every day, I grow irritable. I find I need walking the way I used to need food."

Jennifer intends to lose twelve more pounds. And she will, and then she'll be a svelte 125 pounds. Already she's been promoted in her job. "Since I've lost weight, I've noticed that I'm treated with more respect. I present my ideas more forcefully. At first as I began to lose weight, I was scared. After all, I'd been fat all my life. I didn't know what it would be like to be slender. But thanks to nature's wisdom, the process is gradual and so you learn to adapt."

Dr. Gwinup's study proves that you can lose weight just by walking, and certainly that's good to know. But, personally, I believe that a combination of sensible eating habits and daily walking is the best recipe for losing weight. For obesity is most often the result of careless eating habits as well as inactivity, a disastrous combination. It's never too early or too late to learn sensible eating habits, whether you're overweight or not. Eat for good nutrition. Eat as nearly as possible only the amount of food that your body requires. And walk briskly every day. A program of daily walking, by improving your circulation, will see to it that every cell in your body gets the full benefit of the nutrients in the good foods you take in. Proper diet and proper exercise put you in control of your body. That way you know what it takes to keep it energized and how best to use that energy. Make daily walking, not food, your addiction and you'll be making a quality investment in a longer, healthier, happier life.

CHAPTER

11

WALKING AND DIABETES

"As exercise lowers the blood sugar, it follows that exercise should help control diabetes, which it does."

—Dr. Fred W. Whitehouse, president, American Diabetes Association

THE IDEA OF EXERCISE AS AN IMPORTANT ADJUNCT IN THE TREATMENT of diabetes goes back to the Roman physician and philosopher Celsus (30 B.C.–50 A.D.). Exercise reduces blood sugar just as insulin does. Television star Mary Tyler Moore, who discovered she was a diabetic some dozen years ago, says, "I think I've increased my life span with what I eat and the way I exercise." Says Dr. Whitehouse, "For decades, the litany for good care of diabetes has included diet, insulin, and *exercise*," but he points out in his article in *Diabetes Forecast*, "It's obvious that we still need to learn much more about how exercise lowers the blood sugar."

What we do know, however, is that when a diabetic exercises, he's using his blood fats for energy rather than for stored sugar. And when the fat levels in his blood are decreased, he becomes less diabetic. But it's exercise that is not fatiguing that has the most beneficial effect. Furthermore, writes Dr. Eliott P. Joslin of the Harvard Medical School in his book *Diabetic Manual*,* "It is exercise day in and day out which counts rather than an hour or two once a week . . . and by exercise I mean working about the house or yard, walking up and down stairs, back and forth to school or work. . . ."

Walking has been shown to be particularly beneficial to patients who have developed light to moderate cases of the disease in middle life. Eric Lyss, a retired podiatrist, was fifty-eight when he discovered he had diabetes. Fortunately, his could be controlled without medication by strict diet and regular exercise alone. "Diet and exercise are, of course, essential parts of a diabetic's life," he says, adding, "I firmly believe that regular physical activity is as important as the proper diet to a diabetic, even at my ripe age of seventy-one."

Eight other diabetic patients with histories similar to his walked every

* Published by Lea & Febiger.

day, four times a day, for thirty-minute sessions each, under the supervision of Dr. F. J. Boys of Potchefstroom University in Transvaal, South Africa. A daily record was kept of the foods they consumed, and monthly tests were given for glucose tolerance and insulin response. After a period of eight months, during which this habitual daily walking program was followed, all but one of the eight patients had lost all symptoms of diabetes. Not only that, but two patients who had been taking phenformin, a drug used in the treatment of diabetes, were able to discontinue its use. And, not surprisingly, all eight had shed some unwanted weight.

Like heart disease, diabetes is much more common among sedentary, inactive people than among those who lead vigorous lives. Four out of five diabetics are overweight before manifesting symptoms of the disease. About 70 percent of all newly diagnosed mature diabetics are overweight. So exercise plays a very important part in the diet program. And of course it's also important that patients choose the kind of exercise they will enjoy, so that it will become a permanent part of their life-style. In the September-October 1978 issue of *Diabetes Forecast*, a feature titled "25 Ways to Think Thin" advised: "Take a walk. . . . Contrary to popular belief, exercise does not increase hunger. It has the added advantage of burning calories and decreasing insulin dosage. It also makes you feel good about yourself, something overeating never does." One of the conclusions drawn from a three-day conference on Exercise in Aging: Its Role in Prevention of Physical Decline, held in October 1977 at the National Institutes of Health in Bethesda, Maryland, was that late-onset diabetes (the disease is ten times more common in people over forty than it is in those under twenty) is almost entirely reversible by exercise if the patient is overweight.

Giving exercise pointers to diabetics, Dr. Whitehouse advises, "Never hesitate to exercise; just adjust to it." And as we've seen in previous chapters, walking is the exercise that most people find easiest to adjust to and stay with. "Benefits of exercise," says Dr. Whitehouse, "go far beyond helping to control diabetes. Exercise has a tonic effect on the body. Your muscle tone improves; your sense of well-being and self-esteem grow. Your weight is easier to control; your step is lighter; your breath comes easier; general tension decreases."

And I can think of no exercise that delivers all those benefits in such abundance as the simple act of walking.

"The way to keep joints mobile is to move them. . . . Walking is good exercise provided the joints of your knees or ankles are not swollen, painful, or stiff."

—Arthritis Foundation

WALKING AND ARTHRITIS

There are estimated to be at least 50 million Americans with some form of arthritis, the nation's No. 1 crippling disease.

Arthritis literally means inflammation of a joint. Rheumatism, says **Dr. John Prutting**, is "a general term that's not used anymore," although in Great Britain it is still used to include most forms of arthritis. "The arthritic has got to keep moving," he says. "Activity is very important. It keeps stretching the muscles. It exercises the joints . . . keeps them from 'rusting.' "

Someone who has had arthritis for some time and hasn't been exercising regularly is often amazed by the progress that can be made in a few months of regular, proper exercise.

And you'll recall, I think, our old friend Edward Payson Weston's statement to the press back at the turn of the century: "Walking is almost a sure cure for rheumatism." His boast was that he'd left his rheumatism on the road and it was still there.

The Arthritis Foundation suggests a Rest and Exercise Mix: that is, a balanced mixture of rest and exercise that may vary depending on how severely the disease is attacking. "There will be more resting and less exercising during an acute stage, and vice versa during improved stages. . . . The key word is 'balanced.' Too much rest can result in stiff joints and weak muscles. Too much exercise can damage joints."

Yet every arthritic patient has to realize that exercise must be followed faithfully. Every day the joints must be moved gently, and the exercise must improve the flow of blood. The Arthritis Foundation also cites the need to maintain good posture and breathing habits. Incorrect posture puts a strain on inflamed joints.

Is it any wonder, then, that walking, the gentlest, safest, most natural of all exercises, is considered a good exercise by the Arthritis Foundation?

> "It would be difficult to conceive of a simpler or more effective protection against undue internal blood pressure than walking."
>
> —DR. ALVAH DOTY, *Walking for Health*

WALKING AND HYPERTENSION

It's been known for decades now that in societies where simply to live requires a great deal of physical activity, hypertension (high blood pressure) is almost unknown. The Masai tribesmen in Kenya, for example, show almost none of the increase in blood pressure with age that is seen in modern Western man. As a child the Masai individual tends herds of animals and in the course of a single day walks miles—and the distance grows as he grows.

The New Guineans' blood pressure doesn't go up in middle age as ours does, but usually drops about ten points. Heart disease and strokes are all but unknown in New Guinea, just as they are in primitive societies where automobiles haven't replaced legs and feet as the principal means of locomotion.

Certainly walking alone can't cure diabetes, arthritis, hypertension, or any of the other degenerative diseases, but it can play a pivotal role in both their prevention and the reversal of their symptoms. Dr. Prutting, for example, reports cases of multiple sclerosis where the patients were barely able to walk, "until walking and physiotherapy was encouraged, and then they walked better . . . and better . . . and better, until they were almost able to disguise the instability which they had before." Walking he regards as an important part of the rehabilitation of many people suffering a degenerative disease.

12

WALKING AND LONGEVITY

"I want you to walk and walk and walk—with long, long steps—everywhere, every day of your long, long life."

—GAYELORD HAUSER, *Look Younger, Live Longer*

THE SEVENTY-FIVE-PLUS AGE GROUP IS THE FASTEST-GROWING IN AMERICA. By the year 2000 there will be 30 million elderly Americans—an estimated 15 percent of the population—and nearly half of them are expected to be over seventy-five. God willing, I'll be ready to join the seventy-five-and-over group the following year.

Genetically, my family tree is extremely lopsided so far as longevity is concerned. On one side most of my forebears died in early middle age; on the other side most lived to what used to be called a ripe old age. They were the farmers who worked hard, ate fresh, homegrown foods, and walked everywhere. I should imagine that in many ways the life they led was not much different from the life-style found today in those pockets of longevity around the world where hard physical work and vigorous daily walking are still necessary for survival.

I particularly remember a great-grandfather named Worden Tarbox who lived past one hundred, and referred to a female of, say, fifty-five as a girl and one of seventy as a young woman. Before he sold his farm in an upstate New York hamlet and moved to a home in the county seat, among his neighbors had been the Rockefellers, who hadn't yet struck it rich. Years later, John D. Rockefeller, by then an ancient and fabulously wealthy man, would visit the county seat . . . pass out shiny new dimes to the children . . . pass the time of day with Worden Tarbox . . . and then go and pay a visit to his former schoolteacher, a bright-eyed lady who had passed the century mark.

People in that part of our country lived to a great age. And they were all walkers. One of my boyhood memories is of a man who had been one of Teddy Roosevelt's Rough Riders. Years later he still dressed the part, and strode the streets and country roads bursting with energy and good cheer—a carbon copy of Roosevelt himself, I should imagine. I recall hearing him say one day to someone in the post office, "I feel so good, I attack the day!"

Today, whenever a doctor sees a so-called senior citizen who has retained that kind of zest for living, who is super-alert, he or she is almost always physically alert too. Dr. Ernst Jokl, director of the Physical Education Research Laboratory, says, "We have discovered an age-inhibiting factor so important in forestalling the effects of old age that it can be called the anti-age antibiotic. This anti-age antibiotic is regular daily exercise."

Dr. Paul Dudley White, the world-famous cardiologist, thought walking the perfect exercise, because "it can be done without equipment except good shoes, in almost any terrain and weather and into very old age. The reason that there are centenarians," he concluded, "is that most of them walked and still do walk."

Does walking actually increase your life span? The experts don't claim that it will, but they do say that with brisk daily walking you can remain youthful in condition if not in chronological years.

"We think there probably isn't just a single factor which contributes to long life," says Dr. Alexander Leaf, chief of medicine at New England's prestigious Massachusetts General Hospital, who has traveled the world studying people who are living a long life in sturdy health. "Genetics are important—if your mother lived to be ninety-eight, you may live to old age, too—but they're not as dominant as perhaps environment and dietary habits." The individuals Dr. Leaf has examined who enjoy vigorous health often long past the century mark he found to be great walkers. "If you want to live a long, long time in sturdy health," he concludes, "you can't go wrong in forming the habit of long vigorous walking every day . . . until it becomes a habit as important to you as eating or sleeping."

The trick to becoming a walker is *motivation*. Pure and simple. And what better motivation than this?

"When an older person rests (s)he rusts," says Dr. David Stonecypher, fellow of the American Geriatrics Society.

"Your body will atrophy if you don't use it," warns Dr. John Prutting.

Sluggish circulation. Thin, fragile bones. Weakened muscles. Retard the aging process: *Walk.* Walking is to aging what food is to life. It nurtures and refreshes body, mind, and spirit.

"It is impossible to walk too much," Dr. Joseph Beninson of Detroit said during an address at a health seminar in 1975, adding that, in his opinion, only walking satisfactorily promotes blood circulation. Furthermore, exercised bones don't demineralize but stay dense and strong, and so are far less likely to break. Now, add to that the fact that practically every muscle in your body is exercised when you walk, and you can understand why I say walking retards the aging process.

Remember, too, that walking improves circulation to the brain as well as the heart and skeletal muscles. Mental alertness is thought to improve when larger amounts of pure oxygen are delivered to the brain cells, which are the few types of cells that do not replicate throughout life. At age ten we have billions of them. By thirty we start to lose them, scientists estimate, at the rate of 100,000 or so daily. Clinical psychologists at the Veterans Administration Hospital in Buffalo, New York, administered pure oxygen to senile patients placed in a pressurized chamber. After two pure-oxygen treatments daily for a period of fifteen days the patients' scores on standard memory tests jumped as much as 25 percent!

Should you need more motivation than that, consider some of the great walkers of our time. Harry Truman, for example, was known to the media world as our "Walkingest President." He took a daily pre-breakfast walk every day of his life and often told reporters half his age who were having a difficult time keeping up with him, "I believe walking will make me live longer."

Rose Kennedy, who will celebrate her eighty-ninth birthday on July 22, 1979, walks four to five miles a day. And I can tell you that it's a *brisk* walk, for I've seen her covering ground in Central Park. According to a niece of hers, "If you kept up with her, it would be better than spending a week at a beauty spa."

Greta Garbo, past seventy and supremely fit, walks around New York City as though it were a village and she had decided to cover it, end to end, before nightfall.

Dolores Del Rio, a legendary beauty who started her film career back in the 1920s, appeared on a network television program recently to promote her latest film. She looked barely forty-five. The interviewer asked for her secret, speaking, I imagine, for every woman watching the program. "I don't smoke or drink," she replied. "I have never been on a diet. I like to walk but not jog; it's bad for you. I practice moderation . . . discipline."

Today most nursing homes for the aged encourage their ambulatory residents to walk every day. My eighty-one-year-old aunt (a maverick from the short-lived side of my family, who was still walking to and from her place of business—a distance of a mile and a half—until, at seventy-eight, she fell and fractured her hip on an icy pavement) lives in such a nursing home. Unfortunately, she walks infrequently, and when she does it's with the aid of a pronged cane. She requires a sedative in order to get a good night's sleep. But Mark Brite, who lives in the same nursing home, makes it a point to walk outdoors every day, and I recall his disappointment last winter when heavy snows kept him indoors. But even housebound, he insisted on walking the hallway outside his room for a half hour each day. Mark Brite recently celebrated his hundredth birthday, and he falls into a sound sleep each night as soon as his head hits the pillow.

The three-day conference on Exercise in Aging, held two years ago at the National Institutes of Health in Bethesda, drew physicians from all over the United States and Canada, as well as Spain, Sweden, Denmark, and Czechoslovakia. After their papers were presented, it was generally concluded that walking is the safest, most efficient form of exercise for the aged.

The conference began with introductory remarks by C. Carson Conrad, executive director of the President's Council on Physical Fitness and Sports, who champions the idea of daily walking ("Everyone has a fitness regimen right outside their door"). Dr. Herbert deVries of the Gerontology Center at the University of Southern California reported on a study made with volunteer subjects, men and women, at the Laguna Hills Retirement Community in California. During a progressive walking program, participants who had begun by walking one mile in twenty minutes were, on the ninth day, walking three miles in sixty minutes, and four miles in sixty-four minutes on the eighteenth day. It was clearly seen, Dr. deVries stated, that walking is the exercise that the aged can handle with the least "cardiac effort."

Dr. Harry J. Ralston of the San Francisco Medical Center, University of California, reported that walking is even less demanding on the heart than bicycle exercise, and concluded that "walking is the most desirable type of exercise for older subjects."

"I will never be an old man. To me, old age
is always fifteen years older than I am."

—BERNARD BARUCH

"So much of staying young is mental," says Richard Passwater, former
director of research at the American Gerontological Research Laboratory.
"Long-lived people tend to live for today and tomorrow." And I have yet
to meet a dedicated walker of any age who wasn't doing exactly that. A
newspaper reporter recently commented that "Rose Kennedy isn't getting
older, she's getting busier."

At eighty-four Gayelord Hauser is far too busy with his work to write
the memoirs his publisher has been asking for. Perhaps, he thinks, at ninety
he may take a sabbatical, retreat to his home on the shore of Sicily, and
start writing. Meanwhile, his work schedule has him flying around the
world. The last time I saw him, he'd just returned from Japan, where he
had unveiled his life-size statue erected by the people of Kyoto in the newly
named Hauser Square to honor "The Father of Modern Nutrition." But no
matter where in the world he happens to be, "no day ever passes without
walking. I walk an hour—*fast*. Nonstop. It's a heart massage."

When she was fifty-six, the singer Hildegarde wrote a book titled *Over
50, So What?* Now over seventy, it's still "So what?" "I'm seventy-two, but
I reverse it and make it twenty-seven. After all, I *feel* twenty-seven. I get out
and walk every day, rain or shine, blizzard or flood. I have to do it. I have
to get that action—the legs, the arms, the bloodstream. Sometimes when
I'm in my apartment alone, I'm a little on the depressed side. I don't know
what it is; I have a sweet little home. But the minute I step out on that street
and walk, my morale goes up! I like to visit churches and so I say my
prayers in a different church every day. If I want to go to the fruit market,
I'll walk to the furthest one. I've walked all my life. I love to take off my
shoes and stockings and walk on the beach in Florida. In Orlando I've
walked around the whole lake every day. I've walked the hills of San
Francisco, and that takes a bit of doing. You have to will to take care of
yourself. If you don't, Mother Nature will overpower you and you'll become
old and stagnant."

Certainly "the dear that made Milwaukee famous" isn't. When I last
talked to her, she'd just recorded a new album of songs. And apparently her

256

personal philosophy is always framed as a question. To any new turn in her career, any new challenge, her response is "Why not?"

I visited with Robert Henderson on his last day as librarian at New York's exclusive Racquet & Tennis Club. The previous week—Christmas Day, 1978, to be exact—he had celebrated his ninetieth birthday. Time to retire, he figured. But not to stop walking. Never stop walking, he counseled me. "If you want to live long and die happy, walk every day and breathe deeply." Clear-eyed and erect, he walks two miles a day, inhaling and exhaling to the rhythm of eight steps while maintaining a military cadence of 120 steps to the minute.

He came to New York City from England in 1910. The following year he found employment in the newly opened Public Library on Fifth Avenue and Forty-second Street, and walked home each evening to his apartment on 107th Street. Three years later he was hired to build a sports library at the Racquet & Tennis Club, and today that library is one of the finest of its kind in the nation. His thirty-five-year-old assistant has moved up to fill his chair. "I introduced him to walking eight years ago," Robert Henderson says, "and now his doctor tells him that he's in the best shape he's ever been." And that pleases them both, particularly since Henderson feels you have got to have a philosophy, and his has always been "to leave people feeling better than they felt when I met them."

Janet Flanner, who wrote—under the name Genêt—the Letter from Paris for *The New Yorker* for half a century, died in 1978 at the age of eighty-six. She was an inveterate walker, and so it was appropriate that she should spend her last day on earth enjoying with close friends what her beloved magazine described as "an idyllic walk in Central Park during which she took in the autumn foliage with the eyes of a child and expressed astonishment and gratitude that it could be as beautiful as it was. . . . Her eyes never became jaded, her ardor for what was new and alive never diminished . . . and she was a stranger to fatigue, boredom, cynicism."

As the philosopher Jean Jacques Rousseau put it, "Life is not breath but action, the use of our senses, mind, faculties, every part of ourselves which makes us conscious of our being."

Walking will do that for you. It will also keep you young in body and spirit. And if it helps to lengthen my life too, I'll regard that as a bonus. Meantime, I rather suspect that the best way to add years to your life is to enjoy life. And I know of no exercise, no sport, that adds more enjoyment to life than walking.

WALKING AND THE NEWBORN CHILD

"He begins to walk early—sometimes at nine or ten months."

—"The Way to Raise a Bright Child," *Coronet,* 1957

I THINK BABIES ARE MOSTLY UNDERRATED. THE GENERAL FEELING STILL seems to be that the most important things you can do for them are to keep them fed and dry, meanwhile overlooking the very important fact that a healthy child is kin to a healthy young animal. In their desire to protect their young, many parents inhibit them physically and, in turn, psychologically as well.

Dr. Jaroslav Koch, of the Institute of Care of Mother and Child in Prague, Czechoslovakia, who has been described as a "devoted baby advocate," believes that there is a definite link between the physical fitness of an infant and his psychological and intellectual progress, and that an unsuspected and exciting potential for development lies "hidden and untapped within infants." But all too often many opportunities for development are lost because parents don't give them a chance. "Parents," he wrote in his book *Total Baby Development*,* "may even remove such opportunities from their babies without realizing it." But, given a chance, babies "easily—even playfully—acquire far more than what parents, pediatricians, and standard guide books consider 'normal' capabilities."

Writer-teacher Joseph Chilton Pearce maintains that many of our traditional approaches to child rearing have an alarmingly negative effect on our children, as contrasted with the child-rearing practices found in other, more primitive cultures. The following is an excerpt from an interview with him that appeared in *New Age* magazine (October 1976):

> In Europe and America, our infants do not smile for two months; in fact, they have no sensory motor control for about two and a half months —they are total vegetables. Just about all they do have is the sucking instinct, and some prehensile grip, which means that their fists stay clenched all the time. If they are not asleep (and they're asleep more than they're awake for the first four months), they're crying or feeding.

* Published by Wyden Books, 1976.

That's about all, and we take this limited behavior as axiomatic.

On the other hand, if we look into Marcelle Geber's studies of Ugandan infants, we find that they are smiling within minutes after being born, and within forty-eight hours they're sitting up beautifully with the slightest bit of support. Their head balance and eye focus are perfect, and they're participating enormously in their world: they sleep about one-fourth as much as our children do. The six-week-old Ugandan infant sits up on its own without any support, and crawls all around, and is a highly mobile, extremely intelligent functioning unit. The six-month-old Ugandan infant walks and has achieved what is called "object constancy," which is the ability to retain the memory of an object when it is removed from sight. In our culture, this doesn't occur until somewhere around fifteen months of age.

Now this is simply an indication of what human intelligence can do at an extremely early age. Ugandan infants have a well-developed verbal system at one year; they're speaking beautifully, with a large vocabulary. Now what makes this fantastic difference? The Ugandan mother massages the infant immediately after birth. She takes her cue from the infant, and every time the infant starts to move, she makes sure that move is successful. This has a very definite effect on the mind-brain system: immediately that kind of movement can be patterned in and brought into full sensory play, and so the infant has an extraordinary intellectual development.

What happens to that intelligence later on is another matter. At around age four the Ugandan child is literally abandoned by its mother and forced to bond to the cultural taboos. Thus all intellectual development is stopped cold in its tracks for a number of years.

Now, while all intelligent children are not early walkers, it's interesting how many of them are. Writing in *Coronet* magazine over twenty years ago, the principal of a highly respected eastern high school offered readers a composite picture of the bright child drawn from various sources, including the famous Stanford University studies of gifted children. The first of eight characteristics was: "He's an early starter. He begins to walk early—sometimes at nine or ten months."

Psychologist Philip R. Zelazo, co-director of the Center for Behavioral Pediatrics and Infant Development at the New England Medical Center in Boston, reports that all children are born with a stepping reflex that permits them to begin walking earlier than our society allows. If this desire to move the feet in a stepping motion—which begins in the second week of life—was given an opportunity for expression, Dr. Zelazo believes that it could be maintained until independent walking began, which would undoubtedly be some weeks before babies "normally" walk unaided, since the infant whose stepping reflex had been exercised would spend less time in the crawling and stand-up stages preliminary to independent walking. And early walking means early learning as the child, unaided, starts to explore his world.

"An infant needs to establish contact with his environment as soon as possible and gradually become acquainted with it," says Dr. Koch. "If he is to learn to use his body—mainly his motor and sensory organs—and establish contact with the outer world, then he needs gradually and gently to be led out of this state of inhibition and activated. The evocation of reflexes in the first three months is one important way to activate your baby."

The walls of Dr. Zelazo's outer office are covered with children's crayoned art. Picture books are everywhere, along with an array of plastic toys. It's a child's environment, and that is certainly appropriate for the workroom of a behavioral psychologist. Tall and neatly bearded, the doctor looks barely old enough to be the father of a thirteen-year-old son. He recalls that when the child was born, despite his professional expertise, he was much the typical new father. "I was concerned about how fragile he was, and I remember thinking, 'How can I relate to this baby?' "

Then when the baby was only a few weeks old, he saw his wife holding him under the arms as he stood on the flat surface of a tabletop, "and I noticed this phenomenal response. The baby began the motion of taking steps—literally marching along. It was a remarkable thing to see. Of course, it's routine knowledge among neurologists, as it was for my wife, who's a pediatric nurse, but I didn't know about it at the time. 'Isn't that incredible!' I thought. 'Such a clear, obviously reflexive response. What would happen if you gave the infant an opportunity to use that reflex?' The belief at that time was that after a few months—usually from eight to, say, sixteen weeks —the reflexive response disappears. So the question was: If you allowed the baby an opportunity to use that response, would it be maintained?"

Dr. Zelazo and his wife decided to give their infant son an opportunity to exercise his stepping reflex every day. The behavior was maintained, and the baby walked at the age of seven and three-quarters months. "He walked early and developed beautifully," says Dr. Zelazo, like any proud parent.

A few years later the Zelazos decided to undertake a controlled study involving twenty-four infants, all males. Eighteen were one week old, and six were eight weeks old at the start of the seven-week study. The babies were divided into four groups of six, with the first group receiving twelve minutes of daily active exercise: eight spent supporting the infant under the arms while allowing his bare soles to make contact with the flat surface along which he would be moved, and four minutes of dragging the upper part of his foot against the edge of the flat surface so that he would lift and "place" his foot on the surface itself. The babies in the second group received daily passive exercise—their legs and arms were gently exercised in a pumping fashion while they sat in an infant seat or lay in a crib. Infants in the third group received no exercise at all, but their stepping reflex was tested once every week during the seven weeks of the study. Infants in the fourth group received no exercise either, and their stepping reflex was tested only once: at eight weeks of age, which is when the reflex usually starts to disappear ("winding down gradually," as Dr. Zelazo puts it).

The first group were taking seven or eight steps per minute at the start; at the end they were averaging about thirty steps per minute, with two of them doing fifty steps or so. The second group began with an average of 7.8 steps per minute and declined to an average of three steps per minute. Infants in the third group, who were not exercised, also declined to an average of three steps per minute, but their decline was not so striking, since they began with only 5.4 steps per minute. The fourth group of babies averaged less than one step per minute—near zero—at the time the study ended, leaving the Zelazos to conclude that not only does the reflex response disappear somewhere between eight and sixteen weeks of age, but —on the basis of the fact that at the finish of the seven-week period the reflex of the children in the second group (passive exercise) matched that of the children in the third group (no exercise)—so-called passive exercise is of no value in maintaining the stepping reflex.

Will children who receive early training like that given to the infants in the first group walk alone sooner than other children? Well, the babies in the first group who were averaging thirty steps per minute at the conclusion of the study did walk sooner than the babies in the other three groups, taking their first independent steps at about ten months, a full two months before the babies in the fourth group. It was also noted that the children smiled during the last weeks of their stepping exercises, leading Dr. Zelazo to conclude that "it was a fun experience."

More recently he and his wife conducted another study at home, this time with their identical twin daughters, Suzanne and Seanna. Nancy Zelazo started training one child at the age of two weeks, while training for the other didn't begin until the age of seven weeks, close to the time that the stepping reflex, if not exercised, starts to fade away. Still, when the second baby started her training, she began at a reasonably high level of stepping, much to her parents' surprise. And by the age of eight months each little girl, when held by the hand, was managing over one hundred steps per minute. Both children started independent walking the same week, at the age of eight and three-quarters months—well ahead of the norm. All of which led the Zelazos to conclude this time that, since the two babies' daily training had been no more than two one-minute sessions, it doesn't take much training to retain the stepping reflex pattern.

Now, not only does early walking bring the baby into early contact with his environment, but if walking develops into a habit—a way of life—it almost inevitably leads to successful participation in other longer-endurance-type sports, such as swimming, skiing, and cycling. For successful walking, with its rhythmic motion and good breath control, is the absolute groundwork of every aerobic sport.

During my first visit to Denmark, in 1958, I was intrigued with the way Danish women exercised at home with their preschool children, after which they would usually go for a long, brisk walk—the mother always seeming as agile as a child herself. I made some notes of the exercises, which were almost always in the form of games: stretching, squatting, rolling, and kicking, in imitation of, say, a rabbit hopping, a glider tipping its wings, a giant stretching. Eventually I incorporated some of them in the book I wrote on what I consider to be the Scandinavian genius for physical fitness, adding, of course, that family exercise isn't confined to the Danes; in Sweden, for example, they have a word for it: *Mamabarngymnastik* (mother-child gymnastics). And I was delighted to discover, twenty years later, that Berit Brattnäs, who wrote *Fit for Fun*, then married an American and settled in this country, was doing similar exercises at home every day with her five-year-old son, Frederick.

I had the pleasure of watching them exercise together one day recently. They kicked off their shoes, Berit put a Swedish exercise record on Frederick's phonograph, and the two of them went at it, exercising, nonstop, for the next twenty minutes. The musical accompaniment captured the spirit of each exercise, and when an exercise required some extra effort, "The Volga Boatman" was played as a kind of whimsical signal for the child that a tough one was coming up. As soon as the record ended, Frederick dashed for his hat and coat and they were off for their morning constitutional, with him so full of energy now that every block or so he would sprint ahead to the corner. Berit says, "If Frederick doesn't get his exercise every day, he doesn't feel balanced." In *Fit for Fun* she wrote,

"The best time to start exercising, is to start *early*." Now a consultant to the President's Council for Physical Fitness and Sports, Berit is training her own child according to that very sensible rule.

And apparently it's never too early to start, although the goal is not to force the child to develop faster but rather to give him every opportunity to realize his potential.

Dr. Koch has worked with babies and small children for the last twenty-five years at the Institute of Care of Mother and Child in Prague, Czechoslovakia. He has made little ladders available to infants who, at the age of five months, have reached out and held on to them. At eight or nine months they've climbed up those ladders unaided. And within one to two months they were walking without assistance.

Dr. Koch has experimented with fifty infants who were from two to three weeks old. Each day twenty of the children were brought to the institute, where he and his staff followed a program which was followed at home by the parents of the other thirty infants: for one to two hours each day the babies were stimulated with special games and exercises. When the development of these fifty babies was compared to that of a control group of one hundred other babies raised under so-called normal family conditions, Dr. Koch found the results "fascinating."

> Almost invariably, the exercised boys and girls had good appetites and had no difficulties during the feeding. They learned to be active while awake and to sleep quietly at sleeping time. They doubled their birth weight in the fifth month; the control group in the sixth—and the accelerated weight gain was in muscle, *not* fat. . . .
>
> But their excellent psychological growth is best shown by their rapid development of language ability. At one year, the exercised children had an active vocabulary of twenty words and used them in their daily contacts; the control group used only five.

"And why not?" concludes Dr. Koch. "The entire process of physical stimulation makes good anatomical sense; as he becomes motivated to move physically, the exercised infant's brain is supplied with more than the normal unit of blood; the increased blood supply, in turn, makes the child more receptive to stimulation."

The essence of good baby rearing, says Dr. Koch, is the sincere love of the parents for their baby. I can't think of a nicer or wiser guide to good parenting than that. Nor can I think of a more loving gift to give a child than the opportunity to stand on his own two feet and establish contact with his world as soon as possible.

WALKING AND TODAY'S WOMAN

"Walking for women is the best thing in the world for them."

—EDWARD PAYSON WESTON, 1910

OUR OLD FRIEND WESTON WAS RIGHT, OF COURSE, BUT BACK IN THOSE days most women didn't walk so much as saunter. It would have been unseemly for a lady to really stride along—head up, arms swinging at her sides. And furthermore, the voluminous petticoats and whalebone corsets of the period weren't designed for a free and easy gait.

But as anthropologist Margaret Mead has suggested, the nature of femaleness is more a question of social custom than genes, and so today's woman wears loose, soft clothing, comfortable shoes, and *really* walks. She also knows why it's important that she should.

Walking relieves tension.

And with more and more women joining the nation's work force, she's getting to know firsthand what a hard day at the office means.

Walking improves appearance.

Stepped-up circulation freshens the complexion, and a long, steady stride trims hips and thighs, makes legs more shapely. And walking is a whole lot more interesting and a lot less expensive than joining a gym.

Walking aids digestion, promotes a good night's sleep.

And when you feel better, you look better. You gain poise and self-confidence.

Walking clears the mind, improves the disposition.

Which, in turn, helps make you a more efficient, more attractive individual.

Walking is good for the heart.

It helps it pump blood. And in some quarters it's thought that taking the Pill makes a woman more susceptible to coronary problems. Also, it's a known fact that after the childbearing years a woman's natural protection against heart attack is gone. So daily walking is preventive medicine.

Walking can be enjoyed every day of the month.

It will certainly diminish a woman's discomfort or inconvenience from menstrual cramps.

Walking is the best exercise for the pregnant woman.

Childbirth calls for good muscle tone. Place both hands on your abdomen as you walk and feel those muscles exercising. That's why most obstetricians urge the expectant mother to walk a comfortable distance every day during pregnancy.

Walking is the best exercise after childbirth.

The woman who walks every day regains her figure sooner than the woman who doesn't walk, because brisk walking exercises practically every muscle in the body—especially the muscles in the abdomen, thighs, and hips, where most of the trimming and firming is needed.

Walking is a sociable exercise.

And one of the best ways of staying close to a man is to join him in exercise.

Walking is an aerobic exercise.

That's the best exercise there is—natural, rhythmic, effortless motion. Furthermore, a woman's metabolism is even better adapted to this kind of longer-endurance-type exercise than a man's.

Walking makes you better at sports.

By building good breath control, body coordination, and endurance, walking improves your skill at aerobic sports such as swimming, skiing, skating, and cycling—sports you can enjoy alone or with someone you like.

Walking is great exercise for the entire family.

No one, no matter how non-athletic, has to be left out. And how many other exercises can promise you that?

Walking is an exercise for a whole life span.

Because it does so much for both body and mind—without strain of any kind—walking is the best way known to achieve what we all want: *ageless* aging.

PART IV

WALKING TOURS OF TWELVE GREAT AMERICAN CITIES

> "To enjoy city walking to the utmost you have to throw yourself into a mood of loving humanity."
>
> —DONALD CULROSS PEATTIE, *New York Times Magazine*, April 5, 1942

As I WROTE AT THE START OF THIS BOOK, THE ONLY WAY TO REALLY know a city is to walk its streets. A city walk should not only stretch your legs but your mind, too, as you explore new vistas or get a new perspective on a familiar one.

Nowadays museums, historical societies, even individuals are conducting walking tours of their cities. Here in New York, for example, I know of an actress who takes small groups on walks through the theater district, a highlight of which is a visit backstage to chat with a performer. And the Kinney Shoe Corporation, in cooperation with the President's Council on Physical Fitness and Sports, has created a series of Walking Tours of America, sixty in all, and they will be out in book form sometime during 1979.

Here, now, are my walking tours of twelve cities. Each one takes you through a downtown area where the city's future is being built and some of its past lovingly preserved. But since a city is a mosaic of its neighborhoods, each tour is meant to whet your appetite to know more—much more—about the city.

ATLANTA

The first time I stood on Peachtree Street a grand parade was in progress, part of Atlanta's annual Dogwood Festival, part of the tradition still found in this city that manages the miracle of projecting the charm of the Old South while growing upward and outward at a dizzying rate of speed. In 1960, Atlanta had a population of 1 million. By 1983, Atlanta is expected to have a population of almost 2 million. It already has the second busiest airport in the nation. A walk up this supercity's famous Peachtree Street is the best way I know for anyone to understand what the New South is all about.

Start your tour of Atlanta at the Central Avenue Viaduct, where, for twenty-five cents admission, you'll gain entry to Underground Atlanta, a four-block area that's a collection of mostly boutiques and restaurants, whose decor is often designed to fill a visitor in on the dramatic history of the city. The Metropolitan Atlanta Rapid Transit Authority (MARTA) is at work building Atlanta's first subway system, and, as a result, a small portion of the Underground has been temporarily vacated, and the Zero Milepost, which marked the original site of the railroad town that, in 1847, was officially chartered as Atlanta, is for the moment safely stored away somewhere else.

Return to street level, turn right on Central Avenue, and head for Georgia State University, born thirty years ago in the small dandelion-colored brick building that's still standing. Facing it, turn left and head up Exchange Place, passing Central City Park, a setting for noontime concerts. Cross the street, and you're at historic Five Points, today the hub of Atlanta's financial district and one of the busiest traffic intersections I've seen anywhere in the world. Near here on Alabama Street at White-hall was an old gaslit lamp, a cherished landmark that, like the Zero Milepost, is in storage until MARTA finishes its work. From here walk six blocks west on Marietta Street to the corner of Techwood Drive and the Omni International complex.

Here you'll understand what's meant by "futuristic." A six-acre, fifteen-story enclosed megastructure, Omni International includes a five-hundred-room hotel, a pair of office buildings, six theaters, an Olympic-size ice-skating rink, and dozens of shops and restaurants, along with a 17,000-seat sports arena and the Georgia World Congress Center, a convention center. You could spend an entire weekend sampling the delights of Omni International, but since this is a walking tour, proceed back to Five Points and turn onto Peachtree Street. On your left you'll see the Equitable Tower and on your right the seventeen-story Candler Building, a diminutive structure by today's standards, but when it was built, in 1904, it was one of Atlanta's first skyscrapers. Its exterior has marble panels with carvings of such ancient notables as William Shakespeare and Michelangelo, and in the lobby there are marble portraits of personages that were particularly dear to the heart of the builder, Asa Candler, founder of the Coca-Cola Company.

Continue walking north on Peachtree and be prepared to play the gawking tourist when on the corner of Cain Street you gaze for the first time on the Peachtree Center Plaza Hotel, the tallest building in the Southeast and the tallest hotel in the world. A glass cylinder with a lobby containing a half-acre lake, it's crowned with a revolving triple-tiered lounge-restaurant to which patrons are expressed in eighty seconds flat by elevators speeding through glass tubes. From up there one can look out to the Blue Ridge Mountains.

Moving on up Peachtree, you'll pass the Peachtree Center complex, another futuristic network of office buildings, shops, restaurants, and a dinner theater. Continue walking until you come to the Hyatt Regency Atlanta Hotel. Built in 1967, it was the city's first major luxury hotel. It caused an around-the-world stir when it first opened its doors and visitors stepped into the twenty-three floor atrium lobby that transformed all of its hallways into balconies open to the "eye" of the rocket-shaped elevators, designed like pieces of lighted, moving architecture to whisk patrons up to the revolving restaurant sitting on top of the hotel and looking like a grounded UFO saucer.

Walk north on Peachtree, and when you come to a tiny pie-shaped park, turn right and continue walking until you come to the intersection of Peachtree and Ponce de Leon. There you'll see the "Fabulous Fox," the legendary Fox Theatre, which began life a half century ago here at 660 Peachtree Street, N.E. It was a movie palace in the grand tradition, with a wrought-iron-trimmed courtyard and a star-studdded, blue-sky ceiling across which white clouds floated. During its heyday the Fox's silver screen blacked out each spring when a touring company of the Metropolitan Opera took over the theater. About ten years ago the building was about to be razed, but at the ninth hour it was given a reprieve, and today the "Fabulous Fox," its razzle-dazzle intact, is a highly respected auditorium.

Pay special attention to the grand old hotel located across the street from the Fox. It's the Georgian Terrace, built in 1911, and when the Metropolitan Opera played the Fox each spring, its stars resided here. Catercorner are the Ponce de Leon Apartments, which, in 1913, presented Atlanta with its first penthouse.

Continuing up Peachtree, you'll soon step into a section known as "The Strip," a name given to this once fashionable area by Atlanta's hippies, who claimed it as theirs. Only fairly recently has the city's drive to revitalize the downtown area poked its way here, but it's fairly safe to predict that come 1983, if the city's population is swelling toward the 2 million mark as anticipated, many Atlantans will be living in the nearby residential sections, where restoration has already begun.

The Atlanta Memorial Arts Center stands on the northwest corner of Peachtree and Fifteenth streets. A truly magnificent structure, it's a fitting home for the Atlanta Symphony Orchestra, the Alliance Resident Theatre, and the High Museum of Art, as well as a memorial to the memory of the 128 Atlanta art patrons who perished in a plane crash at Orly Airport in Paris some fifteen years ago.

Nearby Ansley Park is enjoying a renaissance. Some of Atlanta's young professional couples have moved into the old homes there and restored them with loving care and a great deal of taste. During my visit I had the great good fortune to attend a dinner party in one such home—a splendid place with a winding staircase and a Tiffany glass window at the top of each landing. While walking through Ansley Park, be sure to see the Devereaux McClatchey mansion, which later became the Governor's Mansion and remained so until 1967, when the governor took up residence in a new home on West Paces Ferry Road, on land that before the Civil War was part of the plantation of Colonel Hardee Pace.

End your walking tour with a visit to the seventeen-room Rhodes Mansion on the northwest corner where Peachtree Circle rejoins Peachtree Street. Amos Giles Rhodes was a wealthy furniture dealer with a passion for the Bavarian castles he saw on a tour of Germany. The Rhodes Mansion, a composite of the castles he'd seen along the Rhine, and now the property of the Georgia Department of Archives and History, is well worth a visit.

You could walk farther, because Peachtree Street doesn't stop here. But from Underground Atlanta to the Rhodes Mansion is about five miles, which makes this the longest walk of the twelve cities covered in this book. Furthermore, I can't imagine a finer place to end your tour of this supercity that so neatly balances futurity with nostalgia than outside a turn-of-the-century mansion that's still a viable part of the Atlanta of today.

BOSTON

When you walk through what in my college days was affectionately called "Bean Town," you are quite literally walking through whole chapters of our nation's history. And Bostonians have made it easy for you to do that; the Freedom Trail, with its painted footprints, guides you at least part of the way. A city that is both cosmopolitan and cozy, venerable and yet amazingly youthful in spirit, Boston attracts young people from all over America who come here to put down roots.

Begin your walking tour near the top of Beacon Hill on the side of Boston Common. Up ahead you can see the gold-domed New State House which, despite the name, dates back to 1795. Near the corner of Park Street you'll see a memorial dedicated to a Civil War colonel. The day I passed it, a soggy placard was propped up against it, reading, "Do you know where your taxes are tonight?" Turn right at the corner and walk down Park to Tremont. Turn right again and make your way to the Old Granary Burying Ground. Stroll its narrow paths and inspect the gravestones that were carved by hand. America's best-known Revolutionary War heroes are buried here: Paul Revere and John Hancock, to name just two. The ancient headstones are barely readable in most instances, but I did manage to copy the following:

Here lies buried the body of Mr. William Hall, leatherdresser, August 16, 1775. Age 75. First known President of the Charitable Irish Society founded in Boston, 1737.

Leaving the Old Granary Burying Ground, head for Washington Street, which lies straight ahead, running parallel to Tremont. I suggest you approach it down Bosworth Street, which has an old stone staircase. Once you're on Washington, with its glass and wrought-iron galleria, walk to the Old South Meeting House on the corner of Milk Street. This rose-colored brick building was once the gathering place of major colonial meetings, including the Boston Tea Party. From here bear to your right until you come to still another rose-colored brick building—the Old State House, which in 1963 was designated a registered National Historic Landmark. Built in 1713, it was the headquarters of the colonial government until the day the Declaration of Independence was read from its balcony. Exhibits inside include revolutionary memorabilia.

At the corner, to the right of the Old State House, on a little square island, there's a cobbled ring marking the site of the Boston Massacre of 1770, where, on March 5, British soldiers and some townspeople ran afoul of each other and five citizens lay dead afterward.

It's at this point that you pick up the Freedom Trail, following its terra-cotta footprints across the street and down the broad steps toward Faneuil Hall, which is guarded by a statue of Samuel Adams, who's buried in the Old Granary Burying Ground. The base of the statue identifies him as the patriot who organized the Revolution.

The hall, a gift to the city from Peter Faneuil, a wealthy merchant, was Boston's first market and meeting hall as well as the center of its seaport trade. Today it serves principally as the entry to Quincy Market, a warren of restaurants and stalls where you can enjoy every kind of food imaginable, from a Jewish potato knish and Texas barbecue to Syrian and Chinese fare. Flanking Quincy are the North Market and the South Market, each with its gallery of shops, benches, and potted flowers.

Trace your steps back to Faneuil Hall and pick up the Freedom Trail, which will guide you to Paul Revere's house, standing on its original site in what is now the city's Little Italy. This is a zigzag walk across the Fitzgerald Expressway and then down narrow streets past old buildings with carpeted stoops. Built in 1670, Revere's house is the oldest house in Boston. A silversmith, he lived here on North Street for thirty years, and it was from this house that he left on his historic ride toward Concord. The house is open to the public.

Follow the trail to Paul Revere Mall and the Old North Church, with a statue of Revere standing out in front. It was here on the night of April 18, 1775, that the "two if by sea" lanterns were hung when the British set out for Lexington and Concord.

The Freedom Trail guides you back across the busy Fitzgerald Expressway. But before you leave Little Italy, I suggest you take a slight detour to Hanover Street to see the garden outside St. Leonard's Church, with its extraordinarily lush floral embankments lining the path leading up to the church.

Back at Faneuil Hall, cross the street and walk in the direction of City Hall and the eight-acre Government Plaza. Bear left and pick up Tremont Street again. When you come to the renowned Parker House, turn right and start up the hill toward the New State House, and once again you'll be in the picturesque Beacon Hill neighborhood of Federal and Greek Revival homes, graceful gardens, and squares. Explore the streets there, and then cross Beacon Street and walk down into the Common. Follow the paths to your right and pass on into the Public Gardens, a haven of trees, flowering shrubs, and, in season, swan boats on the lagoon. Find a bench and sit down. Your tour has taken you about five miles. You deserve a rest in these idyllic surroundings.

CHICAGO

Chicago became known as the "Windy City" courtesy of a New York reporter, who, back in the 1890s, called it that not because of the gusts of wind blowing off Lake Michigan but because of what he considered the Chicagoans' braggadocio. Years later Carl Sandburg christened it the "City of Big Shoulders." And at about that same time a song titled "Chicago" referred to it as "that toddlin' town." But I think, with Chicago now boasting three of the world's five tallest buildings, it might best be described as High, Wide, and Handsome. Certainly it has become one of the most architecturally exciting cities in the United States. The Great Fire of 1871 all but reduced Chicago to ashes, and then, from 1883 to 1893, there was a frenzy of building, and a new type of construction soon became known simply as "Chicago Construction": an iron skeleton with an overlay of such architectural innovations as the horizontally elongated window that, in turn, became known simply as the "Chicago Window." So it seemed only fitting and proper that the skyscraper should be born in the city's downtown area known as the Loop.

Like many of our larger cities, Chicago can be cut up into relatively small slices and enjoyed piece by piece, step by step. So let's divide your walking tour into two parts: the city's "Magnificent Mile," a dazzling network of shops, boutiques, and galleries cheek by jowl with some of Chicago's oldest and newest architectural triumphs; and for another day, perhaps (unless you're feeling especially energetic), a walk through the Loop, where the Sears Tower, "Big Buck," the world's tallest building, stretches 110 stories into space.

The Magnificent Mile.   Start your tour outside the gleaming white Wrigley Building at 400 North Michigan Avenue. At night, when the building's baroque terra-cotta embellishments are flooded with powerful lights, it's a stunning sight to behold. Built in 1921, it has an annex constructed three years later, and between the two is a small plaza. In a city that contains three of the world's five tallest buildings, the Wrigley Building (yes, it takes its name from the chewing-gum family) is an ornate reminder of Chicago's earlier days.

Cross the street to Pioneer Court, seven acres of fountains and marble benches running alongside the Tribune Tower at 435 North Michigan Avenue. Close to the entrance of the court, embedded in this Greek Revival skyscraper, are pieces of other famous buildings from around the world: Westminster Abbey, the Taj Mahal, and so on. Farther on, you'll come across front pages from past issues of the *Chicago Tribune*, telling of everything from Abe Lincoln's assassination to man's walk on the moon.

Continuing north, take a close look at the Radisson Hotel. Built in the 1920s to house a Masonic Temple, it's now undergoing a $20 million renovation. The mahogany walls of its dining room wear old mosaics the way dowagers used to wear tiaras. Pay a visit to the hotel pool, which resembles a Roman bath; it's awash with mosaics too.

Cross the street and you enter still another phase of the city's architectural life: the Chicago Marriott Hotel, which opened in May 1978. Built on the site of the Time-Life Building, this white marble edifice contains 1,200 rooms and a lobby full of overstuffed chairs and sofas that some

Chicagoans consider "charming" and others dismiss as "tacky."

Next come the elegant shops that have earned this mile of real estate the adjective "magnificent": Gucci, Bonwit Teller, Saks Fifth Avenue, and so on.

At 800 North Michigan Avenue stands the Water Tower, a Chicago landmark for over one hundred years, having survived the Great Fire of 1871. Closed for an unconscionably long period of time, it was renovated and reopened in December 1978 as the Water Tower Visitors Information Center. Its façade has been maintained, and the park beside it has been spruced up with new trees, benches, and electrified gas lamps. Around the tower itself is a three-foot-high brass fence salvaged from another ancient building that, unlike the Water Tower, didn't survive the march of progress.

Diagonally across the street at No. 835 is Water Tower Place, a seventy-four-story castellated high-rise with a seven-level shopping atrium, adding a whole new dimension to the Magnificent Mile.

To the north is the famous I. Magnin emporium, and across the street at No. 875 is the hundred-story John Hancock Center, a commercial building with apartments on its top fifty floors. When it opened its doors in 1969, "Big John" was Chicago's tallest building; now it's the third tallest. Step over to the curb, crane your neck, and note the way its builders chose to cope with the city's mighty winds: huge cross-bracing steel members form giant X's on each side of the aluminum and tinted-glass exterior, with the X's gradually growing smaller as the thousand-foot-high giant tapers toward its top.

As you proceed north toward the Playboy Building at 919 North Michigan, note the Gothic-style church across the street from "Big John." The Fourth Presbyterian Church, it was built in 1912 of carved Bedford stone. With a grass plot on three sides and an arcade on the fourth, it provides dramatic contrast to the sky-high giants casting their shadows along the Magnificent Mile.

The thirty-eight-story Playboy Building began life in 1929 as the Palmolive Building and became an instant celebrity by way of its revolving Lindbergh Beacon at the top. When "Big John" with its posh apartments came into the neighborhood, it became necessary to build a shield to shut off the revolving light.

Walk one block north and you'll come to the Drake, grand dame of the city's hotels. Built in 1921, it's a mere ten stories high, but there are many people who wouldn't think of staying anywhere else when they come to Chicago. Among its other luxuries, the Drake is famous for what some Chicagoans say is the world's most beautiful powder room, with a seventy-foot-long makeup mirror, marble walls, recessed lighting, and a marble washbasin in each stall.

You're standing at Oak Street beach with a view of Lake Michigan, and up ahead is North Lake Shore Drive, certainly one of the most beautiful residential streets in all America. Here your tour of the Magnificent Mile concludes.

The Loop. You start at the Art Institute of Chicago on South Michigan Avenue, which is actually on the perimeter of the Loop. A famous pair of bronze lions guard the entrance to what looks like a royal palace, and what is unquestionably one of America's finest museums. In fact, some Chicagoans refer to their city as "Museum City." One local reporter wrote recently, "In some museums I believe curators would prefer that you not look at the exhibits, because you might get fingerprints on the glass. Exhibits in Chicago museums talk to you, move for you. There are buttons to punch, gizmos to turn and bells to ring. Our museums develop exhibits that communicate with you." Among the treasures you'll see in the Art Museum are one of the largest collections of French Impressionist paintings in the world and an outstanding Oriental collection.

Leaving the Art Institute, walk one block south and four blocks east and you're in the Loop at the Monadnock Building on the southwest corner of Dearborn and Jackson. In 1893 its sixteen stories made it the tallest office building in the world, as well as the highest commercial building with outside walls of masonry construction.

Across the street at Adams and Dearborn is Mies van der Rohe's Federal Center, completed in 1974. The plaza outside is dominated by Alexander Calder's huge orange metal sculpture *Flamingo*, which stands fifty-three feet high and weighs fifty tons. In fact, there's such a profusion of giant sculpture outside or just inside the city's skyscrapers that some visitors have referred to Chicago itself as an outsize museum.

Walk five blocks west and there it is—the 110-story Sears Tower, "Big Buck," the tallest building in the world. Go into the lobby and see Calder's mobile *Universe*, and then take the elevator to Skydeck, the observation deck on the 103rd story with a view that, besides Chicago, also takes in portions of Indiana, Michigan, and Wisconsin.

Back on terra firma, go back three blocks in an easterly direction and you'll come to the Rookery at 209 LaSalle Street, a long-time architectural landmark and now a National Historic Landmark. Named for the flocks of pigeons which used to roost there, the Rookery (1886) is the oldest remaining steel-skeleton skyscraper in the world. Pass through the arching entrance into the exquisitely detailed gold and ivory courtyard designed by Frank Lloyd Wright, who remodeled part of the building in 1905.

Continue three more blocks to the east and stop at the Marquette Building (1893), whose lobby is a treasury of Tiffany mosaics.

Walk one block north to the First National Bank Building at Monroe and Dearborn. In the plaza there you'll see Marc Chagall's brilliant mosaic mural *The Four Seasons,* and then go two blocks farther and you'll be at the Richard J. Daley Civic Center Building, in front of which is Pablo Picasso's fifty-foot steel sculpture placed there in 1967, a gift from the artist.

Two blocks east, at 111 North State Street, is the famous Marshall Field block-long department store. (By October 1979, State Street's mile-long shopping mall, the longest in the United States, is expected to be completed.) You can walk from the State Street entrance through the store to Wabash, or go from Washington Street to Randolph. At the latter two ends of the store are open courts covered by skylights: the one at the Washington Street end is a slightly arched dome of blue and gold Tiffany mosaic. While the court at the Randolph Street end is less spectacular, it nevertheless is the setting each year for the store's mammoth Christmas tree. And unless it will interfere with your diet in some way, I suggest you take time out at this point to sample one of the homemade sundaes in the store's *fin de siècle* Crystal Court ice-cream parlor on the third floor.

Next, walk one block south to the Carson Pirie Scott store at South State Street and Madison, an intersection known as the "World's Busiest Corner." The elegant building you see there is the result of three stages of construction: 1899, 1906, and 1960. Actually, it wasn't purchased by Carson Pirie Scott until 1904, but when their architects enlarged the building, they showed respect for its original design, and the most recent work done also lovingly followed the plan of Louis Sullivan, the original architect. Consequently, the result is an architectural masterpiece whose ornate cast-iron work over the entrance was put there, according to Louis Sullivan, "to crown women with a laurel wreath as they entered the store, to make them feel fashionable and special by shopping there." And today, almost ninety years later, the old Chicago Style architecture is still working its magic.

CLEVELAND

Ohio's largest city, this was the first city in the United States to boast outdoor electric lighting and free mail delivery and, more recently, the first American city with an airport-to-downtown rapid-transit system.

General Moses Cleaveland founded the city on July 22, 1796, and, appropriately enough, it carried his name until one day the first "a" was scissored off. But the Connecticut-born lawyer is still a dominant figure in the form of a life-size bronze statue standing atop a granite pedestal in the Public Square, where the first electric streetlights—not only in the United States but in the world—were lit on April 29, 1879. A very good place to begin a walking tour, since all Cleveland's principal thoroughfares fan out from there.

Standing in the square, face the southwest and you'll see on a corner there what, when built in 1928, was the second tallest building in the nation: the fifty-two-story Terminal Tower, whose elevators will take you at a speed of eight hundred feet per minute to the enclosed observatory on the forty-second floor, from where, on a clear day, you can see a good thirty miles. In the lobby there are marble-walled ramps leading to lower-level shops and the downtown rapid-transit station, from which you can ride out to the Cleveland Hopkins International Airport in twenty-one minutes.

Directly across from Terminal Tower is the Sheraton Cleveland Hotel, standing on a historically prominent tavern and hotel site that dates back to 1815, when a log cabin called Mowrey's Tavern stood there.

On the north side of Public Square is the Old Stone Church. Erected in 1834, it was destroyed by fire in 1853. The present structure was completed in 1855, and many of its stained-glass windows were designed by Louis Tiffany. I suggest you go inside and take a close look at the unusual chairs for the elders that flank the offertory table.

The northeast corner of the square leads out onto the Mall, a three-block park ending with a fine view of Lake Erie, from where, looking in an easterly direction, you can see the heroic-looking War Memorial Fountain, a thirty-five-foot bronze figure on a large sphere symbolizing man's immortal spirit rising above the flames of war and reaching toward eternal life and peace. Around its base are the names of men who perished in World War II and the Korean War. In the same easterly direction across the Mall, you'll see a statue of Abraham Lincoln outside the Board of Education Building. Paid for by schoolchildren's pennies, it was erected in 1932 not far from the place in the square where, in 1861, en route to his first inauguration, he addressed a huge crowd and where, only four years later, his coffin lay in state.

Continue your walk around the square and on your left you'll see the Old Federal Building, built in 1900 as the city's Main Post Office. Go inside the lobby and inspect the historic tablet honoring Joseph Briggs, the postal clerk who created and installed Cleveland's free mail delivery and collection, and was then appointed by the postmaster general to do the same for the rest of the country.

Cross Superior Avenue to the southeast quadrant of Public Square and pay a visit to the Soldiers and Sailors Monument, a Civil War memorial dedicated in 1894. Built of black granite, stone, and bronze, it stands 125 feet high and houses a small museum open to visitors weekdays and half day on Saturdays. Admission is free.

Walk on to Euclid Avenue, the city's principal shopping thoroughfare and once upon a time its grandest residential street. Proceed south across Euclid and you'll come face to face with the bronze plaque marking the birthplace of Dr. Harvey Cushing, "A Great American Surgeon, Scholar, Teacher, Bibliophile, Artist," who won a Pulitzer Prize in biography in 1926. Walk a little farther up Euclid and you'll see still another commemorative plaque, this one marking the site at the corner of East Third Street where, in Studio 12 on the fourth floor, Archibald M. Willard completed his first version of his famous painting *The Spirit of '76*, the finished version of which can be seen in the rotunda of the Cleveland City Hall.

Cross Euclid at the corner of East Fourth Street and enter the Old Arcade. Known as an architectural marvel when it opened in 1890, it's still an awesome structure. Extending north to Superior Avenue, it's four hundred feet long and its glass roof is one hundred feet high, with 112 bazaarlike shops between office towers on five floors. The Old Arcade is still the largest structure of its kind in the country, and its interior of marble, brass, and wrought iron is a masterpiece of Victorian decor.

Exit onto Superior Avenue, and across the street stands the Cleveland Public Library, the fifth largest library in the nation, which Clevelanders remind you is generally regarded as America's second greatest municipal library. Now in two buildings separated by the Eastman Reading Garden, where there are free noonday concerts of recorded music (May through October), the library has the distinction of being the first "open shelf" library in the world.

Continue across East Sixth Street and you'll see the Federal Reserve Bank on your left, a Goliath of a structure that resembles a Florentine fortress. When it opened on August 27, 1923, it had the world's largest vault. In fact, everything about it is outsize including its giant stone figures: Security and Integrity at the entrance, and Energy on the Superior Avenue side. Francis X. Bushman, a silent-screen star famous for his finely chiseled features, posed for them.

Turn onto East Ninth Street and walk a few short blocks, and on your left you'll see the new Federal Building, a thirty-story tower completed in 1967. Its official name is the Celebrezze Federal Building, in honor of Cleveland's former mayor, Anthony J. Celebrezze. On the building's Sixth Street side is a new city landmark, a bronze statue of a rather youthful George Washington wearing a tricornered hat. Unveiled in 1973, it stands on what was officially named Washington Square four years later.

From here walk north to Lakeside Avenue and cross East Ninth Street to City Hall, a classic Greek-columned structure housing Willard's *Spirit of '76*, which the city's Department of Tourism regards as "the most inspirational patriotic picture ever painted."

Cross Lakeside Avenue, bear west, and you'll arrive at the Cleveland Convention Center. More specifically, you'll have come to the main building, Public Hall; the rest is underground and reachable by ramps. The convention hall is one of the largest in the country. Continue along the west side of City Hall north to the Pulaski Cannon Memorial, with its cannon dedicated in 1937 to Count Casimir Pulaski, the Polish general who served under George Washington. Here you can see the Cleveland Stadium, one of the eight largest municipal stadiums in the world. Completed in 1931, it seats eighty thousand spectators.

West of the Mall is the Cuyahoga County Courthouse, completed in 1912 at a cost of $5 million. Walk inside and up its spiral marble staircase to inspect its murals on the second floor. On the west side of the courthouse is Fort Huntington Park, the site of Cleveland's only stockade, built there in 1813.

Proceed south on Ontario South, and on your right will be the city's $135 million Justice Center, opened in 1976. Consisting of a twenty-story tower and an adjacent building, it's situated on a full city block and is graced (disgraced, say some Clevelanders) with a highly controversial piece of modern sculpture. Now continue south on Ontario and you'll be back where you began, at Public Square, the hub of downtown Cleveland.

HOUSTON

The fifth largest and fastest-growing city in the United States, Houston, according to a recent magazine article, "literally glitters and glows in the light of its achievements." The *Wall Street Journal* calls it "the golden buckle of the 'Sun Belt.'" *New York Times* architecture critic Ada Louise Huxtable calls Houston "the city of the second half of the twentieth century." The median age of its citizenry is twenty-six and growing younger. Houston has the third busiest port in the nation and probably has more millionaires in proportion to its population than any other large American city. It also has a world-famous medical center, a fine symphony and opera, and excellent universities. Eighteen new skyscrapers are expected to be decorating the skyline by 1980, and thirty-four new hotels have either been announced or are under construction. In short, Houston, founded 142 years ago, is still a boom town.

Your tour starts in Sam Houston Park, where the buildings, under the protection of the Harris County Heritage Society, tell you something of the city's history. A walk through the park costs you nothing, but if you want to see the interiors of the buildings (and I recommend that you do), the admission is two dollars.

"The Old Place," a log cabin, was Houston's first commercial structure (1824), a combination town hall and barbershop. Among the other buildings in the park, I think you'll particularly enjoy the Kellum Noble home. Built in 1857, it was the city first brick dwelling, and it later saw duty as a zoo and then as an elementary school. Before you leave the park, pay a visit to "The Long Row," a string of shops that are replicas of some of the city's mid-nineteenth-century shops and sell appropriately nostalgic merchandise.

Walk through the park to Allen Parkway and Bagby and, outside the park now, continue two blocks south to Allen Center Building No. 1 at the corner of Dallas and Bagby. Proceed two more blocks east to Allen Center Building No. 2 and take the escalator down to the three-mile-long Downtown Underground, an air-conditioned network of tunnels and malls —a subterranean world of stores, boutiques, and restaurants. Explore, and then walk to the mall beneath 1 Shell Plaza, the city's tallest building, and take the escalator upstairs to the lobby. (At this writing, three skyscrapers are under construction that will be taller than Shell Plaza.)

Walk north on Smith Street to the Alley Theatre, the oldest permanent resident theater in the United States. It got its name for the good reason that the original theater was located in a fan factory in an alley. The present two-stage theater was completed in 1970.

Catercorner from the Alley Theatre is the Jones Hall for the Performing Arts, a $7.4 million home for the city's grand opera, ballet, and symphony, with a seating capacity of three thousand, walls of teakwood, and a flexible ceiling to provide a more intimate atmosphere for, say, a concert of chamber music. View the lobby's abstract sculpture from the top tier of the lobby; from that vantage point the thousands of yards of gold-plate cable holding silver and aluminum rods resemble a fabulous jet stream.

Walk a short distance north on Louisiana Street, look up, and you'll see some of the greenery growing in the garden of what has been described as the penthouse apartment of the late Miss Ima Hogg, daughter of a former governor of Texas. Actually, the lady never resided there. The fifteen-story office building was owned by her two brothers, millionaire oil developers, and she simply used the sumptuous penthouse for entertaining her friends. Landscaped gardens with a gazebo framed the area around the apartment, and it's some of those trees you can see from the street below.

Walk one block east and you're at the park leading into the Old Market Square. A plaque there will give you the history of this, the oldest and once the most notorious section of Houston. At 813 Congress Street, a pub called La Carafe is the oldest commercial building in the city still standing on its original site. An extremely narrow two-story building constructed in the early 1800s, it was first an Indian trading post and then a stagecoach inn (General Sam Houston once slept there).

Walk one block east to Main Street and then three blocks south to the corner of Texas, where you'll find the Rice Hotel occupying the former site of what, for a very short time, was the capital of the Republic of Texas. Walk west two blocks on Texas, turn left on Milan Street, and go south one block to Penzoil Towers, an architectural fantasia consisting of two glass-faced high-rises connected by glass arcades awash with trees and flowers. Go into the lobby and take the escalator down to the Underground for the second time. Walk about four blocks south to the Hyatt Regency Hotel mall, take the escalator up to the thirty-floor-high lobby, and then proceed onward and upward to the Spindletop revolving bar-restaurant named in honor of the first Texas gusher. The view is superb and so's the food, which, I think, is a good reason why you should consider making yours a morning tour so that you'll end up there in time for luncheon.

LITTLE ROCK

In 1722, a Frenchman named Bernard de la Harpe was exploring the valley of the Arkansas River, trying to establish trade with the Indians in the region. He came to a shallow ford in the river, marked by an outcrop of rock on the south bank. There were some larger rocks on the north bank a few miles upstream, so he called the smaller one *la petite roche*, "the little rock." Today, Little Rock calls itself "The Coming Place." For years, it says, Arkansas was undiscovered and unappreciated by the rest of the nation. No more. Over 135 of *Fortune* magazine's top five hundred U.S. companies have chosen locations in Arkansas. Little Rock, its capital city, is growing up and growing out. It has a fabulous new airport, a new $5 million pedestrian mall opened in downtown in October 1978, and its symphony orchestra is rated one of the best in the United States. Little Rock people boast of the quality of life in their city. And rightly so. Burns Park in North Little Rock, for example, is one of the largest municipal parks in the nation; it has a wildlife trail, a camping area, and a twenty-seven-hole golf course, and it's a scant ten-minute drive from downtown.

Your tour begins outside the Little Rock Bureau for Conventions and Visitors, located at the corner of West Markham and Broadway. This is the city's hotel area, with hotels to the west, east, and north of you. Walking east toward the Old State Capitol, you'll pass the construction site of still another new hotel, the Hyatt Regency, which will be opened early in 1981.

Little Rock is the only city in the nation with three capitols. This one at West Markham and Louisiana streets is the first one, and it's been so faithfully restored that it's recognized as one of the nation's outstanding historical restorations. A Greek Revival structure with wrought-iron gates and ancient cannons on its lawn, it served as the capitol from 1836 to 1911. Today it's a museum of Arkansas history, and among its permanent exhibitions are the restored legislative and executive areas, and glass cases containing the inauguration gowns of the various governors' wives. During my visit, the second floor was showing an exhibit of furniture and assorted memorabilia collected from one of Little Rock's most distinguished nineteenth-century hotels.

When you leave the Old State Capitol, you'll be facing south toward Center Street. Cross over and walk down Center Street, turn left on Third Street, go four blocks to Cumberland, and there you'll be at the Arkansas Territorial Restoration. Visit the two-story log house that was once the home and print shop of the founder of the *Arkansas Gazette*. Today it's a museum of Arkansas' pre-state history.

Next, walk west on Third Street just two blocks and you'll find yourself entering the city's new $5 million Metrocentre Mall, with its sculpture by Henry Moore and its fountains, benches, and potted trees. Two blocks wide and six blocks long, it was privately financed by a group of business leaders and opened with a week-long celebration. If you stand in the center of the mall and face west, you can see the present State Capitol about a mile away. Majestic and gold-domed, it's constructed of white marble and bears a distinct family resemblance to our national capitol.

From the center of the mall turn east and walk four blocks on East Capitol Street to Trapnall Hall at No. 423. Built in 1843 and restored in

1963, it's listed in the National Register of Historic Places and serves now as the governor's official receiving hall. Beautifully furnished in antiques of the period in which it was built, it's not only open to visitors but is also available to the public on a rental basis.

From Trapnall Hall go left a half block to Rock Street, and then south four blocks to MacArthur Park, named in honor of General Douglas Mac-Arthur, who was born in a building there when it was the Little Rock Arsenal and Little Rock was still a territory. On your walk from Trapnall Hall you'll pass through the picturesque Quapaw Quarter, the city's oldest section. Only a few short years ago, its fine old homes were in a state of decay, but now the antebellum homes and Victorian mansions are being restored. Twenty-three of these buildings have been designated National Historic Landmarks. One particularly affluent newcomer to the Quapaw spent some $250,000 refurbishing his home.

The former arsenal in MacArthur Park is now the Museum of Science and History and is surrounded by magnolia trees. Among its exhibits is a fascinating one of Indian ceremonial objects, and on the day of my visit some schoolchildren were there busily grinding corn—all the better to understand the life-style of the American Indian. Before you leave the building, I suggest you take a trip down to the basement, which is home for the animals, birds, and reptiles the museum brings to local schoolrooms. I stood and watched, fascinated, as a fourteen-year-old volunteer fed minnows to a baby alligator while an owl observed.

Behind the museum is the Arkansas Arts Center. Here, within a space that might fill only a wing of some other museums, the fifteen-year-old Arts Center houses five exhibition galleries, a 389-seat theater, nine studios, a comprehensive art library, a four-thousand-record collection of early American jazz, a volunteer-operated restaurant and gift shop, and three charming courtyards replete with trees and sculpture. Most Little Rockers refer to the center not as a museum but as a "happening." Convinced that the time to start building an appreciation of the arts is in childhood, the director initiated the "Yellow Space Place," an exhibition area set aside as a children's gallery, where, every Sunday, while parents are enjoying themselves elsewhere in the center, their youngsters are working away at a "make-a-thing" activity.

Walk back to the museum on Ninth Street and from there walk three blocks west to Scott. Turn left and walk four blocks to No. 1321 Scott, the Villa Marre. An Italianate Victorian house built in 1881–83, it is open to the public most afternoons. A tour of its plush interior costs two dollars.

Walk back along Scott and turn west on Eighth Street, right on Louisiana, and then left on Spring. The spot where your tour began is close by, and I recommend just one more stop before you call it a day. Outside the entrance to the Camelot Inn on West Markham and Broadway is a replica of the famous Wild Boar of Florence. Legend has it that the Boar is a protector of children. Rub his nose, make a wish, and drop in a coin. It will go to the Arkansas Children's Hospital.

LOS ANGELES

In 1796, a party of Spaniards set up camp on a riverbank near what is now the Los Angeles Civic Center, and one of them wrote in his diary: "It has all the requisites for a large settlement."

Today the settlement is spread over 464 square miles and is more populous than half of the union's fifty states. And it's still growing. Newcomers stream into Los Angeles at the rate of about 25,000 a year. And one thing is for certain: No one can be indifferent about this dynamic city. In 1906, the *Los Angeles Times* observed, "Life in Los Angeles is a tonic. Optimism, hopefulness and courage are in the air. As one comes downtown in the morning one feels ready for the day's battle, like a giant refreshed with new wine." In *Playboy* magazine (1972), a writer declared, "If someone had given an imaginative, impatient, pleasure-prone adolescent $100 billion and told him to build a city that would gratify all his divergent urges, he would have built something very much like Los Angeles."

Begin your tour at the Plaza, where the city was founded on September 4, 1781, and which contains remnants of the original pueblo from which Los Angeles grew. It's only a stroll from Union Station, which we've all seen in more early talkies than we can possibly count. Enter the Plaza from Olivera Street, a former alley turned pedestrian mall full of food stands, restaurants, and vendor stalls selling everything from paper flowers and pottery to religious statues. Among the antiquities of Olivera Street is Avilva Adobe (1818), the oldest house in the city and open to visitors.

In the center of the Plaza is a lacy wrought-iron bandstand, and around the perimeter huge fig trees and bushes cut in the shape of animals. Here from a barrel-top fruit stand you can buy a mango sliced and skewered in the shape of a flower. Dominating the Plaza are the old Plaza Church, built in 1820, and restorations of the historic Pico House hotel and the city's first fire station.

Leave on the right side of the Plaza and walk south to the Los Angeles Mall. Descend the stairs, go past the fountains and tropical plants and into the lower-level two-block complex of shops, boutiques, and restaurants.

Cross under Temple Street and ride the escalator to the street level. City Hall is across the street on your right. I understand the tower at the top offers a fantastic view. Sorry to report that I didn't get up there, but I think you should.

From here proceed southwest to Third and Broadway. There you'll discover a cluster of the city's favorite landmarks: the Bradbury Building, the Million Dollar Theatre, and the Grand Central Public Market.

The five-story Bradbury Building, built in 1893, is on the southeast corner, and inside, for an admission price of one dollar, you'll be given a three-page tour sheet replete with a mini-history of the building and a floor plan enabling you to act as your own tour guide. The building is described as "a tour de force, a student's dream, Los Angeles' most pleasant surprise." And indeed it is.

While the brown brick exterior is nondescript, the interior all but defies description: the five-story skylit center court with glass roof; two open-cage elevators; offices opening onto ornamental cast-iron balconies surrounding the court. Take one of the elevators to the top floor and walk down the marble staircase, peering over each landing as you go. Each of the spacious elevators contains a table with an antique telephone, and each landing a huge potted fern.

Across the street, the Million Dollar Theatre is still another landmark that requires no little concentration. The venerable old theater (1918) has been disfigured with a bold red and white marquee (it was playing a Mexican skin flick on the day of my visit), but, unlike the Bradbury, its claim to fame is its façade, which features a sculpture gallery of famous theatrical personalities of the past.

South of the theater is the entrance to the Grand Central Public Market, a block-long beehive of produce, grocery, meat, and specialty vendors (chilis, tortillas, sausages, spices, and so on, since this area of the city has the largest population of Mexican descent to be found outside of Mexico City). Walk through and exit on Hill Street. Cut across Pershing Square and visit the renovated Biltmore Hotel, its front door manned by two gents in swallowtailed coats and black top hats. The giant lobby with vaulted ceiling and elegant columns smacks of the Golden Age of motion pictures, which, incidentally, was the heyday of this grand hotel. Guided tours of its public rooms are available on weekdays, but you must phone ahead and make a reservation.

Walk around the corner to 630 West Fifth Street and look inside the Los Angeles Public Library, a handsome buff-colored stucco building. Most Angelenos refer to it simply as the Central Library. Make a point to visit the second-floor rotunda, with its great high walls covered with murals de-picting California history.

Walk west on Fifth and visit the rather intimidating-looking Arco Tow-ers on Flower Street. It has a two-tiered subterranean shopping area, and the space between is festooned with silver kites. Ride the escalator back up to Fifth Street and cross the footbridge leading into the Bonaventure Hotel, a collection of five mirrored-glass cylinders with a six-story-high lobby and glass-capsule elevators that zip you up to the revolving bar-restaurant on top.

Finding your way out of the Bonaventure isn't all that simple (at least, I didn't find it so). Go to the eighth level and take the footbridge leading into the World Trade Center. Take still another footbridge from its en-closed mall across Flower Street to the block-long Security Pacific Bank. Ride an escalator from the concourse level to the street and a park you'll recognize for its stunning red Calder mobile. Walk south and then north on Hope Street and you'll find yourself at the Music Center. This is an impressive grouping of three separate buildings: the imposing Ahmanson Theatre, the smaller Mark Taper Forum, and the Dorothy Chandler Pa-vilion, which is the winter home of the Los Angeles Philharmonic and in summer the Civic Light Opera. The view from here will have you turning in all directions.

This isn't a very long walk, but it has so many sudden and dramatic shifts of scene and the city is so spread out that you may feel you've walked twice the distance you actually have (about three and a half miles). So don't hesitate to stop for some rest and refreshment whenever you feel like it.

NEW ORLEANS

For years the closest I got to New Orleans was a Tennessee Williams play. And the last one I saw was titled *Vieux Carre*, meaning "Old Square" —the French Quarter. I guess I felt it was high time that I saw the *real* thing. Over the years friends had come back from there starry-eyed. One woman kept delaying her return day by day, until finally her money ran out and she simply had to come home. A couple of years ago I talked with a man who had moved to New Orleans from the Midwest, and he rhap-sodized about how the Vieux Carre Commission, a regulatory agency, was policing the 260-acre area to make certain that the laws protecting its historic architecture were rigorously enforced. He said that even the newest hotels were built in the nineteenth-century style. Now, of course, there's a whole lot more to this colorful Mississippi River city than the French Quarter (the Louisiana Superdome, for example, the largest enclosed stadium in the world), but I found it so fascinating—and I think you will, too —that I've chosen it for your walking tour.

Start outside the Tourist and Convention Bureau, located at 334 Royal Street, and walk to the Manheim Galleries at 404 Royal. The gallery has been in business some sixty years and houses the largest collection of jade for sale in the world. While there are twenty-six showrooms full of such things as Dutch paintings and eighteenth- and nineteenth-century porcelains, the jade room is the *pièce de résistance*, with such treasures as a vase valued at $65,000 and a red jade dragon pendant with diamonds for $8,500.

Until recently your next stop would have been the famous Jazz Museum, with its special treasures, too—such things as Louis Armstrong's trumpet, for example. But, unfortunately, it's shuttered and awaiting a new home in the New Orleans Mint Building.

So remain on Royal Street and head for the Merieult House at No. 533, one of the few survivors of the 1794 fire that destroyed most of New Orleans. Acquired in 1938 by General Kemper Williams, today on its ground and second floors are exhibits containing not only the 1812 Louisiana Constitution but also the Historic New Orleans Collection of prints, paintings, and documents. Admission to the ground floor is free, but a guided tour through the permanent exhibition on the second floor costs two dollars. Before you depart from Royal Street, pay a visit next door to the Pearl Factory store. Here for six dollars you can dip into a bucket and take an oyster that's guaranteed to hold a minimum of one pearl.

Your next stop is only a few steps to the left and down Toulouse Street to the Casa Hove. Built in 1725, it's another of the few survivors of the fire of 1794. Now the residence of Ms. Julie Yochim, the upstairs apartment, handsomely restored, is a treasure cove of antiques of the period and is open to visitors for just fifty cents admission. Downstairs is a perfume shop selling not the famous-name brands but, rather, its own specially blended Vieux Carre fragrances.

From here walk through Pirates Alley, a narrow cobblestoned passageway to Jackson Square, named to commemorate the fact that it was there that Andrew Jackson delivered an address after the Battle of New Orleans. The St. Louis Cathedral, built in 1794, dominates the square, and adjoining it is the Cabido, a complex of five buildings that today is the home of the Louisiana State Museum.

Leave the square and head for Tradition Hall at 721 Bourbon Street just a few blocks away. It's a small, rustic concert hall where jazz is played every night starting at eight. Fine jazz it is too. There is no entrance fee, but a donation of $1.50 to $2 is requested.

Now backtrack to Jackson Square, where, at the lower end, you'll find Moon Walk, a promenade with a commanding view of the city. Walk to its center, stop, look, and then continue on to the dock at the Toulouse Street Wharf. It's from here that visitors leave aboard the *Natchez* for two-hour cruises ($5.50) up and down the river. That might suggest a sleepy little port, but don't be misled; you'll find ships from all over the world here. But the *Natchez*, with repeated blasts of its steam whistle and a pre-departure calliope concert, succeeds in making its passengers feel as if they were in olde New Orleans despite all the international flags fluttering in the breeze.

Now it's probably about time you did some shopping in the French Quarter, which is rife with boutiques, galleries, sidewalk stalls, and antique shops, of which there are some four dozen. The Vieux Carre Candle Shop, at 708 Iberville, and the Toy Village, at 518 St. Peter Street, on Jackson Square, are great favorites with most visitors to the French Quarter.

Trailing off the square along the levee is the recently restored French Market complex of more shops and boutiques, as well as the Café du Monde, famous for its café au lait and beignets—French doughnuts sprinkled with powdered sugar by a most generous hand. If after that repast you're still feeling up to it, I suggest you walk over to 118–32 Royal Street, two blocks up from the market, and take a tour ($2.50) of the Gallier House, built in the 1860s and, like everything else in the French Quarter, lovingly restored.

NEW YORK

A visitor's introduction to this city should start where the city itself started, down at the southern tip of the island. The area is often referred to as Wall Street, although this world-famous street is but a small "V" one mile long and 120 acres in area. Still, it was the foundation for America's first frontier town when, in 1653, Governor Peter Stuyvesant erected a wooden wall here that gave the dirt road its official name. The wall was intended to keep out the British; it didn't, nor did it discourage local residents from hacking away at it for firewood. The wall was knocked down in 1699, but the name Wall Street endured, and so has its reputation as one of the greatest marketplaces of the world.

Begin your walking tour at City Hall, situated in an irregularly shaped park about one mile north of the southern tip of the island, which is the direction in which you'll be walking. Many architecture critics consider this Federal-style building, with its broad steps, Georgian cupola, and clock, to be one of the handsomest city halls in the nation. The cornerstone was laid in 1803, and the building was completed nine years later. Enter through one of the five arched entry doors, and to your right you'll see a life-size bronze replica of the marble statue of George Washington that stands in the state capitol at Richmond, Virginia. The rotunda extends the full height of the building, and its fluted columns and its elegant double-curved stairway are tremendously impressive. The mayor's office and those of his aides are on the first floor. The rooms upstairs are open to visitors weekdays from ten to four.

When you come out, walk south through City Hall Park, which, in early Dutch times, was used as a common pasture and parade ground. Several structures were built in this park: the first was an almshouse for the poor in 1736, and the British built a prison here in 1776 to house captured patriots. When the year was barely half over, however, George Washington was reading the Declaration of Independence to his assembled troops here.

Leaving the foot of the park, bear left, cross the street, and proceed down Park Row, once known as Newspaper Row, since it housed the city's greatest newspapers. On the corner of Ann Street (named for Queen Anne, but somehow the "e" was lost), turn left, and halfway down the block you'll discover Theatre Alley, a narrow lane connecting Ann and Beekman Streets. Stop about two hundred feet north of Ann Street, and you'll be standing about where actors entered the stage door of the Park Theatre, the city's first important legitimate theater, which opened its doors on January 20, 1798, with a production of *As You Like It*. When George Washington died, on December 3 of that year, the Park closed for ten days in tribute. It was razed in 1821 and a new Park Theatre was built on the site. In 1832 it was the scene of a ball given in honor of the visit of Charles Dickens, to which guests came dressed as Dickens characters. The theater burned to the ground in December 1848 (in cold weather two blazing fires were kept up at either end of the wide carpeted lobby).

Return to Ann Street and walk south to Nassau. Go one block to your right and turn left on Fulton Street. Continue on Fulton until you see the lighthouse on the left-hand side of the street that announces you've arrived at the South Street Seaport Museum. Founded in 1967, the museum (actually a collection of buildings rather than a single building) is dedicated to preserving and restoring the buildings, vessels, and piers of this area, once known as the Street of Ships and declared a national landmark in 1977. Restoration starts in the spring of 1979, and then some of the buildings may be closed.

Stroll down nearby Water Street and visit the galleries showing old ship models. Visit the printing shop (this area was once the printing center of the city), and then drop in at the Visitor's Center at 16 Fulton, where all manner of books and postcards having to do with the area, past and present, are for sale.

Wander through the Fulton Market across the street and inspect the stalls that sell everything from pottery and solid-brass plates to fresh shrimp. Cross to the south side of Fulton, and a few doors north of the corner of South Street you'll see the unimpressive entrance to a very impressive restaurant called Sweets. Established in 1845, it's the oldest seafood restaurant in the city.

Move on to South Street, walk a block to your right, and see the ships moored at Piers 15 and 16. Some are there to be inspected free of charge by visitors like you. From May to September the schooner *Pioneer* is available for a three-hour sail around the harbor. The largest sailing vessel ever built is here, too; it's called *Peking*, and to go aboard costs $2.50.

Walk back up Fulton Street to Water Street, turn left, and move on and up Maiden Lane, past the Louise Nevelson Plaza, with a collection of four pieces of her sculpture, and turn left at the corner of Nassau. Go one block, and on the northeast corner of Liberty and Nassau you'll find the immense Federal Reserve Bank of New York, which resembles a Florentine Renaissance palace. Five of its stories are below street level, with subterranean vaults resting on bedrock.

One more block and you're at the corner of Broad and Wall streets, where stands the national memorial, Federal Hall. It was built in 1842 along the lines of the Parthenon, and at the top of the steep steps is a giant statue of George Washington, who, on this site on April 30, 1789, when New York was the capital of the new nation, took the oath of office as president.

On both sides of the gold, white, and blue rotunda are exhibition rooms, where you can view a pair of Washington's shoe buckles; a brown suit ("Persistent family tradition holds that this brown suit 'of American manufacture' is the one President Washington wore for his first inauguration"); and Alexander Hamilton's bookplate, found between pages of a collection of essays written in favor of the new Constitution.

Next, cross to the southwest corner of Broad Street and go to No. 20, the entrance for visitors to the New York Stock Exchange. Take the elevator to the third-floor gallery and watch the frantic activity below, while a young lady at the far end of the gallery delivers a running commentary.

Continue walking south on Broad, and on the southeast corner of Pearl you'll find Fraunces Tavern, where Washington bade farewell to the officers of his troops at a noontime gathering on December 4, 1783. The building was bought by the Sons of the Revolution in 1904. A first-rate restaurant operates on the ground floor, and a free museum is on the second and third floors. You'll see the Long Room, restored in 1971, on the approximate site of Washington's farewell; a collection of clocks and mirrors of the colonial period; nineteenth-century silver (some, I'm proud to say, created by William Gale, Jr., an ancestor of mine); and some letters and documents bearing the signature of George Washington. Weekdays (12:30 and 1:30) there's a free ten-minute audiovisual presentation, "A Colonial Seed Grows a Big Apple," of New York's early history in the Flag Room on the third floor.

Turn left on Pearl and walk to Whitehall Street. Turn right, and in two blocks you'll come to the old U.S. Custom House. Unfortunately, it is open only during the summer months, when it houses free exhibitions dealing with facets of the city's history. It faces Bowling Green, New York's earliest park, a tiny triangle of grass between Whitehall on the east and Broadway on the west. It was leased in 1733 for use as a bowling green at a rental of one peppercorn a year. Here in 1776 patriots toppled the equestrian statue of King George III. They also ripped off the tiny crowns that decorated the fence around the park, but otherwise the original fence is still intact.

Cross over to Broadway, where at the juncture of Wall Street stands Trinity Church. Already a stately eighty years of age at the time of the Declaration of Independence, the church you see now is the third church on the site. The first was a victim of the fire of 1776. The second church, completed in 1790, was razed when heavy snows severely damaged the roof. The present church was dedicated in 1846. By all means wander through the cemetery on the north side of the church. On the weathered tombstones you'll see such illustrious names as Alexander Hamilton and Robert Fulton of steamboat fame.

A few blocks north between Fulton and Vesey streets is St. Paul's Chapel, the oldest public building in continuous use in the city. After taking his oath of office as our first president, Washington went immediately to St. Paul's for prayer. It was here he worshiped during the time he lived in the city, and his pew on the north side of the chapel is marked.

Directly across the street from St. Paul's is the Western Electric Building, on the site of the famous Barnum Museum, which numbered among its attractions General Tom Thumb and Jumbo, the world's largest elephant. The museum burned to the ground in 1865, leaving the carcass of a white whale, another stellar attraction, on Broadway for several days.

No. 233 Broadway is your next and final stop: the Woolworth Building, the tallest building in the world until 1930. When it officially opened on the evening of April 24, 1913, President Woodrow Wilson, sitting in the White House, pressed a button and the brand-new sixty-story skyscraper was suddenly illuminated with 80,000 light bulbs. Considered an architectural classic, it was awarded a gold medal in 1915 by the Panama-Pacific Exposition as the "most beautiful building in all the world erected to commerce." Some people called it a "Cathedral of Commerce." An amusing feature of its three-story-high entrance arcade is a series of carved figures, half portrait and half caricature, nestled high under the supporting crossbeams. Among them you'll see one of Cass Gilbert, its architect, holding a miniature model of the building in his arms, and another of Frank W. Woolworth, the five-and-ten-cent-store tycoon who financed it, counting his nickels and dimes.

Across the street is the southern tip of City Hall Park, where you started your tour. And now if you're feeling too exhilarated to stop, you might consider walking south about eight blocks to the World Trade Center. Take a rocketlike elevator to the observation deck on the 107th floor of the southernmost tower and enjoy one of the world's most spectacular views . . . while you decide what section of the city you'll walk through next.

SACRAMENTO

California's capital advertises itself as "The City That Brought You the Gold Rush." It's referring, of course, to the day in January 1848 when gold was discovered at Sutter's sawmill. Before the year was over, thousands were on their way to Sacramento City to strike a claim. By 1849, according to Dr. John F. Morse, first editor of the *Sacramento Union*, Sacramento was ". . . perfectly crowded with the efforts of landing immigrants and merchandise, and notwithstanding the rapidity with which tents and frame houses were being erected, yet the facilities for storage were totally inadequate, and enormous rates were paid for what could be procured. The bank of the Sacramento soon became lined with vessels devoted to storage, boarding, and lodgings."

Conditions worsened when, in 1850, the Sacramento and American rivers overflowed, flooding the city, and in 1852, when a fire caused damage estimated at $10 mililon. But it wasn't all bad news. On October 15, 1850, the riverboat *New World* arrived with the news that California had been admitted to the union. Four years later Sacramento was designated the capital of the new state.

Sad to report, many visitors to California, myself included, often bypass Sacramento and content themselves with visits to Los Angeles and San Francisco. Happily, however, on my last trip to the West Coast I finally broke that bad habit. Sacramento is a fascinating city, and a great city for a walker.

Start your tour at the Governor's Mansion on the corner of Sixteenth and H streets, where for fifty cents you can enjoy a guided tour conducted by a state trooper every half hour. This mansard-style Victorian home, with a front lawn of ninety-year-old camellia bushes, was built in 1877 and was home to thirteen governors and their families until the Ronald Reagans moved out in 1967. It was designated a state historic landmark the next year. What with fourteen-foot ceilings, six-hundred-pound sliding doors leading to a music room containing a 1903 Steinway piano, white marble fireplaces, a 101-year-old coal scuttle, and bathtubs with silver feet, the mansion is a Victorian extravaganza.

When you leave its front door, walk directly across H Street to the Mansion Inn, known as Sacramento's Garden Hotel and for good reason. In its two landscaped courtyards there are 1,100 varieties of plants in an award-winning botanical garden laced with shady walkways.

Leave the hotel on its H Street side and walk west to Sixteenth Street. Bear right and go to L Street, where at No. 2701 stands Sutter's Fort, established in the 1840s by Captain John A. Sutter, who's known as the city's father and the settler on whose land the gold was discovered that started the gold rush of 1849. (Sutter died penniless in 1880.) Fifty cents will buy your admission to the fort's carpenter and blacksmith shops, prison, and living quarters. Wands, included in the admission price, provide you with complete information.

Adjacent to Sutter's Fort is the State Indian Museum, with exhibits of basketry, featherwork, pottery, dress, dances and ceremonies, and other Indian memorabilia. Admission is only twenty-five cents.

Go back on L Street to Fifteenth, and if it's sundown you'll hear the chimes in the rooftop of the block-long Romanesque Memorial Auditorium playing "The Star-Spangled Banner." Up ahead is Capitol Park, bordered with hundred-foot-tall palm trees. Rather, I should say, bordered with rows of *Washington filifera*, the proper botanical name for these palms that are the only ones native to California. Walk through the park en route to the Capitol and marvel at its forty-acre display of one of the finest collections of trees from every continent and climate of the world: pine, fir, eucalyptus, southern magnolia, redwood, tulip—and that's only the beginning. There are four hundred varieties and species of trees and shrubs. In the rose garden there are eight hundred varieties of roses.

The restoration of the Capitol to make it earthquake-proof was part of California's bicentennial project, and when I visited in the fall of 1978 the work was still going on. There was a special exhibit just inside the entrance that explained the extensive restoration, and a series of fifty-eight glassed-in displays, one for each county in the state.

And now comes the big walk of your tour—down the splendid Capitol Mall, with the State Library and Court Building ("Into the Highlands of the Mind Let Me Go") on your left and the State Office Building ("Bring Me Men to Match the Mountains") on your right. You'll walk from Ninth to Third Street toward Tower Bridge, but just before reaching the bridge turn right and you'll enter Old Sacramento, comprising seventy-eight acres along the Sacramento River. This is the city's historic area and the largest historic preservation project in the West, and it isn't quite finished yet. Take a stroll down its board sidewalks surrounded by gaslights and you'll pass authentic nineteenth-century structures (circa 1850–70) including, as well as shops and restaurants, the Old Eagle Theater, a wooden and canvas structure and the first building constructed as a theater in the state; the Pony Express Monument on its actual 1860 site; a one-room schoolhouse; and the justly celebrated Central Pacific Passenger Station, a reconstruction of the first terminus of the transcontinental railroad (circa 1868). A fifty-cent admission charge provides you with a wand, and you walk through the station to the accompaniment of not only the hiss of steam engines and cries of "All aboard!" but the dot-dot of the telegraph and the squawking of chickens. Among other examples of authenticity are a ladies' waiting room replete with horsehair sofa and an antique baby buggy; the Silver Palace eating stand; a baggage room containing everything from a birdcage and fiddle case to a walnut casket; and, of course, the collection of wonderful old trains, notably columnist and railroad buff Lucius Beebe's private coach, the *Gold Coach*, with its observation platform, fresh flowers on a dining table set with silver, and a silver cigarette case alongside a stack of playing cards.

When you're ready to leave Old Sacramento, hop one of the open trams that for ten cents will ride you back downtown to the Community Center at Fourteenth Street.

SAN FRANCISCO

This is an unbelievably small city: only ninety-two square miles in area, and more than half of that is under water at high tide. Yet, despite its size and comparative youth, San Francisco, with its hilly, watery landscape, is one of America's most cosmopolitan cities, as well as the financial capital of the West. "Everybody's favorite city" is what it's often called. It abounds in superb hotels and restaurants. Furthermore, it's a city virtually without seasons; a warm day in winter is just as likely or unlikely as one in summer. Anything over 80 degrees is considered a heat wave. San Francisco is a twentieth-century city that still has a romantic otherworldly quality. It's been variously described as a sensuous city of perennial Forty-Niners living in a perennial renaissance . . . an electric community of creative, adventurous, independent people . . . America's dreamed-of end of the rainbow . . . and the ultimate in urban human dignity. No city in the world attracts more bouquets than this compact, precipitous city of seven hills and clanging cable cars.

Your walking tour starts outside the venerable St. Francis Hotel opposite Union Square in downtown. Cross the street and walk through Union Square; President McKinley broke the ground here, and the monument you pass is a tribute to the naval heroes who served under Commodore Dewey at Manila Bay. As you come out of the square, cross the street to Maiden Lane, an elegant alley of small office buildings and posh shops. Once upon a time it was called Morton Street and was a notorious area of prostitution. It's been said that the fire of 1906 (San Franciscans seldom call it an earthquake) cleansed the city. In any event, when the alley was rebuilt and renamed, it started life with an unblemished reputation.

As you walk through Maiden Lane to Kearny Street, note the building at No. 140 designed by Frank Lloyd Wright. When you reach Kearny, go left to Post and turn left again and walk two blocks back to Powell Street. Post is one of the city's finest shopping streets, and you'll pass such pedigreed emporiums as Gump's, Abercrombie and Fitch, and the Elizabeth Arden salon, with its lipstick-red door. At the corner of Powell turn left and walk down to Market Street, where the famous Powell Street cable car starts out. At some point every visitor to the city must stand and watch it start its hilly climb to Nob Hill. That's where you're going, and you won't be cheating if you interrupt your walk with a cable ride. Your destination is the corner of Powell and California, and how you get there is strictly up to you.

At the corner of Powell and California, you'll have two of the city's most celebrated hotels on either side of you: the Mark Hopkins on your left and the Fairmont on your right. Walk up California on the Fairmont side four blocks to Leavenworth Street. As you do, you'll be passing through territory that before the fire of 1906 was dotted with the mansions of new millionaires. The Mark Hopkins was the site of the rococo mansion of Mark Hopkins, one of the builders of the Pacific Railroad. The Fairmont stands on the site of the incredibly ornate mansion of James G. Fair (Bonanza Jim), the most colorful of the Big Four of the Comstock bonanzas. Only the Flood mansion, a Goliath of Edwardian architecture, survived, and it still stands across the street from the Fairmont, now an exclusive men's club.

Turn right on Leavenworth and, now on Russian Hill, walk eight blocks to Green Street and revel in its variety: tall apartment buildings with terraces cheek to cheek with wooden houses painted blue, green, lavender. Backtrack to Leavenworth, and between Green and Union you'll find one of the hidden delights of San Francisco—Macondray Lane, a residential alley. Start down its narrow brick road lined on both sides with cottages fronted by all manner of trees and shrubs. The peace and quiet are punctuated by the chirping of birds and perhaps the sounds of a homeowner watering the lawn or pruning a bush. Before you reach the end of the lane, the brick road becomes a wooden walk, and then, suddenly, you're at the top of a steep wooden staircase. Descend with care and you'll find yourself on Taylor Street. Turn right on Taylor and start back up toward Nob Hill.

As you approach California Street, you'll have the Flood mansion on your left and the Grace Cathedral close occupying a square block on the right. The cathedral's chimes ring every hour. Turn left on California and enter the lobby of the Fairmont Hotel at California and Mason. Luxuriate in its miles of flowered carpet flowing between marble pillars of Parthenon dimensions, marble staircases, and gilt exploding from cornices. This should give you some idea of what's meant when San Francisco is called a city of perennial Forty-Niners.

Then walk across the street to the more sedate Mark Hopkins and take the elevator to the Top-of-the-Mark, the super saloon perched on its roof. The view is legendary, and what better time to plan your next walking tour of the city? Chinatown, perhaps; California at Grant Avenue is the very heart of Chinatown. Another day board the Hyde Street cable car at

Powell and Market and ride to Fisherman's Wharf and then walk the Golden Gate Promenade toward the Golden Gate Bridge. In this wonderfully compact city everything is so attainable. Meantime, at the Top-of-the-Mark, on the very top of Nob Hill, you'll feel as though you were sitting on top of the world, and that's precisely the way San Franciscans, fiercely proud of their fabulous city, want you to feel.

WASHINGTON, D.C.

The first time I visited our nation's capital city I was nine years old and Franklin Roosevelt was president. The last time I visited it I brought my nine-year-old niece with me, and I think (certainly I *hope*) she was as thrilled with the city as I remember I was at her age. Washington, D.C., is an experience that every child should know. And no matter how often I visit even now in middle age, I can never take its majesty for granted. I know I always come home feeling very proud and very fortunate to be an American. That may sound corny (does anyone else use that word anymore?), but so be it.

Your walking tour starts on the Mall, which is lined on both sides, north and south, with important buildings. Begin at the National Air and Space Museum, which is home for, among other historic machines, the Wright brothers' *Flyer*, displayed with the following excerpts from *Century Magazine* of September 1908.

"The first flight lasted only 12 seconds, a flight very modest compared with that of birds, but was nevertheless the first in the history of the world in which a machine carrying a man had raised itself by its own power into the air in free flight, and sailed forward on a level course without reduction of speed, and had finally landed without being wrecked. The second and third flights were a little longer, and the fourth lasted 59 seconds covering a distance of 852 feet over the ground against a 20 mile wind."

Walk behind the *Flyer* to the lunar sample that asks to be stroked: "Touch a piece of the moon—cut from a rock picked up from the surface of the moon by the crew of *Apollo 17* in December 1972. It is a very hard, fine-grained basalt produced by volcanic activity and is nearly 4 billion years old." It's arrow-shaped, charcoal gray in color, and feels smooth.

See Amelia Earhart's Lockheed Vega used in 1935 when she became the first person to fly solo from Hawaii to the U.S. mainland; the aircraft that made the first U.S. nonstop transcontinental flight in 1923; and, of course, Lindbergh's *Spirit of St. Louis*, in which, in 1927, the "Lone

Eagle," as he was called, flew solo across the Atlantic to Paris in thirty-three hours thirty minutes.

Across the street is the Hirshhorn Museum, which offers free guided tours of its spectacular collection of American paintings. By all means take the underpass to the Sculpture Garden, with its serene pool and weeping-willow tree serving as the setting for Auguste Rodin's bronze *Burghers of Calais* and *Crouching Woman*.

Your next stop is the Smithsonian Institution Arts and Industries Building, with its entrance watched over by a gilt eagle flanked by eight American flags. Step inside and you're transported back to the 1876 Centennial Exhibition in Philadelphia. For ten cents, buy a copy of the *Centennial Post*, with news stories of December 13, 1876 ("Grant Erred. Regrets Mistakes. President Blames His Aides for Rampant Corruption. His Wife Angry"). Then see an exhibit that ranges from period furniture, olde ice-cream freezers, and rotary ventilating fans to horseless carriages and sleighs, cannons, totem poles, and a letter signed by George Washington, to which is attached a lock of his hair and that of his wife, Martha.

Visit the adjacent Smithsonian Castle (1855). To the left of the entrance is the tomb of James Smithson, whose last will and testament provided for "an establishment for the increase and diffusion of knowledge among men." Smithson died in Genoa, Italy, in 1829, and one of his calling cards, inscribed, "Mr. Smithson, Rue Montmarte No. 121," is framed.

Now walk across the Mall to the north side, to the Museum of National History and Technology, with José de Rivera's sculpture *Infinity* outside, and inside an elegant grab bag of such things as World War I Liberty Bond posters; the patched Star-Spangled Banner that flew "through the perilous night" at Fort McHenry; Bell's telephone; Ford's Model-T; and the rose-colored purse and gloves Mamie Eisenhower wore to the dinner given by Queen Elizabeth and Prince Philip at the British Embassy during the 1957 royal visit.

Next stop on your tour is the National Museum of Natural History. Mounted in its rotunda is an African bush elephant, and once you've gone past it, there are perhaps more fossils and skeletons than you might want to see, but upstairs in the Hall of Gems and Minerals is the 44.5-carat Hope Diamond, the largest blue diamond in the world.

Proceed across Constitution Avenue to the National Archives, with its reminder outside that "The Written Word Endures." Among its milestone documents of American history are the Declaration of Independence, the Constitution, and the Bill of Rights.

Continue in a northerly direction and up Tenth Street to the restored

Ford's Theatre, where on the night of April 14, 1865, Abraham Lincoln was shot by John Wilkes Booth. During my visit the theater was being repaired, but one could walk up to the balcony and from there look down at the flag-draped box in which the Lincolns were sitting on that fateful evening. In an anteroom behind the balcony you'll find framed copies of newspapers of that period describing the assassination and subsequent death of President Lincoln. The *Evening Star*, for example, reported, "At 22 minutes past seven o'clock the President breathed his last, closing his eyes as if falling to sleep, and his countenance assuming an expression of perfect serenity."

In the museum, located in the basement, there's the thirty-four-star American flag that draped Lincoln's coffin on its journey from Washington, D.C., to Springfield, Illinois; a letter written by his widow after the assassination to her dressmaker, "Lizzie" Keckley, an ex-slave who with her earnings from dressmaking bought her freedom and that of her son; and in a glass cabinet some of Mrs. Lincoln's White House china, along with a card informing us that "Food and its embellishments interested him little." Upstairs in the theater a fifteen-minute lecture on the assassination is given every hour on the half hour. As you leave Ford's Theatre, note the modest building directly across the street. It's the Petersen House, to which the wounded President was carried and where he died.

Backtrack to the Mall and visit the National Gallery of Art, which is directly across the Mall from where your tour started. Admission is free. You can't possibly see anywhere near as much as you want to in just one visit. Van Gogh. Cezanne. Monet. Leonardo da Vinci. Wander through the exhibition rooms and make a promise to yourself to return and spend hours there next visit.

Outside, continue along the Mall to the Capitol. Once there, sign on for one of the guided tours that leave from the rotunda every few minutes. Since you've already walked about three and a half miles, you might want to sit down and rest before starting on this last lap of your tour.

"There is nothing more powerful than an idea whose time has come."

—VICTOR HUGO

Perhaps the executive director of the President's Council on Physical Fitness and Sports had Hugo's statement in mind when he said, "Walking is an idea whose time has come." No matter. What does matter is that he was right.

A 1978 study* conducted by Louis Harris and Associates, Inc., America's premier pollsters, the findings of which were released in January 1979, not only documents our increasing national consciousness of the physical and psychological benefits of exercise but shows that *walking*, despite the current boom in running, is the single most popular exercise of adults in the country, with *34 million* adherents. America's 26 million swimmers make swimming the second largest participatory sport.

This study also shows that (1) women are getting involved in sports and athletics at an even more rapid rate than men, and (2) parents' interest in fitness activities has the strongest influence on the children, greater even than the influence of brothers and sisters or friends. And that first point happily calls to my mind a slogan made famous by the *Ladies' Home Journal* back in the 1950s, "Never Underestimate the Power of a Woman."

All things considered, we can expect to see the joy of walking sweep the nation in the very near future. And then we shall see the splendid results: a new generation of Americans walking their way to a healthier, happier way of life. Join them.

Never ride when you can walk.

* *The Perrier Study: Fitness in America.*

INDEX